More praise for *Not Working*:

'Through often fascinating readings of literature, reflections on his own experience and case studies drawn from his psychoanalytic practice, [Cohen] explores the consequences of overwork and the separation of being from doing ... A compassionate and thought-provoking way of thinking about what work is and might be ... A convincing case that human contentment is only possible if we value equally work and non-work, and make space for simply being' *Irish Times*

'A beautifully written and potently argued post-Bachelardian case for reverie, and for stopping to listen to the quieter manifestations of the inner life' Chloe Aridjis

'Gently provocative, intensely humane and exceptionally thought-provoking' *Lady*

'An eloquent defence of the necessity of the daydreamer, the artist and the slacker as part of the essential repertoire of our humanity. Offering the delicious possibility of a world slowly imagined differently and more creatively' Maria Balshaw

'Cohen usefully grounds the more theoretical wrangling of each chapter with a composite case history gleaned from his consulting room ... *Not Working* not only instructs us in the pursuit of aimlessness, it also teaches us about the psychoanalytic process' *Financial Times*

Josh Cohen

Not Working

Why We Have to Stop

GRANTA

Granta Publications, 12 Addison Avenue, London W11 4QR

First published in Great Britain by Granta Books, 2018
This paperback edition published by Granta Books, 2020

A CIP catalogue record for this book
is available from the British Library.

1 3 5 7 9 10 8 6 4 2

ISBN 978 1 78378 206 2
eISBN 978 1 78378 207 9

Typeset in Bembo by M Rules

Printed and bound by CPI Group (UK) Ltd, Croydon, CR0 4YY

www.granta.com

For my parents

Contents

Introduction

For over a decade practising as a psychoanalyst, I have started my day before the beginning and finished it after the end of the standard working day, those hours when most people are not working. This often means a first hour immersed in one person's dread and a final hour steeped in another's exhaustion. Those who come during the time between, meanwhile, are frequently snatching an hour from the office or self-employed work or childcare.

The discontents of work are forever hovering in and around the edges of the session, in the form of stories and complaints about working life, or more indirectly in the intrusive alerts of phones left on vibrate ('Sorry, that's probably work'), as though the patient, consciously or not, wants me to know something of the demands that follow her even here, in this supposedly protected space.

No doubt this gives me a partial, perhaps exaggerated picture of modern working life as plagued by stress, enervation and fatigue, maladies often compounded by a sense of unfulfilment and meaninglessness, of work as not only arduous but empty, bereft of guiding purpose beyond its simply being there to do.

The psychoanalytic consulting room is just one vantage point from which to view a problem whose scope and reach across our lives today are dauntingly broad. As a proliferation of books and articles attest, our age is witnessing a social, economic and political crisis of work. Overwork is one of its most glaring symptoms. The increasing scarcity of jobs is another. Whole sectors of the labour market, including manufacturing (cars and computers assembled by robots), retail (stores manned entirely by computers) and transport (self-driving cars and trains), are anticipating or already experiencing their eventual full automation. 'Higher-level' cognitive and intellectual work is by no means immune – artificial intelligence will take over many of the jobs we had come to think of as irreducibly human, from marketing to investment banking, from preparing legal contracts to teaching maths.

The shrinking labour market impacts those with work as much as those without. Competition for jobs drives down wages, while imposing ever greater demands for efficiency and dedication. An army of potential workers is on hand to replace us if we slip or slide, intensifying pressure on the job and closing down escape routes from it, giving rise to feelings of resignation, despair and entrapment. Many of us, caught in the struggle to maintain a decent standard of living, or simply to survive, find ourselves stuck in, or chasing after, stressful, unfulfilling work.

This impending crisis of work has given rise to the development of a loose network of 'post-work' thinkers and writers addressing the economic, social and political consequences of a future world without work. The idea of a universal basic income (UBI), the provision of a liveable, non-means-tested income for every citizen, is now enjoying support in mainstream as well as radical social policy circles, and has become a central pillar of post-work policy and debate.

But as many post-work authors argue, the questions raised by a post-work future are as existential as they are political and pragmatic. A world in which the place of work is no longer central compels us to ask where life's meaning lies. What, if not work, makes life worth living? And what kind of beings are we if not fundamentally working beings?

This book is the result of years of reading and thinking about this question. Since childhood, the value of work as the primary meaning and aim of life has never felt self-evident to me. The reason I didn't pursue a career in law, accountancy, finance, corporate management, the civil service or any other respectable middle-class profession, beyond serious doubts about possessing the requisite abilities, was that they all seemed to assume a belief in work as its own justification. Professional life struck me as full of obligations to do things not because they were stimulating or enjoyable, but because those were the responsibilities of the job. That quality of self-denying maturity, it seemed to me, was what real work was, and why I was bent on avoiding it.

The cartoon heroes of my childhood and adolescence – Snoopy, Bagpuss, Garfield, Homer Simpson and, later, their live-action successor Lebowski – lodged in my consciousness as dissidents from the imperatives of productivity and purpose conveyed to me each day by family members and teachers. They justified my conviction that the window always held more interest than the blackboard, that few teachers' lessons could hold their own for long against my daydreams.

Many years later, as adulthood loomed, the lures of daydreaming ran up against the laws of necessity. As I relate in the chapters that follow, literature and later psychoanalysis offered me ways of reconciling the two; I found in them vocations reassuringly hospitable to the refusal of productive activity, ways of making a living in spite of my aversion to the demands of external reality.

But beyond gifting me a working life I could bear and even enjoy, art and psychoanalysis helped me in different ways to question the primary value our culture places on action and purpose. This book is the outcome of that questioning. As our society is confronted increasingly urgently with the question of how to live without work, the time has come to ask whether the essence of our humanity doesn't lie elsewhere than in the fact that we act and produce. This despite the transformative power of human work, and our drive to perform it, in the history of the world. In modern Western culture, our individual day frequently becomes one long attestation to our desire not to work. Many of us, even when working hard, turn in hope and comfort to the prospect of stopping, spending large parts of even our most productive days fidgeting, staring into space, distracted by the window or the computer screen. Distraction is usually a form of disguised lethargy, a way of emptying activity of any content, of stopping without really stopping. It is a form of non-work, but one that tends to induce a state of nervous exhaustion rather than rest.

We often see this impulse not to work as an embarrassing or superfluous accident of our make-up. I am a substantial being in so far as I achieve some definite, objectively useful end, not in how I doodle or invent a private scheme of rhyming slang. But what if we have this wrong? My contention is that not working is at least as fundamental as working to who and what we are.

The first basis for such a claim is hinted at in the fabric of our physical reality. Newton's first law of motion, also known as the law of inertia, states that a body in motion will stay in motion unless acted upon by an unbalanced force. Lurking behind the quest for perpetual motion that has so fascinated scientists since the Middle Ages is the fantasy of overcoming this law, of going on without ever having to stop.

The law of inertia is a cruel master. The ball we throw will hit a wall, the clock's mechanism will run down, our feet will stop dancing: whatever the body in motion, animate or inanimate, infinitesimally small or cosmically large, some or other 'unbalanced force' will sooner or later impede its progress.

In this respect we are physical entities like any other, subject to the burden of our own weight. We can only move so far and do so much before we are forced to stop.

Here lies a clue as to why children are sent into raptures by the sensation of weightlessness. They love bubbles and balloons and being swung in the air, and dream of floating above the earth. They perceive that gravity is a thief of such dreams. Gravity keeps us riveted to the ground and ensures that our bodies can move only by waging a battle against an invisible counterforce. It makes hard work of walking, running, swimming, and an impossibility of flying.

As we grow older, bigger and less nimble, we recognize gravity as an inexorable law. We renounce levitation, first as a physical aim and eventually as a mental state. Being 'in the clouds' is code for a childish evasion of worldly reality and its demands. Clouds will not help us pass exams or find gainful employment.

But acceding to the law of gravity means facing up to the limits it imposes on both body and mind. The wonder that birds induce in us stems from the impression they convey of tirelessness. Although they are no less prone than any other animals to wear and tear, they do not collapse, exhausted, at the end of a long flight.

From its gestation through roughly the first half-year of life, the human animal is carried weightlessly, spared like a monarch in a sedan chair from the indignity of bearing her own heft. It's only when she begins to crawl that she discovers this weight, but the strain is compensated for at first by the thrilling novelty of independent movement. A child's weight is liable to become a bitter source of resentment to her only once she realizes it is permanent. Then, encouraged to walk to the park, she will implore you to bear the burden of her cumbersome body so that she doesn't have to, a frequent source of parental exhaustion as well as exasperation.

In saying no to the labour of walking, the child registers her discontent with the law of inertia. The adults around her have the task of teaching her that no one escapes it, that she must learn to carry the baggage of her body and feelings and anxieties.

Sigmund Freud's postulation of a 'death drive' in 1920, perhaps the most controversial of his concepts, offers us a kind of psychic recoding of the law of inertia. The death drive is associated with a desire for total quiescence, a destructive tendency and a pattern of compulsive repetition of traumatic experiences. But it also signals a more basic truth: that human beings are resistant to activity, that they cannot start anything, including life itself, without at some point having to stop it.

Freud often looked to ancient mythologies (most famously, of course, the Oedipus narrative) to confirm the universality of the patterns he unearthed in unconscious psychic life. He did not seek such support for the death drive, though had he done so he would have found it in abundance, most strikingly in different theogonies, or genealogies of the divine order. In any theogony, the gods serve as embodiments of specific emotions and modes of existence – love, hate, war, art and so forth – thus correlating the terrains of the cosmic order and the inner life.

The most famed narratives of the gods, such as Hesiod's *Theogony* or the *Mahabharata*, recount their febrile creative and amatory exploits, intrigues and internecine battles. But a more subterranean region of the divine order is peopled by a distinctly more inertial constellation of gods. In the Hindu theogony, Lakshmi, the creation and consort of Vishnu and the personifica-tion of good fortune, purity and elegance, is cosmically balanced by her sister Jyestha, goddess of ill fortune. Fat, unkempt and ugly, Jyestha represents a kind of divine slackness, registered even in her abundant, drooping flesh, as though her body itself is manifesting a refusal to hold up the world or maintain its appearances.

Greek theogony, meanwhile, reserves a particularly full and variegated portion of the cosmos for the gods of night, sleep and lassitude. According to Hesiod, the original Chaos that preceded the creation of earth engendered the couple Erebos (Darkness) and Nyx (Night), who in turn gave birth to Hypnos, god of sleep. With Pasithea, goddess of relaxation and hallucination, he fathered the three lords of the dream kingdom, Morpheus, Phobetor and Phantasos, each assigned rule over, respectively, the changeable, fearful and fantastical regions of dream life. Guarding Hypnos's court is Aergia, literally 'inactivity', goddess of sloth, born of the union of Gaia, broad-bosomed Mother Earth, and Aether, or Air. The two primordial life forces merge to create an anti-life force, a cosmic protector of sleep and lassitude.

The order of the universe, according to these accounts, cannot beget life without simultaneously begetting a brake on life. Freud conceived of the life drive, the death drive's more boisterous counterpart, as seeking to override this enforced brake, preferring to know nothing of the limits of the mind and body. The life drive strives for more of everything. Through sexual reproduction and hard work, it ensures that the species renews itself and that new life can be sustained. Through curiosity, imagination and practical application, it creates new territories, ideas, communities, technologies and cultures. The life drive would go on without stopping if it could.

When Freud suggests that the death drive insinuates itself quietly and invisibly into the life drive, seeking to inhibit its forward movement, he reminds us that even in the most manically expansive and ambitious periods in the life of an individual or a people, there is a moment of sluggishness, Aergia's or Jyestha's voice of lassitude whispering: Really? Can you be bothered? Wouldn't you rather stay in bed?

This book explores our troubled and ambivalent relationship to this voice. In the contemporary West, our lives are subject to a constant, nervous compulsion to activity that brooks no pause. The emblematic image of our culture is the panicky phone-checker, filling in any interval of rest or silence, on the train or at the family dinner table or in bed, with emails and work documents, or else with social media updates, addictive games and viral videos. Nervous distraction provides the only relief from a perpetually incomplete to-do list. Not working becomes at least as tiring and incessant as working. We know we have no choice but to stop, yet doing so makes us so fearful, scornful and guilty.

Our perpetual busyness is fuelled by a culture that derides or trivializes the need to stop. An ethos of anxiously competitive workaholism ensures that millions of men and women spend a vast proportion of their lives at work. Ads for energy drinks and flu remedies promise to power through illness and exhaustion and spare us (and our employers) a day off.

There is a link between these fantasies of superheroic dedication and magical immunity and the malevolent conspiracies sniffed out by our tabloid media and demagogic politicians, of welfare scroungers and migrants enjoying easy lives at the expense of decent, hard-working families. Our resentment and envy are aroused by the thought that someone may not feel bound by the imperative to keep going at all costs.

In recent decades, Western governments both left and right of centre have been increasingly zealous at keeping us working regardless of our circumstances. The receipt of welfare entitlements in the UK, USA and elsewhere is subject to ever more stringent criteria, most obviously the active search for work. As the post-work theorist David Frayne writes, 'Even groups that have been traditionally exempted from the duty to work, such as single parents and people with disabilities, have found themselves under scrutiny in the drive to move people off welfare and into employment.' Disability allowances are being denied and withdrawn on the back of often brutal bureaucratic assessments of the applicant's fitness to work.

The justification for this relentless drive to reduce the non-working citizenry is well known: the financial burden of an ageing and expanding population renders the current welfare bill unsustainable in the long term. If countries are to avoid bankruptcy and terminal decline, they must plug all gaps in productivity and turn economic waste into surplus. The ideal state and economy of the future would thus triumph over the law of inertia – no 'unbalanced force' will intrude to block or inhibit the perpetual mobility of the economy.

The problem is that Western economies have long shown themselves to be anything but exempt from the law of inertia. Whatever solutions they find to clear obstacles to their dynamism just generate new problems. Automation increases output and efficiency only to drive down employment and wages. The pressures resulting from job scarcity ensure that both the state and the wider economy lose billions each year to stress-related illnesses such as fatigue, burnout and depression. Trying to override the law of inertia guarantees only that it asserts itself more implacably. But the scornful moralizing about work from commerce, politics and the media would count for little if it didn't find ready amplification in our own minds. Many of us are all too vulnerable to being embarrassed by having to stop.

Psychoanalysis offers various thoughts about why this might be. We carry within ourselves an idealized self-image, or 'ego ideal' in Freud's terminology, that presses us to do and achieve more. The ego ideal is the residue in us of an unconscious belief, transmitted to us by our parents from earliest infancy, in our own perfectibility. While it can serve as a spur to ambition and creativity, it is also liable to become insidiously punishing, inducing feelings of shame and inadequacy at the gap between who we are and who we feel we should be.

Where the ego ideal assures us, 'You can', the more famous agency of the unconscious mind known as the superego dictates, 'You must', provoking punitive guilt at our low levels of conscientiousness and responsibility. The interplay of external and internal messages ensures that most of us experience some level of anxiety regarding our limits: no sooner do we come to a stop than voices assail us from without and within, demanding we start again.

The ego ideal is an irresistible sitting target of today's culture of work and employability, with its unrelenting demands and incentives to maximize our potential. 'Each worker,' writes Frayne, 'is taught that he or she can always be *more*, and employability becomes a tragic path whose travellers declare a constant war on themselves, questioning the suitability of their personalities and achievements, never quite satisfied that they are spending their time sensibly enough.'

Our discomfort with stopping, with time unfilled and unspoken for, also gives rise to a mode of constant distraction, the perfect twin of the imperative to work and produce: the moment we come to the limit of our capacity as producers, we can activate our capacity as consumers. The eyes, ears and nervous system of a child born today will be assailed from the first by an unbroken flow of images and information beaming from television, tablet and mobile screens. His physical presence in tangible spaces such as the home, office or street will be absorbed by the virtual networks of digital life and their unremitting pressures to follow, like, update, stream, buy. The intervals away from his devices will induce feelings of abandonment and emptiness.

We are nervous of pressing the off switch on our machines and minds, as though fearing the void that might be made visible. And yet this wariness coexists with an intense yearning for silence and reclusion, a break in the unremitting flow of noise. More than one patient in my consulting room will regularly express a wish for the world, or themselves, to dissolve. They speak of the bliss of catatonic exhaustion, of a weekend morning spent vacantly, of staring at a single line of newspaper until it acquires the perfect emptiness of a Buddhist koan.

We find ourselves suspended between a compulsion to do too much and a wish to do nothing. The distractions of net-surfing are a kind of weird convergence of these impulses. Comparing twenty-three minor variations on a white T-shirt, consuming dozens of viral cat videos or scrolling through metres of social media feeds, our frenzied overactivity becomes a way of wasting our (or our employers') time and damming our productivity.

Our complex and ambivalent relationship to activity and purpose thus suggests one reason to doubt the conception of human beings as primarily working beings. Another is the existence of art.

Art has a central place in this book. This is partly because the lives and work of literary, visual and cinematic artists offer a rich array of thoughts and representations of non-working states of mind and body: apathy, laziness, indifference, dreaminess and so on. But more fundamentally, the very fact that art exists attests to a dimension of us that rejects active, purposeful life, what we might call the tyranny of doing.

After all, what do artists *do*? Inhabiting the realm of the imagination rather than practical reality, directing our gaze away from truth to fiction and illusion, artists do very little in the way of concrete action, rendering them an object of persistent suspicion for those who seek to promote virtue and honesty. In *The Republic*, Plato has Socrates banish artists from the ideal state for various reasons, but above all because they have nothing to contribute to, or tell us about, right living and action. Even Homer, laments Socrates, the most loved and revered of all poets, cannot claim to have authored a constitution, waged a successful war, invented a practical device or devoted himself to public service. He may be irresistibly entertaining, but as a guide to life he is worse than useless.

Around 2,300 years later, Oscar Wilde inverts Plato's hierarchy of values, promoting this uselessness as the artist's supreme virtue. By resisting the compulsion to be active that holds everyone else in its grip, the artist throws off the limits of our reality and finds his way to the limitless, airy region of dream life, 'a life that has for its aim not doing but being'.

Despite their opposed positions, Socrates and Wilde converge on the same insight: the making and enjoying of art express an implicit refusal to understand life's aim as doing. The fact that works of art exist points to a kind of gratuitous, even useless dimension of human existence, a resistance to purposeful action. It is hard to discern any direct practical effect in reading a poem or looking at a painting.

The obvious counter to this argument is that the arts are a highly profitable industry, while works of art can be and are mobilized by those who make and consume them for all kinds of political and personal uses. Art, in other words, is part of our living, worldly reality, not a private kingdom split off from it. This is surely why the arts today are constantly having to justify their use of public resources – money, space, time – in terms of commercial value or social utility. Art has to be shown to do something financially or socially profitable.

We can certainly try to get works of art to do and say all sorts of things. But the sneaking suspicion remains that what defines a work of art is that it 'does' nothing. 'Art,' writes the French writer and critic Maurice Blanchot, 'acts poorly and little ... as soon as art measures itself against action, immediate and pressing action can only put it in the wrong.' Blanchot's contemporary the German philosopher and critic T. W. Adorno argued that art – or at least the kind of art he considered most worthy of the name – is politically subversive not because of what it 'says' but because it 'says' very little; the profound effect of a play by Samuel Beckett or a painting by Pablo Picasso is to alienate the empty modes of language and communication imposed upon us by modern capitalist society.

What if, instead of measuring it against action, we cherish art as the one region of life where that measure doesn't apply? In a provocative passage, Blanchot suggests that the Romantic myth of the artist as divine creator, taking over the place vacated by the ancient gods, misses the most sacred of all divine functions: in almost all myths of the world's origin, but especially the Genesis narrative, the divine entities not only create but *rest*. The Romantic artist mistakenly imagines his divinity consists in assuming 'the least divine of the god's functions ... which makes of God a laborer six days a week'.

Authentic divinity consists not in working, which anyone can do, but in not working, the prerogative of a god. Like the god, the artist is not a 'laborer'; where a builder's use of stone makes a wall, a bridge or some other useful object in the everyday world, the sculptor's use of stone gives rise only to an object in the imaginary world. However hard he might seem to work, from the perspective of real utility and purpose, the artist does nothing. The formula projected in light onto various buildings by the artist Martin Creed – 'the whole world + the work = the whole world' – concentrates this insight beautifully. 'The work' is essentially superfluous – it neither adds nor subtracts from the overall sum of the world's contents. People who call themselves taxpayers and artists useless layabouts are making the same point – the world doesn't 'need' artists in the sense it needs bricklayers or doctors.

It is in this sense, rather than in the Romantic sense of divine creativity, that we might say an artist resembles a god. In taking a day's rest, God asserts His freedom from any external imperative or demand. The Sabbath, explicitly sanctifying non-work, encourages us to imitate this divine lassitude; its disappearance from contemporary life may have as much to do with the sacralization of work as it does the secularization of society. The elevation of the Sabbath to sacred status hints to us that being is a higher mode of existence than doing. Perhaps art is the last vestige of the sabbatical dimension of us human beings, putting us in contact with the experience of living without explicit aim or purpose.

In 1999, the world beset with millennial anxieties, Tracey Emin drew teeming crowds of intrigued, baffled and angry viewers to the Tate Gallery in London to see *My Bed*. Quickly established as one of the most emblematic and notorious artworks of our age, it painstakingly re-created her bed as it appeared after an alcohol-fuelled breakdown, triggered by the end of a relationship.

A disordered tangle of used and dirty stockings, towels and sheets, the undersheet spilling freely over the bed's base, was bordered by the accumulated debris of an exhausted life: used and unused tissues, bloodstained knickers, a lonely cuddly toy, empty vodka bottles, tampons, condoms, Polaroid selfies, crushed cigarette packets, old newspapers and condiments.

My Bed triggered a storm of tabloid ridicule and disgust,

breathing a new urgency and life into that worn-out question, what is art? In what sense, asked its detractors, did the term apply to this unedited presentation of a life's raw mess, this indulgent and ugly act of self-exposure? How can we confer the status of an artwork on an object that brazenly refuses the terms of both art and work?

The Greek word *poiesis* defines the creative act, whether in natural or human life, as a *making*, a transfiguration through work of one thing into another. Not coincidentally known as Emin's 'unmade bed', *My Bed* seemed to be the statement of a defiant refusal to make anything. Instead it left the formless detritus of her disintegrating life undisturbed, strewn with no thought to its harmonious arrangement, or to inducing aesthetic pleasure in her viewer.

The lassitude on display in *My Bed* evoked not so much the restorative Sabbath that prepares our return to the service of God, work and family, as the profane Sabbath of the *tohu va-bohu*, the terrifying 'waste and void' that preceded the Creation. Through the microcosm of a single image, it stages a return to the original chaos of the universe.

Emin's bed provokes a horrified recognition of a scene playing itself out invisibly and secretly in each of us, a spot in us that, amid our purposeful lives of action and progress, would surrender to entropy, to the dissolution of all order and meaning. And yet its impression of abject sloth and neglect was the effect of much painstaking work, in which the distinction between making and unmaking was artfully blurred. Rather than sounding the death knell of the imagination, inertia and lassitude served for Emin as a creative resource.

My Bed documents a specific experience of depressive iner-tia. Its roots in Emin's personal history made it a lightning rod for ad hominem (or rather, given the barely coded misogyny of many of the attacks, ad feminam) denunciations of her supposed narcissism and cynicism. But this confessional aspect is only the springboard for the much broader connection it makes between art and inertia: it isn't the work of a quasi-divine creator, in which the elements of a broken self are gathered and integrated, conferred with pictorial or narrative shape. It is an exercise in art as doing nothing, bent upon (Blanchot again) 'culminating in a work which *is* and nothing more'.

Still, *My Bed* isn't a work that realizes the Wildean aspiration of an Art purified of, as he puts it, 'the sordid perils of actual existence'. It delivers us not to the dreamy contemplative space of pure feeling which for Wilde was the essence of the aesthetic life, but to a murky region of incoherence and lethargy. The aim to be rather than do, and its allied renunciation of action, is more ambiguous than Wilde wants to allow. It might just as easily entail the soul's descent into exhausted indifference as its ascent to the sublime heights of contemplation.

Emin's bed isn't a place of sabbatical rest, airy dreams or frenzied coupling, but of illness, exhaustion and despair. The intoxicants and contraceptive devices convey not a lively appetite for excitement, but a quest for physical and psychic numbness, for the discharge rather than the heightening of feeling. The scene plunges us into what French sociologist Alain Ehrenberg calls 'the weariness of the self', a state he diagnosed, in his seminal 1998 book of that title, as the essential malaise of our time.

The weariness of which Ehrenberg speaks is expressed in a feeling of radical inhibition, a chronic incapacity to act. In our contemporary consumer society, the places where we work, conduct relationships and consume arouse intense competitive and rivalrous impulses. Enervated by perpetual demands to choose and to act, we are prone to slip into a debilitating paralysis of will and desire. 'Holding back, freezing, braking, suspension of activity, and so on,' writes Ehrenberg, 'are all part of the language of apathy.'

This list of synonyms could serve as a striking caption for Emin's scene of a life ground to a halt. But the list also evokes the nature of art and its difference from what we call real life. An artwork, writes the French philosopher Emmanuel Levinas, one of the few modern thinkers to question the morality of art, is a freezing of its object in 'an eternally suspended future'. Where a living face is a vehicle for emotional expression in all its variety and changeability, the subject of a portrait is caught forever in a single moment of her inner life: 'Eternally, the smile of the Mona Lisa about to broaden will not broaden.'

'The characters of a novel,' meanwhile, are similarly 'shut up, prisoners. Their history is never finished, it still goes on, but makes no headway.' To be a fictional character is to be condemned to an eternal Groundhog Day, compulsively repeating a story we can never escape. Even the characters in a film, for all their appearance of live movement and response, are stranded in the same story, the same changeless physical and verbal gestures, for all time.

We do not need to assent to Levinas's argument about art in all its particulars to recognize a striking truth in it. The famous insistence of children on hearing the same stories repeated incessantly, without any deviation from the original version, makes a similar point: art gives us access to a world in which things remain stubbornly as they always have been and will be, a condition which can be experienced as both reassuring and hellish.

From this perspective, *My Bed* starts to look not simply like an artwork whose theme is inertia, but a meditation on art as a kind of protected reserve of inertia. In an interview with Julian Schnabel, Emin spoke of the work's origin in the moment she returned from her bathroom to see the chaos of decay and filth her bed had become, only to imagine the very same scene transposed to a white gallery: 'And at that moment I saw it, and it looked fucking brilliant. And I thought, this wouldn't be the worst place for me to die; this is a beautiful place that's kept me alive.'

This transfiguration of deathly horror into life-affirming beauty is effected not by any physical intervention, but by her thought of the scene's transposition to a white gallery. The imagined shift from a life space to an art space radically alters the meaning of the scene without it changing its appearance. A good part of the work's impact may be the eerie sense it gives us of a moment thick with real pain and confusion having been teleported fully intact to a place it doesn't belong.

The paradox of *My Bed*, then, is that it transforms an experience by doing nothing to it, by letting it be exactly what it is. Imagine yourself in Emin's place, returning from the bathroom and being shocked out of your catatonic lethargy by sheer horror at the chaos that has spread around you as you've surrendered to your grief and suffering. The more conventional response might be to clear up the room and yourself, go out for some fresh air, perhaps meet up with a friend. Seeing that life has ground to a halt might induce us to get it started again.

Emin points us to a different way of relating to our inertial feelings. Instead of getting rid of them by tidying the mess and pulling herself together, she honours them, presenting them to us in the same formless state in which she found them, and seeing beauty in it. She awakens from her nightmare not by forgetting it, but by preserving it as faithfully as she can.

A moment at which life has come to a stop is itself fixed indelibly. Instead of turning away from the scene in reflexive disgust, we are invited to recognize in it an image of the law of inertia as an inescapable fact of our lives. We are not perpetual-motion machines, Emin reminds us; we cannot simply override the gravitational force of sadness or exhaustion. At some point, we just have to stop.

It is only when we stop that we attain a sense of how we might float free of gravity's pull. In that moment of revelation, Emin saw a scene of deathly chaos morph into one of beauty and affirmation. The possibility of artistic transformation instantaneously relieved the scene of its oppressive heaviness. Art is an antigravitational force.

The denunciation that inevitably accompanies apathy and weariness of the self has a long and venerable history. The two Testaments of the Bible abound with prickly reproaches to the non-working. The authors of the biblical book of Proverbs, observing the human inclination to gluttony, drunkenness and sloth, warn repeatedly that poverty and an early grave await the person who persists in idle ways. Paul's Epistle to the Thessalonians declares, 'If a man will not work, he shall not eat.'

The Bible was the foundation for a Western morality of work that continues to govern even our own, thoroughly secularized culture. The malaise known as acedia, a state of tormented spiritual doubt and loss of will endemic to monastic culture, was linked by medieval theologians to sluggishness of both body and soul. Not merely one sin among others, sloth was the gateway to all sin, for it relaxed the inner discipline and vigilance required to resist temptation.

Severe as it may sound, this morality at least leaves some room for flexible interpretation. It insists that we must work, not that work should be the horizon of our lives. Only in the modern period did work become something that must not simply be done, but be loved and cared for as a divine gift.

In his seminal 1905 study, *The Protestant Ethic and the 'Spirit' of Capitalism*, the German sociologist Max Weber traced the history of the move away from what he calls a 'traditionalist' economy, in which the worker's concern is with work as a means rather than an end. In the past, the aim of work was simply to provide sufficient income 'to live in the manner in which he is accustomed to live'.

For most citizens of the modern West, it is hard to imagine a relationship to work and income so free of ambivalence and anxiety. So thoroughly have we internalized the sweet and bitter fruits of work as the measure of our worth and significance that the traditionalist conception of work as a means of satisfying basic needs and comforts has been consigned to an unimaginable past.

Inside and outside the consulting room, people who spend their days wrestling with MRI scans or opaque financial instruments or knotty points of human rights law tell me they fantasize about being farm labourers or bricklayers or shelf-stackers, knowing that however arduous or dull their working hours might be, they could go home and rest their tired bones, confident that the day was truly done. But radical life changes of this kind remain at the level of fantasy, and not simply because of their financial liabilities. Work has acquired a privileged and fraught place in self-understanding that is not lightly surrendered.

Weber's masterly analysis tells us why. He shows how, over the course of three centuries, psychology and culture entrenched the modern work ethic deep in the self. The various Protestant movements to emerge from the Reformation infused the secular order of work and wealth with a new spirituality. The key word in the Protestant lexicon is 'calling' (*Beruf*), which transforms work from a pragmatic means to a sacred end in itself.

There is an unmistakably Freudian resonance to the word 'calling', with its connotations of an enigmatic voice addressing the self from within. Both the cheerleading ego ideal and the persecuting superego exhort the besieged ego to fulfil its calling, tasking it to realize its potential as well as its responsibilities to the world. Once work becomes a calling heard from within, rather than a necessity imposed from without, it is much more difficult to stop it without feeling inadequate or guilty. Gordon Gekko's 'Lunch is for wimps' is the logical conclusion of the elevated status of work.

In sacralizing work, Protestant movements such as Calvinism brought a new imperative of method and purpose into everyday living, one of the most important consequences of which was to invest time with the highest value. Weber quotes the Puritan minister Richard Baxter enjoining his flock to 'Keep up a high esteem of Time; and be every day more careful that you lose none of your Time, than you are that you lose none of your Gold or Silver'.

To esteem time in this way is to keep a tight leash on the direction of your daily life, not to stray, meander or idle into some unexpected detour, especially if it has no discernible profit or purpose. For Baxter and his counterparts across Protestant Europe, writes Weber, 'According to God's unambiguously revealed will, it is *only* action, not idleness and indulgence, that serves to increase his glory.'

Clear-sighted action is the sole antidote to the malaise of waste and idleness. So successful was capitalism, the secular inheritor of this ethic, in establishing the sovereign status of work in our culture, it no longer needed the support of its religious foundations. Over the last two centuries, it expanded itself instead through the spread and growth of cities, technologies, corporations and consumer culture.

These radically new and alien forces took their toll on physical and psychic life. The excitements and anxieties of the accelerated, hyper-stimulating culture of the modern industrial city resulted in a global epidemic of nervous exhaustion, or, in the coinage of the American neurologist George Beard, neurasthenia.

Neurasthenia manifested in a diffuse proliferation of symptoms, including, as Beard wrote in 1869, 'debility of all the functions, poor appetite, abiding weakness in the back and spine, fugitive neuralgic pains, hysteria, insomnia, hypochondriasis, disinclination for consecutive mental labour, severe and weakening attack of sick headache, and other analogous symptoms'. In neurasthenia, these symptoms have no organic basis, but are the effect of the overloading of the nerves by the unmanageable rush of sensations, demands and anxieties generated by modern life.

Combing Beard's list, it is hard not to be struck by its contemporary resonance. Eating disorders and sleep deprivation continue to disturb the everyday functioning of body and mind; the massive expansion of a sedentary white-collar workforce has ensured chronic back problems remain widespread, while giving rise to new forms of musculoskeletal and nervous injuries such as RSI. We can also recognize the signs of our neurasthenic culture in migraine and exhaustion. 'An entire battery of psychopathologies,' write post-work theorists Nick Srnicek and Alex Williams, 'has been exacerbated under neoliberalism: stress, anxiety, depression and attention deficit disorders are increasingly common psychological responses to the world around us.' To Beard's list we can add the various compulsions and addictions that have proliferated in the online age – the permanent distraction of social media updates, the ever present, instantly accessible lures of gambling, pornography, newsfeeds, shopping, each scratching at the most vulnerable and anxious spots of our inner lives, exciting us with the promise of transformative gratifications while yielding only deflating disappointments. The sources of chronic enervation may change, but the symptoms remain strikingly consistent.

Of course, the hedonistic consumer capitalism of our day seems the obverse of early capitalism, whose moral severity was under-pinned by 'an ascetic compulsion to save' and a disdain of luxury. Consumerism, in contrast, extols the pleasures of indulgence and waste. But there is continuity as well as dissonance between these attitudes. Take a day at the shopping centre, sold to us as an invig-orating break from the rigours of work. Does it not feel more like an extension of it, blurring the line between work and 'free' time? When I wander beneath the cavernous white ceilings of Europe's largest shopping centre, the consumerist cathedral of Westfield, I experience a creeping exhaustion and irritability rather than a heady rush of consumerist desire, a mounting, anxious pressure to complete my designated tasks. Merging zombie-like into the stream of shopper-ants while strains of Bieber scramble my hear-ing and shopping-bag handles cut into my fingers, I am struck by how much it all feels like hard work.

Our bodies and minds are overworked by more than work. They are subject to a culture that relates to every moment as an opportunity to produce or consume. It is no coincidence that today's lifestyle pages are preoccupied with sleep disorders. Sleep, as Jonathan Crary argues in his fiery polemic *24/7*, is the one state in which we cannot be put to work; little wonder that corpor-ations and the military are so interested, and financially invested, in finding ways to minimize the need for it.

The principle of inertia established the impossibility of perpet-ual motion as a law of nature. Our knowledge of this law is coded deeply in our biology and psychology. But so, it seems, is the urge to defy it, to insist that we don't have to stop if we don't want to. This pull of contradictory impulses creates an irremediable divi-sion at the heart of our selves. We dream of building, expanding, conquering, of becoming masters over an ever larger territory of possessions and people; but in the midst of this heroic ambition lurks the yearning to crawl back into our beds and stay there. In the chapters that follow, we will find this yearning confirmed in a range of expressions of psychic and social exhaustion.

In his great late essay *Civilization and Its Discontents* (1930), Freud saw this conflict between work and the wish to stop it as the fundamental predicament of human culture. Life urges us to take command of some portion of reality, and work presents itself as the readiest way of doing so. And yet, he observes, work signally fails to make most of us happy; the near-universal distaste for work he finds among his fellow human beings leads him to speak of a 'natural human aversion' to it.

Twenty-two years earlier, in his short but suggestive paper on 'Creative Writers and Daydreaming', Freud had hinted at why we prefer art to science. Art spares us the slow and laborious path to gratification which science cannot avoid. Because the scientist's quarry is reality, she has no option, if she wants to get anywhere in her enquiries, but to learn, test, deduce, wait. The artist, in contrast, is not beholden to reality; if he wants infinite riches, brilliant adventures or beautiful women, he need only imagine (or 'daydream') them.

In the great, much-retold legend of Faust, the scientist finds a way to exploit the real world in exactly the way the artist uses the imaginary world – as a playground for the realization of his every wildest wish. By taking all the effort out of science, Faust courts disaster.

Faust throws into dramatic relief the paradox of 'civilization'. He labours through a lifetime of obsessive scholarly work whose final aim is to acquire the power to do and have whatever he wants without having to work. A similar paradox animates our own culture of frenetic overwork. It too drives us to incessant hard work in the hope of realizing the fantasy of an effortless life. The habits of the gambler and the drug addict, to take two among many possible examples, are fuelled by the same Faustian wish to leapfrog the labour involved in attaining one's desires.

It is culturally acceptable for us to complain aloud about how busy and how tired we are, as though in doing so we reassure the world that we fully acknowledge our moral and social obligation to work and contribute. Acknowledging the need to stop is more difficult, for it implies a shaming admission to being weak-willed, lightweight and not quite up to it.

When I raise the secret desire to do nothing in conversation with friends, I find I elicit a stream of confessions of secret vices: procrastination, laziness, gluttony, slovenliness. It is as though the fact that such habits can be thought about gives them a substance and meaning never previously suspected. The licence to think of sloth as a universal human tendency, rather than as a furtive indulgence of their own, induces a gleeful relief; my interlocutors on the subject have needed little encouragement to share their expansive inventory of ways of doing nothing.

We might be inclined to place clinical psychoanalysis on the side of active, purposeful life. It seeks to restore a sense of aliveness, to mine the currents of unconscious life that animate creativity and desire. But as I'll argue in this book, it achieves these aims not by infusing us with some sense of panicked urgency, but by slowing us down, encouraging us to think and speak in the rhythm unique to us, rather than to adapt ourselves to someone else's notion of the best way to live.

One of Freud's most important and paradoxical discoveries is that the circuitous, aimless detour is the most reliable way of reaching the truth. The concept of 'resistance', one of the best known and least understood in clinical psychoanalysis, is helpful here. In caricatural versions of psychoanalytic treatment (sometimes propagated by psychoanalysts themselves), resistance is simply the patient's wilful recalcitrance, which the analyst must decisively overcome, in the face of their unconscious (sexual, envious, murderous) desires and impulses.

Perhaps the physics of electricity offers a better way of understanding the term. Resistance here is what impedes the flow of the electrical charge. Electrons constantly bump up against fixed atoms in their conducting material, blowing them off course as they stream towards their destination. Similar obstacles obstruct us when we try to hear and voice the flow of our own thoughts and feelings. Psychoanalysis came into being when Freud recognized that neither he nor his patients could simply override their resistances. Like electrons, the contents of our mind cannot get to their destination without crashing into recalcitrant material along the way.

Short-term cognitive psychotherapies seek to show the patient that this recalcitrance can be overcome by more positive thinking. In this view, the inertial forces that obstruct our progress through life – despair, inadequacy, lassitude, apathy – are mere errors to be corrected and removed. The progress of psychoanalysis is long and meandering and its outcome uncertain because it sees those same forces as fundamental to who and what we are, fixed atoms in the structure of our selves.

Those fixed atoms are the subject of this book. The four chapters at its heart are organized around a typology of the inertial character: the burnout, the slob, the daydreamer and the slacker. Each of these types, by volition or necessity, has stopped working, or at least working blindly. Their lives involve some or other combination of loss of interest in the external world, lazing about, withdrawing into a room, forsaking all worldly ambitions and refusing any schedule or agenda not one's own. They are different models for inhabiting and resisting the modern malady of weary overactivity, pointing to a range of possibilities for living differently. By a model I mean a version rather than an ideal of life. As we will see, in resisting work as an imperative, each type is liable to fall into one or more impasse: depressive exhaustion, listless entitlement, loneliness or marginalization, among others. These four types, in other words, offer not so much instructions about how we should live as provocative and fruitful questions about how we do live.

These types by no means exhaust the descriptive vocabulary of non-work, nor are they strictly marked off from one another – on the contrary, they frequently and inevitably overlap. I have extracted them from a soup of my own memories and reflections, from immersion in culture and ideas and from clinical experience.

The four types are divided into two pairs, one coming under the heading 'Gravity', the other 'Antigravity'. The division was sparked by a passing thought of the Icarus myth, in which the great artisan Daedalus is imprisoned in the Labyrinth he had himself built for King Minos of Crete, for the crime of helping Theseus, Minos's enemy, to escape it and defeat the Minotaur. Crafting wings from wax and feathers for himself and his son Icarus to escape, he counsels Icarus to steer a course between the sun and the sea. But after soaring excitedly towards the sky, Icarus's wings are melted by the sun, sending him falling into the sea.

Daedalus imagined and created a way out of the imprisoning structure of his world; but its success depended on a subtle mediation between defiance and acceptance of gravity's law. Should Icarus submit too readily to that law, or too arrogantly defy it, gravity would be sure to take its revenge.

The first pair of types could be described as slaves of gravity, hovering too closely above the sea, weighed down by their own physical and emotional weight. The burnout, subject of Chapter 1, is the most reactive of these types. Driven for all his life by the blind impulsion to act and achieve, he is derailed by a sudden and overwhelming need to stop, to which he can only blankly surrender. Chapter 2 centres on the slob, who willingly embraces that same need, turning lassitude, gluttony and entitlement into an elective way of life.

The second pair court the opposite risk, seeking to escape or defy the world's inertial force. The daydreamer of Chapter 3 tries to elude the burdens of daily life by taking flight into the far reaches of the imagination. In contrast, the slacker, the subject of Chapter 4, finds ways to turn this aversion to the real world and its demands into a concrete ethos and lifestyle.

Each chapter ends with a brief clinical case history, exploring some resonances between the given type and the individual patient. Writing about clinical work confronts every psychotherapist with the irreconcilable claims of the patient's right to confidentiality and the reader's expectation of clinical truth. I have weighed heavily on the side of confidentiality; each case is in fact a composite of cases, disguising most of the relevant aspects of the patients' histories. My justification for this choice is that I'm writing for a general rather than a collegial readership; in this context, confidentiality is imperative and cannot be compromised (one cannot be 'a bit' or 'mostly' confidential). Clinical truth, on the other hand, is a more flexible notion. My hope is that these little histories convey something of the spirit and texture, if not the specific detail, of the psychoanalytic process.

These chapters alternate with biographical sketches of four major figures in the modern history of art and literature who channelled feelings of indifference, slothful indulgence, withdrawal and boredom into remarkable cultural achievements: Andy Warhol, Orson Welles, Emily Dickinson and David Foster Wallace. While each figure correlates loosely with the preceding type, there is no strict correspondence between them because there are no pure types. In each of them, different facets of each type are mixed in greater or lesser proportion.

All four are distinguished by an almost freakish level of creative prolificity and obsessiveness. This is precisely my reason for choosing them; what is striking about these men and woman is that they each found a way to mobilize their scepticism towards action and purpose for imaginative life. This is an importantly different point from the commonplace (and unobjectionable) notion that taking time out benefits creative work, and the general counsel of a healthy 'work–life balance'. The purpose of such counsel, frequently endorsed by gurus of business and commerce, is always to recover maximal efficiency and focus, to return from rest fully restored for work.

Emin did not emerge from her catatonic breakdown to make her bed, but to preserve it unmade. For her as for Warhol, Welles, Dickinson and Wallace, it isn't a matter of transforming the inactive state into an active one. The creative act consists, paradoxically, in sustaining the inactive state. In each case, as we'll see, exhaustion, sleep, gluttony, waste, dreaminess and slackness become the strangely compelling substance of both life and work.

Not working has almost always been valued only to the extent that it serves the cause of work. It is time we spoke up for not working, in all its creative possibilities, as its own value.

PART ONE

Gravity

Chapter 1

The Burnout

Years ago, for a few wintry months before he lost his head to a fox, I was lumbered with the daily care of a rabbit named Rr. It wasn't long before I found myself resenting it all – the resinous little pellets forever trailing his tail, the clumps of sodden hay and sawdust pasted to the base of his hutch. And then there was the problem of Rr himself.

The rabbits I'd known in childhood had sprung from the pages of Lewis Carroll and Beatrix Potter, and the animations of Disney and Tex Avery, entrenching deep confusion about the humanity of rabbits that I'd failed to slough off with adulthood. I didn't expect Rr to be mischievous, kindly or overanxious, but was it too much to ask for some minimal gesture of animal sentimentality – a glance of welcome, a grateful brush of my cheek from his reaching paw?

Perhaps it's because we're so unnerved by their blankness that we feel the need to remake rabbits in our own wishful image. Rr showed me just how pointless a tendency this is. For all the warm undulations of his furry flesh over my forearms, he conveyed no sense of inhabiting the same world as me, offered not the slightest twitch of recognition, nor any sign of goodwill, hostility, curiosity or concern. I began to understand the rage I'd witnessed in toddlers when domestic pets or new babies didn't respond to their attempts to initiate conversation.

1

For a while, I bristled at Rr's indifference to me, and at my own inability to relieve the distance between us. Even as his velveteen body huddled into mine, I couldn't imagine meaning any more to him than the splintery wood of his hutch.

This indifferent mode of being has much in common with the bovine torpor famously described by Nietzsche in his early essay on the uses of history. The grazing cow, he writes, is 'fettered to the moment and its pleasure or displeasure, and thus neither melancholy nor bored'. Like that cow, Rr endured neither regrets for the past nor anxieties for the future, lived free of the burdens of memory and anticipation, meaning he neither missed me when I was gone nor welcomed my return. For all he depended on me for his basic daily needs, for all the space he took up in my mind, I meant nothing to him. It seemed strange that a creature so guileless could be so ruthless.

It was partly a problem of bad timing. I was in the midst of a gruelling psychoanalytic training while continuing to hold a full-time academic post, shifting between different physical and psychic locations from one hour to the next. I was tending to Rr in a state of exhaustion, resentful about why I was dedicating time I didn't have to the care of some dumb ingrate rabbit.

But in time, the exhaustion that was causing my resentment began slowly to transform it. I began to experience a new feeling of affinity with my silent charge. Sitting alongside his run, drained by the day's demands, I would watch him shuffle across his parallel universe and make contact with the same secret, self-enclosed blankness in myself. I related to his incapacity to relate to me. Losing myself in his empty stare and aimless busyness, I felt empathy, and a little envy, for his indifference to the world's and my existence.

As I registered Rr's exemption from the labours of internal growth and change, my fascination for his world deepened. The moment we humans enter the world, we're bound to a process of cognitive and emotional development from which we can't opt out. The cornerstone of this process is learning to discriminate and prefer. This, Freud suggests, is how we first become selves; things come to us from the external world through the mouth or eyes or nose or skin, which we duly welcome or reject. We become who we are by *judging*, by saying yes to this, no to that.

Rr, I thought as I sat on the damp decking, hugging my knees and losing myself in the stop–start rhythm of his scrabbling paws, is untroubled by this burden of having to say yes or no. He experiences impersonal needs, but not personal feelings. He lives without self-consciousness, and so is free of the intrusions and disturbances of desire.

Perhaps this absence of desire seems difficult to square with a creature who's a byword for irrepressible sexual appetite. But 'fucking like rabbits' surely means fucking indifferently, less out of authentic desire for a particular body, an automatized response to an indifferent body. The makers of the best-selling Rampant Rabbit vibrator presumably chose its name and shape to signal just this efficient depersonalization of sex.

And what about the Duracell Bunny, with his clockwork motion and dead-eyed grin? Irritating yet compelling, he hints at the automated state into which our own lives threaten to slide. He goes on and on, powered not by any personal aim or desire, but by an inexhaustible supply of impersonal energy. Behind his rictus grin lurks the unmistakable figure of the zombie, ubiquitous emblem of our apocalyptic pop culture, trapped in the purgatorial grip of blind forward movement.

I hear echoes of my lapine reverie every day. My consulting room resounds with stories of reclusion from the world, with fantasies of a cessation of doing, wanting, feeling, of total liberation from the everyday mental labour of being human. In tones untinged by bitterness or morbidity, a patient will say, 'I've no wish to kill myself, but just for a while I'd like to be dead', or, 'Sometimes all I want is for the world to disappear.'

They say this in awareness that the world will once again bear down on their overburdened minds and bodies the moment they leave the room, arousing in them the same curiosity, confusion, care, rage, passion and hope as it did yesterday and will tomorrow.

They suffer an all too human predicament: their impulse to live, to expand their presence in the world by participating in and contributing to it, also begets the opposite impulse, to contract and withdraw into the indifferent neutrality of a rabbit. But no sooner do they begin to sink into oblivion than they once again feel the scratch of worldly demands and desires.

To be pulled between these extremes is debilitating, and can sabotage work and rest alike. Sufferers of this condition of exhausted busyness will often refer to feeling 'burned out', a term that locates their malaise in the external pressures of working life rather than in the turbulences of the inner world, thus circumventing the stigma of depression. 'Burnout' was first used in a psychotherapeutic context by the German–American psychologist Herbert J. Freudenberger in 1974, to refer to the growing phenomenon 'physical or mental collapse caused by overwork or stress'.

Freudenberger, notes Anna Katharina Schaffner, observed that people with 'burnout' had a tendency to 'depersonalize' working relationships, being indifferent to the sensitivities and needs of co-workers and clients. Drained of positive commitment to their own role and to those around them, burnt-out workers were running on empty, depleted of all but the most minimal internal resources. The exhaustion of burnout leads to an intense yearning for a state of rest alongside the sense that it cannot be attained, that there is always some demand or anxiety or distraction that won't let them go.

This experience was vividly depicted in Graham Greene's 1960 novel *A Burnt-Out Case* (the title likely helped bring the term into general circulation). Greene parallels the mental and spiritual burnout of his architect protagonist, Querry, with the 'burnt-out cases' of leprosy he witnesses in a Congolese leper colony. Just as feeling in the limb stumps of the lepers around him has been extinguished, so Querry believes he's 'come to the end of desire' and is waiting out the rest of his life in a state of weary indifference, his emotions cut off like amputated limbs.

Yet for as long as he's alive, Querry cannot 'come to an end'. There will always be something or someone to stir or disturb him. The consulting room resounds with echoes of this bind: the patient's wish for a cessation of all the feelings that intrude on his peace, alongside the painful awareness that the world is still there and that the emails and voicemails and other demands and distractions have been accumulating, even during our fifty-minute session.

For Greene, the burnout's malaise is fundamentally a spiritual one, a draining of his faith in a meaningful universe. Burnout is a modern, secularized iteration of what the medieval world called acedia, or 'spiritual crisis' – a genealogical link confirmed by Schaffner in her history of exhaustion.

Medieval theologians derived the term from the Greek word for indifference or apathy. It was the most spiritually perilous of states, for it corroded not simply this or that article of faith, but the basis of faith. To experience the world as poor in meaning and hope was to empty it of God's presence. This posed a mortal threat to monasteries, convents and other religious communities, and could sap the spiritual and physical reserves required to keep them alive.

Losing the single-minded focus of the devotee, the acediac monk was victim of a lethargic aversion to activity and a state of agitated distraction. He lacked the will, discipline and energy that drove faith and prayer, killing time with aimless activities, like idle chat and snacking, that exacerbated his anxiety and obstructed his contact with God. 'Just like neurasthenics and the burned-out,' writes Schaffner, 'those afflicted by acedia vacillate between sluggishness and restlessness.'

The figure of the monk remained a constant in understanding lethargy, even as the naming and understanding of the affliction changed. The diagnosticians of the late nineteenth century coined the term 'neurasthenia' to designate the same malaise, now conceived as the overburdening of the nervous system by the daily onrush of stimuli – muscular, mental, sensory, opiate and sexual – generated by modern urban, industrial society.

Among the most celebrated neurasthenic case studies is the sickly aristocrat Jean Des Esseintes, the fictional protagonist of J.-K. Huysmans's classic 1884 novel *A Rebours* ('Against Nature'), whose tragicomic trials centre on his desperate attempts to return his body and mind, ravaged by sexual and narcotic debauchery, to a state of undisturbed peace.

Des Esseintes transforms the ground floor of his villa in the Paris suburbs into a massive *trompe-l'œil* that combines the appearance of monastic asceticism with the feel of decadent luxuriousness. Des Esseintes himself, hints Huysmans, is a modern version of the acediac eremite, or monk: 'Like an eremite, he was ripe for solitude, exhausted by life and expecting nothing more of it; like a monk again, he was overwhelmed by an immense weariness, by a longing for peace and quiet, by a desire to have no further contact with the heathen . . .'

A patient who fantasizes about a temporary retreat into death or disappearance is usually speaking from this same state of agitated weariness, an ambiguous zone between starting and stopping. They too are longing for a total reprieve from the surrounding world and the charged internal states it arouses.

Freud, following a suggestion of the British psychoanalyst Barbara Low, named this longing the 'Nirvana principle', acknowledging the Buddhism that long preceded him. In various Buddhist traditions, nirvana – 'extinguishing' or 'quenching' – is the mind's ideal horizon, a radical detachment from the three fires of passion, hatred and delusion that animate and trouble the everyday self.

Rr for me was an image of this benign indifference, released as he was from the daily torments of feeling. His twitches registered not love, hatred or concern but the pure, neutral fact of being alive. Rr spoke to a yearning in me to undo the knots of desire and dependence in which life entangles us. I intuited in him the blissful indifference that had bewitched poets and mystics down the ages, the psychic and sensory numbness extolled by Keats in his 'Ode on Indolence':

> Pain had no sting, and pleasure's wreath no flower:
> O, why did ye not melt, and leave my sense
> Unhaunted quite of all but – nothingness?

Keats knew that we cannot make a home in this nothingness and that the intrusions of pain and pleasure lurk ominously in the wings. The eventful lives we lead as differentiated individuals are a world apart from the anonymity of the rabbit's existence. And yet we are all secretly intimate with this animal inertia. It is this that speaks to us in Keats's evocation of the indolence at our very core. Concealed in the anxious pursuit of our desires is a craving for their extinction.

This craving, or 'desire for non-desire', in the words of the French psychoanalyst Piera Aulagnier, is a 'major scandal', the most puzzling enigma of our inner lives. How could it be that our deepest desire is to put an end to desire? How does such a claim square with the blind tenacity with which so many of us pursue our passions?

'The desire for non-desire': the phrase, rather than setting the two terms in contradiction to one another, brings out their mutual entanglement. It points us to a frustrating paradox of human experience, that even the wish for nothing is still a wish.

Another medieval monk, in this case the twelfth-century Japanese Buddhist Kamo no Chōmei, captures the paradox in a brief and beautiful memoir of his attempt to carve out 'a little safe shelter in this world'. He tells of the ten-foot-square mobile hut he built himself and settled on Mount Hino, a refuge from the menaces of the natural and human worlds. Living in the city, he had witnessed how ordinary lives were bedevilled by fires and floods, whirlwinds and earthquakes, apocalyptic phenomena that could wipe out entire populations, in addition to the petty caprices of the ruling class. These calamities showed Chōmei the vanity of the desires which attach us to worldly existence. In the hard-won peace of his hut, he could retreat into the quiet joys of gardening, music and walking, and take in the sublimities of the surrounding mountain landscape.

As it turned out, things weren't so simple. Having sung the pleasures of his mountain idyll over the preceding pages, Chōmei closes the memoir with a stinging self-reproach: 'The Buddha's essential teaching is to relinquish all attachment. This fondness for my hut I now see must be an error, and my attachment to a life of seclusion and peace is an impediment to my rebirth. How could I waste my days like this, describing useless pleasures?'

It is a bitterly comic irony: withdraw from all attachments only to realize you've become attached to your withdrawal. You can't seek non-desire without getting caught in the snares of desire. This is why I envied Rr – without effort or self-consciousness, he could live without aims or projects; whereas for me even living without projects had to be a project. This is what makes Chōmei so frustrated. To renounce all desires is very different from never having had any in the first place, as different as human from rabbit.

Rr, as far as I could see, was constitutionally indifferent, never having acquired the capacity or inclination for judgements or preferences. His serene emptiness is denied to the human being at the moment of birth and can't be attained even by a master of the highest spiritual discipline in the solitude of a mountain retreat.

And if not in a mountain retreat, then certainly not in our networked world, where we experience an indifference more akin to the Duracell Bunny's than to Rr's, as mindless as the real rabbit's but lacking his untroubled quiescence. In our culture of perpetual work and distraction, our indifference takes the form not of nirvanic peace but of manic deadness, or what the writer Ivor Southwood calls 'non-stop inertia', a state of perpetual motion concealing the 'underlying stasis' of our souls.

The desire for non-desire is today considered (to recall Aulagnier's phrase) the 'major scandal' of social as well as psychic life. What more scandalous response is there to the white noise of social media than to declare yourself not bothered. Permanent mental activity, enforced by the screens that surround us at work and in the home, have made an outlaw of silence and indifference. In the words of the Italian social theorist Franco Berardi, we inhabit 'a cognitive space overloaded with nervous incentives to act', the non-stop inertia of the Duracell Bunny rather than the organic inertia of the real one.

We are bombarded daily with an avalanche of data and stimulation, which exceeds our capacity to process or navigate it. If I open my computer now, I can be travelling within seconds through a landscape of far-right campaigns, pay-day loan companies, celebrity diet secrets, S&M fantasies and jihadist networks; enter one of many social media applications and follow, like, comment, update, upload and link to a limitless array of friends and strangers; or download one of many dating apps and swipe through never-ending vistas of beauty, sadness, guile, anger, vice and hope.

Our new neurasthenic landscape calls upon us perpetually to choose, to agree, to join, to prefer. Under these conditions, it is near impossible to sustain even the most minimal contact with the pitch of our own desire. Subjected to what the Slovene philosopher and social theorist Renata Salecl has called 'the tyranny of choice', our faculty of desire, like a damaged internal organ, burns out, shuts down and begs to be spared the crippling anxiety of choosing.

The consulting room confirms the force of this daily tyranny. Every day, prospective and current patients talk over the impossible dilemmas of marriage, career, family and friendship. This churn of thoughts, often accompanied more by appeals for me to extricate them from indecision and ambivalence, rarely brings relief or resolution. Indecision, together with its accompanying anxiety and enervation, has become the soul's ether, the element to which it has adapted itself.

There's nothing new or unusual in a patient bringing a life dilemma to the consulting room. Indecision is a good deal older than psychoanalysis, as old as human freedom itself. Yet when I hear these painful rehearsals of the same impasses, my analyst's chair feels like a listening post for a malaise which is specific to our time. This malaise is audible in the monotone weariness of the voices that speak them. I sometimes feel that this vocal tone expresses the secret aim of my patients – not to make a choice, with all the loss and upheaval this will entail, but to do nothing, to reach a zero point of action, a state of non-desire.

In recent years there has been a plethora of popular books,

articles and TED talks addressing the ever greater proliferation of public and private decisions that confront us in the networked age, suggesting remedies for our inertia in the face of the choices they impose, offering to usher us through the thicket of our anxious uncertainty to the discovery of what we really want. None of these contemplate the possibility that what we really want is to be allowed to choose nothing. So thoroughly internalized is the spirit of compulsory activity governing our culture that we cannot let ourselves hear or even imagine the wish to put a stop to it. The consulting room provides, if nothing else, one place where that wish can be heard. In early-morning and evening sessions, before or after the patient's long day in the high-pressure cauldron of corporate finance or law, I've heard it expressed in the same flat voice: 'I'm so tired, I may just fall asleep'; 'I'm fed up with it all. I just want to stop.'

The words I hear in the consulting room are frequently cross-hatched by words (and images and feelings) etched into my mind by both life and literature. When I hear this wish to sleep, for example, to nullify all demands for action, the refrain of Herman Melville's cadaverous legal copyist Bartleby comes to me unbidden: 'I would prefer not to.' More than an association, the phrase is a kind of gift from my unconscious to my conscious ear, hinting at how to hear what the patient is saying.

These messages from the interior are embedded in the memory of my relationships with the books in which I found them. If the famous phrase from 'Bartleby, the Scrivener' comes to mind, so too do the few sultry months of inactivity between school and university when, suddenly bereft of aim or direction, my bookshelf became a fragile life raft on an unnavigable sea.

When I left the A-level exam room for the last time, I looked into the blazing June sun and saw a cosmic affirmation of my plans for the year to come. Following the trail blazed by many before me, I would work, save and travel before returning, brimming with newly minted knowledge of the world's many ways, to take up my university place.

Within a few days, my confidence had yielded to blind panic as I came face to face with the painful truth that imagining and doing are not the same thing. I'd devised my gap-year plan without a thought for the business of actually carrying it out, and my complacency had caught up with me. Having failed to secure meaningful work, I was looking down the barrel of nine months of the exasperation of retail managers with hopelessly airy types like me, nine months during which I might save just enough of my risible hourly pay for a return flight to Hanoi or Bratislava. I had no companion or, it dawned on me, any desire to travel. I visualized myself wandering the vestibules of Rome, the wats of Chiang Mai, the beaches of Goa, and felt only the heavy downward pull of indifference.

When I phoned my university and was told I could take up my place that autumn, my lungs filled with sweet relief, commingled with sour defeat. Now what? For the ten weeks before term started, I was free to do anything or be anywhere. I floated aimlessly through London, falling out of bed at noon to wander towards one park or another, carrying one book or another. From my current place in the middle of my fifth decade, deep in the mire of adult responsibility, it's hard to imagine an existence more blissfully in tune with the blank contentment of Rr's daily life. But for my adolescent self, that expanse of solitary days under the white glare of the sky was a plunge into depressive confusion, an unaccountable fall from the grace of self-certainty.

It was a good time to find Bartleby. He appeared in a volume of Melville's stories. It sits to my left as I write this, a 1961 New American Library paperback bearing the chiselled bust of Billy

Budd, its pages pulling away from their binding so I daren't open them at an angle of more than forty-five degrees.

A sudden breeze had woken me earlier than usual that day. Shortly after, I pulled the book from its resting place atop a row of *Biggles* and *Famous Five*s and began reading in the morning shade of the patio. *Billy Budd, Sailor* seemed long and oppressively nautical. I skipped to 'Bartleby, the Scrivener'.

Towards the end of the story the narrator, an unnamed attorney, describes himself as 'thunderstruck ... like the man who, pipe in mouth, was killed one cloudless afternoon long ago in Virginia by summer lightning; at his own warm open window he was killed, and remained leaning out there upon the dreamy afternoon, till someone touched him, when he fell'.

I can remember vividly the effect of these lines, which had me catatonic with fright and excitement. It struck me that I'd joined this chain of thunderstruck men. I had been the attorney for as long as I could remember, guided like him by 'the profound conviction that the easiest way of life is the best', seeking always to restore equilibrium at the slightest hint of its disturbance. This was just what I'd done in cancelling my gap year, as though, intuiting the impending train wreck of my life's story, I had pulled the nearest emergency cord and braked just in time.

Like the attorney, I felt bound by the imperative to keep life going on as usual, not to suffer any turbulence 'to invade my peace'. But I was pointedly unlike the attorney in other respects. I couldn't recognize his compulsion to neutralize all conflict in the name of business as usual, or his advocacy of non-stop inertia, of an undisturbed flow of activity allowing of no interruption.

I felt more like Bartleby, refusing to be absorbed into this tyrannizing flow. From the moment he arrives at the office, the cadaverous, 'pitiably neat' young man casts a shadow over this clockwork universe, in spite of his initial insatiable appetite for copying. The problem for the attorney is that his new employee is not 'cheerfully industrious' but writes 'silently, palely, mechanically', exposing an inhuman deadness at the heart of the attorney's seamlessly articulated world.

And then, without warning or explanation, the work stops. When the attorney asks him to examine a paper, Bartleby replies, 'in a singularly mild, firm voice . . . "I would prefer not to"'. With those words, he announces his withdrawal from copying – a preliminary, as it turns out, to his eventual withdrawal from all work and activity.

Since the story's publication in *Putnam's Magazine* in 1853, philosophers and literary critics have puzzled over the meaning of Bartleby's refrain. But all this speculation only demonstrates that he outfoxes every attempt at definitive interpretation. Bartleby is immune to understanding; there is no getting hold of him. He is, observes the attorney, 'alone, absolutely alone. A bit of wreck in the mid-Atlantic.' Only he's not in the mid-Atlantic but at its dry edge, and far from bobbing harmlessly in the oceanic drift, he is quietly corroding the world around him. With his mild insistence on preferring not to, Bartleby collapses the foundations of his world as ruthlessly as Samson dislodges the pillars of the temple.

With Bartleby immobile in a screened corner of the office, the attorney flees to alternative premises, leaving the new tenants exposed to the rage of an angry mob. To prefer not to is to say neither yes nor no, and this quiet disturbance of the binary logic of positive and negative has the violent force of an earthquake. In declining to assent or refuse, Bartleby mires those around him in his grey fog, paralysing their capacity to think or act.

The attorney lives in a world in which everything is expected to slot into place, much like the world I'd lived in before running up against my unsuspected inner Bartleby and being cast adrift in my own mid–Atlantic. I was thunderstruck by the revelation that the course of the world isn't guaranteed, that things need not proceed in the same straight line simply because that's what I expected them to do. Like any good therapeutic intervention, the story didn't so much cure my depression as open up my curiosity.

The unspoken but inviolable rule of the 1980s Duracell ad is that we never see the Bunny running down; just at the point we think he might, he springs back into life, powering through his own threatened demise. That we might as easily stop as continue, that we aren't duty-bound to become the pale copyists of our own lives, forever taking the same steps in the same direction, hardly ever seems to occur to us. This possibility is Bartleby's 'mild, firm' bolt of lightning, the source of the story's startling resonance for me and its many obsessive readers. More than a story of mere defiance or refusal, it hints at some impulse in us to enter a zone of indifference, where the obligation to judge, choose, decide is suspended indefinitely.

And this is why Bartleby 'invades my peace' when I hear a patient say they want to crawl into a hole or to become invisible or to be allowed to stop caring or wanting or feeling, or to remain in a state of indecision. They have reached the point at which to go on as usual feels uncomfortably like going through the motions, copying rather than living one's own life. At the threshold of that fateful summer, my ill-planned gap year suddenly struck me as a stultifying mimicry of someone else's gap year. Only rather than mobilize the insight to forge some new and different enterprise, I let it hustle me into the dubious safety of a no less familiar script.

Perhaps what we call burnout is precisely a crisis of this familiar script, a feeling of sudden alienation from the role with which we've so long been identified. A protracted crisis of this kind befell Melville himself. The commercial success of his first two novels, *Typee* and *Omoo*, brought intense pressure from his publishers, readership and growing family to repeat the generic formula. Driven instead to expand the boundaries and possibilities of the novel, he lost readers and income. Presaging Bartleby, Melville gave up copying his own work.

But – and again like Bartleby – in giving up copying, he courted disaster. Either he could write the crowd-pleasing books the world wanted and end up hating himself, or he could write the strange books he wanted to write and end up penniless. 'Dollars damn me,' he complained to his friend Nathaniel Hawthorne in 1851. 'What I feel most moved to write – that is banned, – it will not pay. Yet, write altogether the *other* way I cannot.'

Melville's way of dealing with this impossible dilemma – to choose a path (in this case art over commerce) without resolving his gnawing doubt, to renounce 'the calm, the coolness, the silent grass-growing mood in which a man *ought* always to compose' – was courageous and very difficult.

So difficult that most of us prefer to sink into the stasis of indecision. In my consulting room, such impossible dilemmas often conceal a desperate appeal: tell me what to do, cause the sky to fall in, do something, anything, so I don't have to choose. With this appeal, a patient might seek to fend off both the unendurable agitation that comes with not choosing and the irremediable loss and pain implied in choosing. Our predicament is that we care about, want, prefer in so many diverse and contradictory ways that we can't help wishing we didn't, can't help getting snared in the desire for non-desire. If only we could be rabbits.

Bartleby's attorney is an adept at making the world he sees coincide with the world he desires.

Before Bartleby arrives, he employs two copyists, Turkey and Nippers, both of whom are prone to fits of irritability and nervousness, the latter before noon, the former after. The attorney remarks of these half-time employees on full-time salaries that 'their fits relieved each other like guards. When Nippers' was on, Turkey's was off; and *vice versa*. This was a good natural arrangement under the circumstances.' In seeing the problem through this magically reparative lens, the attorney eliminates the negative, conjuring a seamless whole out of two fractured and fractious halves.

Unlike his colleagues, Bartleby doesn't disrupt, complain or protest. He stops working, but not in the name of some right or principle (for dignity, say, or against exploitation). The phrase 'I would prefer not to' announces a withdrawal from the world of intelligible motives, from shared rules of communication. I found this withdrawal hard to endure in a rabbit. In a young man it would reduce me, as it did the attorney, to stunned silence.

Bartleby's withdrawal brings to mind the Boston psychologist Edward Tronick's famous 'still face' experiment, in which a mother engages in lively face-to-face play with her baby, attending lovingly to all his vocal and physical cues. She then abruptly turns stony, devoid of expression in the face of all his attempts to bring her back to life. His initial agitation turns rapidly to despair. His posture collapses, he turns his face aside, a picture of bewildered hopelessness, until the mother resumes her previous responsiveness. If we were to attempt a translation of this baby's experience into adult language, we might hear in the baby's despair a realization that the world in which he'd hitherto been so invested had revealed itself as a hollow fiction. The same world which a moment ago seemed so alive, so various, so brimming with live objects to identify, differentiate and care about, has become a coldly indifferent wasteland.

Hearing Bartleby's 'I would prefer not to', we experience something like this baby's shock. Our unthinking faith in the meaningfulness of the world and of our actions falls away, making visible a shadow world in which it doesn't matter whether life goes on or comes to a halt. I sometimes wonder if this is what the attorney is groping towards with the lament – 'Ah, Bartleby! Ah, humanity!' – that closes the story.

Some commentators have caught in Bartleby's refrain an echo of Pyrrho, the founding figure of philosophical scepticism, who was born around the middle of the fourth century BC. Pyrrho's name and ideas were claimed for the first century school of Pyrrhonism, later to become known as scepticism. His life and teaching exist for us only in the second- and third-hand transmissions of later writers, who inevitably interpreted both to suit their own interests and agendas. Travelling with Alexander the Great through the East, he encountered Indian mystics and philosophers, who had a profound effect on his thinking.

Much of the folklore of Pyrrho's life was gathered over five centuries later in Diogenes Laertius's famed but unreliable *Lives of Eminent Philosophers*. The disputed anecdotes have Pyrrho wandering through the world, taking no care to avoid the hazards of 'wagons and precipices and everything of that sort', from which he was saved only by the solicitous friends following him close behind.

His indifference to danger, it's said, was fully matched by his indifference to drudgery. In a society which placed the greatest value on nobility and high-mindedness, he would do laundry, clean furniture and take poultry to the marketplace. We're told 'he carried his indifference so far that he even washed a pig'. Pyrrho evidently lived the ataraxia (unconcern) he taught. During a fierce sea storm, he remained calm and comforted his frightened fellow passengers by staying on deck to eat a pig, 'saying that it became a wise man to preserve an untroubled spirit'.

Pig, cow, rabbit – these are the blank animal screens onto which we project desire for the non-desire we ourselves can never attain. This wisdom, Pyrrho suggests, lies in his intuiting the truth of *ou mallon*, that any given entity is '*no more* one thing than another'. With this phrase, all judgements and all determinations are suspended at a stroke, and all clear distinctions collapse. As the later Pyrrhonists saw it, 'a thing can never be apprehended in and by itself, but only in connection with something else. Hence all things are unknowable.'

If all things are unknowable, there is no special reason to halt at the cliff edge, or to pay more attention to the storm than the trough; the instinct for life over death becomes mere prejudice. If life is a condition of irremediable ignorance, it is folly to care about it, to prefer rather than prefer not to. Wisdom lies instead in a progressive divestment from life, though it's worth recalling Chōmei's caution at this point – even as we try to detach ourselves from life we somehow fall more deeply into it.

'According to some authorities,' says Diogenes Laertius, 'the end proposed by the Sceptics is insensibility; according to others gentleness.' Pyrrho is said to have striven always to maintain the same insensible countenance, regardless of how he was feeling or what was going on around him. His aspiration to total indifference fascinates me, though lurking somewhere in my fascination is a baby's terror of the still face and the void it exposes.

No one today is spared the shrill imperative voiced by politicians, advertisers and happiness gurus to be active, responsible and positive.

In *Non-Stop Inertia,* a vivid personal account of today's persecutory welfare culture, Ivor Southwood described how, as a claimant of Jobseekers' Allowance, he was required to keep a detailed diary of his efforts to find work, showing evidence of his having done at least '"three positive things per week"', on pain of losing his benefits. Much less important than the content of those three things, he suggests, is the documented fact of doing them. Any deviation from this enforced optimism, any failure to fulfil his quota of positive things, threatened some unspecified punitive measure. However low or defeated he might feel, the jobseeker must adapt himself to the order of compulsory cheeriness.

This culture induces lethargic indifference, then banishes its expression. Our exhaustion has been rendered unspeakable by the persecuting rage of a political class and mass media intent on casting it as a ruse of coddled malingerers, wasters, freeloaders and losers who want to live easy lives at the expense of others. Many of us may be feeling the same inertia, the same chronic seepage of meaning and desire, but in the absence of any humane or curious ear to listen to it, few of us have dared voice, let alone act upon, it.

Perhaps this is how the spirit of Bartleby slowly insinuates itself into our inner lives; denied a direct outlet, inertia expresses itself in ever more extreme forms. The compliant Duracell Bunny will eventually run down; the skeletal young stranger who enters the office and 'silently, palely, mechanically' churns out copy is bound one day to come to a halt. At a certain point, the gap between the relentless onrush of the world's demands and our own capacity to meet them becomes unsustainable.

Succumbing to the indifference and lethargy of burnout may seem like a negative, even nihilistic response to our overworked and accelerated culture. But at the very least it registers a profound discontent, a refusal or inability to continue running blindly towards that culture's hazy promises and ideals.

Going further, Graham Greene points to the ethical possibilities of burnout through his protagonist Querry, who renounces his grandiose architectural designs, in which he can no longer find meaning or virtue, to embrace the more modest and tangible aim of building functioning hospitals for the disease-stricken communities of central Africa.

Querry's exhausted disgust with the acquisitive ideals of the consumerist society around him finds ever more resonant echoes in the discontents of our own time. In recent years Japan, for so long held up as the model of a productive and efficient economy and culture, has seen this inertial spirit take root on a mass scale.

During the early 1990s Saitō Tamaki, a young, psychoanalytically oriented Japanese psychiatrist working as a therapist in a hospital to the east of Tokyo, found himself inundated by requests for consultation from parents of children who had become chronically withdrawn. The stories were strikingly similar even as they proliferated; adolescents and young adults, largely though not exclusively male, were giving up school, work or any other engagement with the world outside and retreating into the privacy of their bedrooms.

In the years that followed, Tamaki devoted himself to clinical and theoretical research into these young people's lives, discovering in the process an epidemic of social withdrawal or *shakaiteki hikikomori*, affecting as many as a million individuals and their families, a figure eventually confirmed in a 2010 survey by the Japanese Cabinet Office. With regular media appearances and the publication of his best-selling book *Hikikomori* in 1998, Tamaki conferred on these lives, now known popularly as *hikikomori*, a place in the Japanese public conversation they have held ever since.

The *hikikomori* phenomenon was first comprehensively documented by the American journalist Michael Zielenziger in his 2006 book *Shutting Out the Sun*, which ascribed the malaise to a specifically Japanese economic and social pathology. Zielenziger saw Japan's rigidly disciplined industrial 'monoculture', along with its culture of shame and principle of *sekentei*, or concern with how one appears to society, as chronically maladapted to the new globalist virtues of flexibility, innovation and individual flair. *Hikikomori*, he argued, were the expression of an impotent and desperate protest in the name of the stifled right of individual difference and dissent.

Tamaki, however, while recognizing the familial and social tendencies, in particular the ethic of unconditional duty of parental care and the cultural force of shame, which gave rise to a specifically Japanese hermetic mode of withdrawal, questioned Zielenziger's claim that this was a phenomenon unknown outside Japan. Stimulating Western professional interest in the phenomenon, he argued that withdrawal is a universal tendency that takes different forms in different contexts. He pointed to a parallel population of so-called NEETs (Not in Education, Employment or Training) in the Anglophone countries, an invisible underclass more likely to be long-term welfare recipients or on the streets than secreted in the family home, as in Japan.

In his book, Tamaki takes us into the everyday psychopathology of social withdrawal. Perhaps the most striking feature of the inner life of the *hikikomori* is the sense of perpetual disquiet. Talking to these young men and women revealed less pacified indolence than tormented inhibition. 'In reality,' he writes, 'they are spending their days assaulted by feelings of impatience and despair over their inability to participate in society.' The difference from the classically depressive picture is that *hikikomori* are less likely to indulge in the false consolations of resigned defeatism. On the contrary, they are perpetually resolving to start again as soon as possible. Barely has this resolution been made, however, than it confronts the sufferer with his failure to carry it out. The impulse towards a new beginning 'just transforms into irritation and despair'.

The *hikikomori* are caught in the hellish non-place of the burnout, unable to attain either the peace of the zero state or the gratification of the active state. Like the tramps of Samuel

Beckett's *Waiting for Godot*, they are condemned to repeat the same sequence of resolving to go and not moving. Social withdrawal, Tamaki concludes, is the exemplary pathology. What keeps the *hikikomori* suspended in this purgatorial grey zone is the illusion, fostered by the Japanese educational system and by the consumer capitalism in which that system is embedded, of their 'infinite possibilities'. In order to do or be something, one has to relinquish the freedom to do or be most other things, and this circumscription of possibility is what they cannot accept. The *hikikomori* can preserve their limitless freedom only by placing themselves in prison.

Are *hikikomori* the collateral damage of our culture of permanent activity and distraction, or an advance guard showing us its only logical universal outcome? Is this culture making *hikikomori* of us all? Granted, most of us haven't taken their drastic measures. But there is a secret corner in all of us in profound solidarity with them, desperately seeking the unbroken peace we can't attain, at least as long as life has us in its grip.

∼

The person sitting at the edge of the armchair of a strange waiting room, waiting for their prospective analyst to open the door for the first time, bears a burden of hopes, anxieties and fantasies about who they're going to meet. Perhaps this is why they so often look startled, as though to say, you're not what I expected, or you're just what I expected, or you're kind of what I expected, only . . . Their expression is the involuntary, noiseless whisper of an apprehension laid to rest (or not), of a curiosity satisfied (or not) – in any case, a signal not to forget that something big is at stake here, even if neither of us yet knows what that is.

Unless, like Sofia, they come as though primed for a game of analytic poker, seeking to outdo the psychoanalyst's surgical neutrality by betraying precisely nothing. Sofia's face lodged no complaint, made no demand, expressed no wish, remained resolutely unaltered by its encounter with mine as she shuffled unhurriedly into the room.

Unexpectedly, I felt a weariness overtake me as she answered my opening question: what brought you to me? She wasn't avoiding eye contact, but gazing with a glassy coolness around the room. It felt as though my presence was just another, indifferent surface for her. Her voice dragged. It conveyed not sadness, which is live and palpable, but weariness, a grim worldly irony.

It was a surprise to hear details of her external life: an impressive career in urban planning that had seen her work in difficult, far-flung locations across the world. It was hard to match the creative energy and exertion demanded by such a life to the sunken figure in black seated opposite me.

It took me some conscious effort to hear the content of her words, to distinguish them from the drone carrying them to my ear. She told me she was in the grip of an overwhelming depression that had set in some weeks after she'd arrived in London. I caught the first discernible uplift in tone as she revealed those first weeks had actually been kind of euphoric. She'd come from a two-year stint in Berlin to take up a new position with a fair degree of prestige. The prospect of an end to the precarity of short-term contracts, coupled with the excitement of discovering the city, had induced a mood of hope and anticipation.

Then, around four months ago, she'd woken up with a leaden feeling, a sense of inner dullness that coloured the whole world grey. If her colleagues were struck by her abrupt withdrawal from the daily banter and after-work drinks, they didn't say so. 'But Londoners are kind of like that, right?'

She was hardly new to depression, but this felt different. In past episodes, she was kept afloat by some quiet sense of being somehow more than her depression. 'I knew it would pass, so I could tell myself it wasn't real. I don't know why, but every time I try to tell myself that now, another voice takes over and says, bullshit, *this* is the only thing that's real. Everything else is just a cute story.'

Her solution was to plunge into work, or rather overwork. 'The weird thing about doing so much is that at a certain point it feels like you're doing nothing. You stop loving the work, or hating it, you kind of don't even notice you're doing it.' It was this permanent state of mindless overactivity that had been holding her together, but she wasn't sure how much longer she could continue like this.

I wondered if her remorseless despair concealed some child-hood trauma, some deep fault line in her inner history. More accurately, and uncomfortably, I hoped it did. I needed to hear the story that would justify her overbearing emptiness, give it some semblance of shape and substance.

Instead she baffled me with an account of her youth in a loving family in a prosperous suburb of Sydney. Her exceptional smartness, creativity and energy were evident from very early on, nurtured by parents who shuttled her tirelessly from school to ballet, art class and piano, providing homework support, nutri-tious meals and cheerleading along the way. Their unvarying message, often conveyed explicitly, was that she could be and do anything she wanted. It is, of course, a (if not the) pervasive message of our culture of achievement, whether in the form of Disney's sunny assurances, Nike's brash imperative or the slo-gans of self-styled management gurus and executive coaches. But Sofia's parents personalized it for her, put emotional flesh on its hollow bones, so that it wasn't merely a generalized formula beamed in from the outside, but a demand stalking her from within.

As she grew older, her parents were careful not to impose their preferred educational and career paths on her. On the contrary, they were brimming with curiosity about her own thoughts about the future, unstinting in their willingness to facilitate work experience, book university open days and introduce her to a diverse range of professionals. Their zeal to explore every passing enthusiasm or vague aspiration made it increasingly difficult to discern where her own wishes stopped and theirs began.

It is neither assuring nor restful to feel you are exempt from the limits imposed by your own capacities and the world's reality. It is different from the demands of the superego, the internal agency that speaks the forbidding dictates of authority – parent, teacher, boss – in your ear. What the social theorist Byung-Chul Han calls our 'achievement society' eschews the force of prohibitions and demands, the ideology of 'you must', in favour of the exhortations of 'you can'.

This is the injunction of what Freud called the 'ego ideal', the imprint in us of our parents' unconscious conviction, transmitted to us from birth, in our unblemished perfection. To our parents we are, in Freud's wry phrase, 'His [or Her] Majesty the Baby'. We counter the bad news, which must sooner or later reach us, that we're not quite so perfect as they used to think by setting up within ourselves an image of that original, now lost perfection we once saw reflected back at us in our parents' loving smiles.

The ego ideal is a strange and ambiguous taskmaster. Setting itself up in us as a loving ally that only wants the best for us, it is harder to resist or defy than the superego (which Freud introduced a decade after the ego ideal). Where the superego denies us what we want, the ego ideal, like the tyrannically loving parent, only wants what we want, perhaps more than we do ourselves. Its exhortations are liable to leave us forever jumping through hoops, anxiously eyeing the next target, perpetually wary of falling short of where one could be. In the shadow of the ego ideal, Han suggests, '*the feeling of having achieved a goal never occurs*' (the emphasis is his).

Sofia would complain that the life she was living moment to moment felt unreal to her. Only the future really mattered, for that was where her ideal life resided. 'If I just wait a little longer,' she remarked in a tone of wry despondency, 'there'll be this magically transformative event and everything will come right.'

This belief, she gradually came to realize, had taken a suffocating hold on her life: 'The longer I live in wait for this magical event, the more I'm not living this life, which is sad, given it's the only one I've got.' Forever anticipating this future event, Sofia had come to view life in the present with contempt, a kind of travesty of the perfect life she could have. The job she was now doing, the man she was now seeing, the place where she was now living were all pale shadows of the ideal she was chasing. The problem with an ideal is that nothing in reality can ever come close to it; it tantalizes us with a future that by its nature can never be realized.

Feeling exhausted and emptied by this chase, she retreated into two contradictory impulses. The first was a compulsion to work, to let the Hydra-headed beast of the office eat up all her time and inner space. But shadowing this compulsion, frequently accompanied by chronic insomnia, was a yearning for the opposite. She would fantasize in our sessions about going home and sleeping, about waking only to periods of blissfully catatonic inactivity over a stream of endless, undifferentiated days and weeks. Occasionally she would in fact steal the odd day in such a state, only for a rising panic to jolt her out of it and back into work. In frenzied activity and depressive inertia, she found twin strategies for escaping the dilemmas of her life in the present.

This escape manifested above all in a paralysis before every decision, as though there could be nothing worse than to choose one thing and so lose the possibility of others. Decisions, after all, involve an inevitable moment of negativity; they intrude brutally into the omniscient fantasy that we can be, do or have whatever we want. As Sofia vividly showed me, the maintenance of all possible futures at the expense of 'the only life I've got' is intensely debilitating, the paralysis of a self ransomed to its own ideal.

Beyond the inevitable themes of her everyday life – her precarious relationships with partner, friends, colleagues, her difficulty resisting any demands and requests, her compulsive fitness routines, her chilliness towards her parents on the phone, as surprising to her as to them – our discussions over six years of three times weekly psychoanalysis returned insistently to her relationship to psychoanalysis itself, and to me.

As the months and years went by, the knots of her indecision seemed only to grow and tighten around her. She began to wonder how long I could put up with her obsessive turning over of the same conundrums, how soon before I begged her to stop punishing us both with the same circular ruminations? 'You must be so darn bored of me,' she said, not without the trace of a smile in her voice.

In spite of the accuracy and insight of what she'd said, I wasn't. The perpetual iteration of the same dilemmas was distressing to witness, a punishment it sometimes felt she needed to visit on me as well as herself. But the dead end of her circular reasoning was always enlivened by the creative bite of her language, the ever more intricate metaphors she invented to characterize her predicament. 'My life,' she said, 'is this great colonial house, and I'm its neglectful tenant. I leave rusted cars on the front lawn and never sweep the porch. Maybe someday it'll be condemned.' Her allusions to books, films, songs, buildings always had the quality of curiosity too unselfconsciously alive to seem anxious or contrived.

She loved our sessions, she blurted out one day with a poignant clumsiness. She specifically loved having three hours a week in which she had no agenda to follow, no demands to answer to beyond the urgings and impulses of her own mind. She then quickly contradicted herself. 'But sometimes I'm convinced I'm doing it wrong, that you'll become exasperated with me for thinking too much, or not thinking enough or thinking the wrong thing or the wrong way ...'

'So the session you enjoy,' I replied, 'is spoiled, like everything else, by being turned into a test you can pass spectacularly or fail abjectly?' She laughed lightly and said, 'That's basically how my life is spoiled more or less every hour of the day. I barely know how to do anything without wondering if I'm doing it well enough.'

She paused. 'Except, I kind of feel I'm learning how to do that here.'

Like Pyrrho before him, Rr lived in blank indifference to the dangers lurking at the edges of his world. He had no solicitous friend to prevent him from squeezing out of his run one morning, or to block his oblivious shuffle into the path of a waiting fox. I can't help wondering guiltily whether he maintained his Pyrrhonian equanimity as he looked up and saw the gaping maw of his nemesis.

I certainly didn't when I found him. But then even Pyrrho's equanimity wasn't invulnerable. When needled for his discomposure in the face of a canine attack, he replied 'that it was a difficult thing entirely to put off humanity'. This difficult thing is the lot of all of us. Caught in the avalanche of excitements, possibilities and dangers that assail us daily, lapine indifference eludes us.

Like the *hikikomori*, I know the yearning for a reprieve from the world in which things happen, in which one is called on to play a part, do stuff. Sometimes I can even experience it, sink for just a moment into the painless, pleasureless nothingness of Keatsian indolence. But the fox is always there, prowling on the other side of my lowered eyelids, ready to spoil it all.

Ah, Rr. Ah, humanity.

'PEOPLE ARE WORKING EVERY MINUTE':
ANDY WARHOL

Among Andy Warhol's most disturbing images is one we'll never see. In 1949 the fledgling commercial artist, newly arrived in Manhattan, painted a series of large canvases which were later lost or destroyed. One, based on a harrowing photograph known as 'Bloody Saturday', originally published in *Life* magazine, showed a lone baby sat among the ashen wreckage of Shanghai's South Station during the Japanese bombing campaign of 1937.

The baby is propped upright at the edge of the platform, his skin blackened, clothing shredded, mouth fixed in a cry of despair as he stares into the ruined vista ahead. According to Warhol's biographer Victor Bockris, 'the painting was horrific yet surprisingly decorative', executed in what would come to be his trademark 'blotted-line technique and pastel colours'.

The painting foreshadows the celebrated 1962–4 Death and Disaster series, but with a striking difference; where in the later images of electric chairs and road accidents, human beings are either ominously absent or grainy corpses indifferently merged into the mechanical wreckage, the Shanghai baby brings us into the traumatic presence of raw and incomprehensible pain.

A young man I treated in analysis over many years had come to London fleeing a childhood marked by the unbounded cruelty of a civil war. One day he arrived having had a minor though potentially fatal cycling accident the previous afternoon. He was shaken less by the speeding white van that muscled him off his bike than by the succession of cars that drove past him as he lay on the pavement. 'I felt like a screaming, naked baby in the middle of the road,' he told me.

Perhaps, Bockris hints, Warhol disowned the painting once it revealed itself to him as an unwitting and shocking self-portrait, an exposure of the darkest and most vulnerable corner of his own self. His commercial work at the time mined post-war consumer culture's deep seam of sentimentality, conjuring an idyll of lush pastel flowers, cherubs and butterflies, an enchanted inner child-hood. Perhaps the Shanghai baby, rendered in those 'surprisingly decorative' colours, was the cherub's unconscious obverse, an unac-knowledged black trauma haunting the idealized, pastel surface.

At every stage of our life, we are conditioned by our earliest experience of total dependence on the adults to whose care or neglect, love or hate we're consigned without choice or consent. To use Freud's term, we are born into a condition of helplessness.

This original helplessness is imprinted indelibly on our psychic and bodily lives. How much it defines those lives will depend on both our subsequent experience and the ways in which we pro-cess it. Physical and mental traumas of all kinds – war, poverty, neglect, accidents, illness – can reactivate this deep-lying layer of vulnerability and exposure.

As a child of four, my patient had woken in the night to find his mother had left the house and himself alone and defenceless against the dangers outside, real and imaginary. He recalled, or perhaps imagined, groping for the walls in the dark while screaming, which felt to him like hanging over the abyss from his fingertips. Was he more scared, he wondered, of the appearance of some nameless monster, or of no one? (Or, I wondered to myself, are these more or less the same?) The helpless baby, naked and screaming, came to life in the panic of the abandoned child, who in turn resurfaced in the young man splayed on the pavement, watching the cars pass him by.

Coloured by illness and grief, Warhol's childhood afforded him little relief or distance from the terrors of infantile helpless-ness. At the age of two, he suffered ocular swelling, treated by his mother with boric acid baths; at four, curvature of an arm bone he'd broken without realizing it; at six, scarlet fever and at eight (the most notorious of these biennial afflictions), recurrent bouts of chorea, or St Vitus's Dance.

Chorea is a disorder of the central nervous system causing its sufferer to lose control of his limbs, which periodically flail in an unpredictable frenzy. The sensation of dispossession would stoke the child's fear that he was going mad. Andy's shaking fits led to the malign attention of bullies, leaving him in terror of going to school, confused by basic tasks of coordination and provoked all too quickly to tears. His childhood had become a story of the traumatic breaching of his bodily and emotional borders.

Prescribed a month's bed rest and constant care, Andy was moved by his mother, Julia, into the dining room adjoining the kitchen, enabling her to attend him round the clock and perhaps beginning the fraught relationship that saw her live with him (though kept increasingly out of sight) through the various homes of his adult life.

In bed, the convalescing patient enjoyed a limitless supply of paper dolls, comic books and magazines procured by his mother, from which he cut the elements of the collages he'd then assemble. Describing the scene in his *Philosophy*, Warhol evokes – knowingly? – the ambience of a factory in miniature: 'I would spend all my summer listening to the radio and lying in bed with my Charlie McCarthy doll and my un-cut-out paper dolls all over the spread and under the pillow.' The convalescent bed shared an essential paradox with Warhol's later Factory, the legendary studio space in which Warhol's manic production mingled with sexual, narcotic and emotional excess and where too the radio would be kept on through the working day: both the child's bed and the adult Factory were places of compulsive productivity and of inertial retreat, of perpetual motion and its cancellation.

Three years later, another bed in the Warhola home housed

the much longer convalescence of Andrej, Andy's taciturn and dependable father. Where Julia embodied a proximity both comforting and claustrophobic, Andrej was a source of physical and emotional distance. In 1939, he returned from what would be the last of his stints of temporary labour away from the family, at a mine in Wheeling, West Virginia. There, along with some fellow workers, he drank contaminated water and was sent back home, confined to bed with jaundice.

The prodigiously hard worker was housebound over the next three years as his condition deteriorated. When he died, in 1942, he was laid out at home for three days in accordance with tradition. This particular form of laying to rest proved too much for Andy, who ran and hid under his bed and refused to see the corpse. He stayed at his aunt's home until it had been safely removed from his own.

The funeral is likely the only one Warhol ever attended – not excluding his mother's thirty years later, from which he stayed away, pleading the same aversion to the presence of death. 'His fear of death,' writes Bockris, 'would lead to a hardcore detachment from anything concerning it.'

On one side of the coin was Julia's intrusive proximity, breaching the membrane of her son's bodily and affective privacy; on the other, Andrej's unbridgeable distance – frequently geographical, always emotional and finally irrevocable. Warhol's subsequent life and work would be conditioned by his suspension between these extremities. Contact, physical or emotional, would be forever excessive or privative, too much or not enough. Perhaps the hypochondriasis he suffered throughout his life, examined in Brian Dillon's *Tormented Hope*, can be understood as the affliction of a body that feels itself at once violated and abandoned; a naked, wounded baby.

*

Cut out from newspapers, the serial images of electric chairs, car crashes, suicides and race riots in Warhol's Death and Disaster series have a disinterested quality, as if taken by an anonymous camera. Saturating them in industrial yellow, green, red, orange, Warhol submerged the traumatic images in a wash of indifference.

These paintings have always aroused in me a queasy shame, as though catching me in the posture of the gawking rubbernecker. When you drive past the scene of a motorway accident, the speed of the cars ahead, and then of your own car, dips to a catatonic slow motion. For those few seconds, the concertinaed fenders, shattered glass, even the blood trails, are drained of human significance, as your eye becomes a coldly mechanical recording instrument.

I experience the same split in perception before the Death and Disaster paintings. The car crash scene is both an eruption of violence, destruction and pain, and an indifferent arrangement of interchangeable objects. I feel at once inhuman and all too human, too far away from and too close to the surfeit of horror.

Warhol's 'hardcore detachment from anything concerning [death]' doesn't preclude compulsive fascination with it. In the grip of hypochondriac anxieties that imagined his skin and internal organs under permanent siege, Dillon suggests, he took refuge in the fantasy of a neutral body, in which all agitation was cancelled out: 'Fearing illness and medicine in equal measure, he imagined that physical well-being consisted in remaining inviolate from both and thought that a healthy body was a body that was unified, self-same, wholly itself and itself alone.'

It is this fantasy of equilibrium that colours the screaming Shanghai baby in dreamy pastels, and that coats the later scenes with a tone of ironic commercial glossiness. The vacant electric chair signifies both the violent shock it will administer and the permanent silence of death that will follow. The artificial colour

washes out these twin terrors of excess and nullity. While commentators have ascribed political meaning to the series, during a
radio conversation with Claes Oldenburg and Roy Lichtenstein
Warhol insisted they were 'an expression of indifference'.

The flattening function of colour gives a more sinister inflec-
tion to the whimsicality of Warhol's comments on painting, more
than a decade later, in his book *The Philosophy of Andy Warhol*:
'You see, I think every painting should be the same size and the
same color so they're all interchangeable and nobody thinks they
have a better painting or a worse painting.' Put differently, the
ideal of painting would be to nullify both its own content and the
viewer's response – saying nothing, soliciting nothing, a moment
of pure non-communication between artist and audience.

Neutrality, indifference, emptiness – these were Warhol's
resources in the struggle against the onrush of disturbances to
his internal balance. He sought, in both life and work, a state of
serene pastel stillness, only to find it menaced on one side by the
threat of pain and shock, on the other by the void of silence and
death. His erotic life oscillated between long periods of asexual
detachment and abrupt bursts of passionate, often hopeless desire,
just as his successive relationships with his Factory 'superstars'
repeated a trajectory of adhesive mutual entanglement ending in
cold indifference and rejection.

Warhol's life and work can seem like an interminable rehearsal
of our most basic predicament: our wish to love and be loved. It
is a wish that arouses need, excitement, yearning and curiosity.
If love promises gratification, care and protection, it also puts us
at perpetual risk of exposure to indifference, neglect and cruelty.
Warhol evidently found this double bind intolerable, leading to
a compulsive oscillation between renouncing erotic desire and
giving himself up to it.

Among his greatest creations was the cultivated emptiness of his persona, a solution to this bind. Visiting Hollywood in 1963, he dreamed (as he writes in *POPism*, his 1980 memoir of the 1960s) of his life assuming the unalloyed vacancy of Hollywood: 'Vacant, vacuous Hollywood was all I wanted to mold my life into. Plastic. White-on-white.'

To attain a white-on-white life is to permanently neutralize the agitations of feeling, to cleanse the face of life of the colours that distinguish it. According to Warhol's friend and biographer David Bourdon, his favourite film of 1964 was *The Creation of the Humanoids*, in which a post-apocalyptic labour shortage is resolved by the invention of humanoid robots. The film's 'happy ending' 'comes when the heroine and the hero discover themselves to be machines'. The disappearance of the human into the machine was the happy ending Warhol sought for himself. Numbness and indifference, the state of Greene's burnt-out case at 'the end of desire', were increasingly Warhol's primary creative resources.

But maintaining this state of non-desire is no less troublesome for Warhol than it was for Chōmei, the Buddhist monk who found himself attached to his wish for non-attachment. Warhol was forever seeking to cultivate his own machinic neutrality only to find himself wrenched out of it by the alien eruption of human desire.

Warhol's manifested persona was an attempt to realize 'the desire for non-desire' as his very essence. Indifference insinuated itself into his gaze, his voice, his comportment: into the texture of his everyday being. Paradoxically, his persona also fed off the creative, emotional, narcotic and sexual excesses flaring around him. A community of artists, drag queens, hangers-on and superstars inhabited the Factory during the 1960s and a febrile cauldron of loves, hatreds, rivalries and yearnings bubbled perpetually around the impassive humanoid at its centre.

*

Perry Davis, one of Warhol's teachers at Pittsburgh's Carnegie Institute of Technology, where Warhol studied commercial art in the mid-1940s, described the adolescent Andy as leaving 'a very sexless impression'. The same observation recurs among the companions and witnesses of his life. One friend, the artist Ruth Kligman, recalls him cautioning that 'Sex takes up too much time.' Another, the key figure and collaborator at the Factory, Gerard Malanga, remarked, 'It was almost as if he was sexless.'

Warhol's writings reinforce this impression of erotic aversion. 'Sex is more exciting on the screen and between the pages than between the sheets anyway,' he wrote in *The Philosophy*. Sex is fine once it is externalized, an artefact to be looked at rather than a pleasure to be felt and enjoyed. Sex belongs on the screen or the page, where it can be generalized and diffused among its viewers and readers. It becomes a waste of time the moment it becomes 'personal': 'Personal love and personal sex is bad,' he wrote. To love personally is to stain the white-on-white ideal of machine-like anonymity.

This apparent erotic detachment emphatically did not preclude an insatiable curiosity about the sex lives of others – on the contrary, it facilitated it. Intimating celibacy, suggests Malanga, 'gave him enormous manipulative power over the magnificently beautiful people he brought together'.

But in withdrawing from the sexual marketplace, Warhol exerted power over his own erotic life as much as he did over those of others. 'You can be just as faithful to a place or thing as you can to a person,' he wrote in *The Philosophy*. Distance and objectification became a form, rather than a simple rejection, of relating.

Warhol's tendency to objectify was evident from the beginning of his adult life. Technical instruments – the phone, the tape recorder, the TV screen and the camera, as well as the pen and paintbrush – provided the means for a mediated closeness, for maintaining a cool distance within even the deepest intimacy. Around 1951, while living alone in Manhattan, he developed a lifelong dependency on the telephone. George Klauber, a member of the circle of Carnegie friends who had moved to New York and Warhol's initiator into the city's subterranean gay cultures, recalls him calling from his bed at two in the morning, demanding all the details of Klauber's night with his new lover.

As Bockris has it, 'Andy was frightened of going to sleep alone but was not able to sleep with anyone else.' Taking a hard-shelled telephone rather than a soft-skinned lover to bed proved an ideal solution to this bind. And the phone was only the first in the chain of erotic displacement – consistent with the voyeurism that shaped both his sexual life and his art, Warhol was being aroused not by his own lover but by someone else's.

According to his account in *The Philosophy*, by the late 1950s, television had begun to take the place of close relationships. But it was only in 1964, with the purchase of his tape recorder (which he called 'My wife'), that he renounced emotional life altogether. 'The acquisition of my tape recorder really finished whatever emotional life I might have had, but I was glad to see it go. Nothing was ever a problem again, because a problem just meant a good tape, and when a problem transforms itself into a good tape it's not a problem any more.' 'Problems' are personal; when they are externalized and reproduced, they are rendered impersonal, things to be dispassionately examined, rather than experiences to be felt.

Warhol's 'marriage' to his tape recorder bore its most conspic-uous fruit in his 'novel' *a*, a sequence of transcriptions of many hours of interminable and often unintelligible conversation between the various players at the Factory, recorded by Warhol's 'wife'. We tend to think of intimacy and coldness as opposites, but reading *a* suggests otherwise; the licence to eavesdrop on the interlocutors' formless, aimless private exchanges is radically alienating. The excess of detail, the absence of any orientation or narrative shape, the insistence on raw presentation without even minimal organization, are all confusing and exhausting. Because its 'author' is an inanimate technical object, the glut of words is stupefying; we take in abundantly while understanding and retaining almost nothing.

Warhol would elicit the same response with his next recorder, the Bolex movie camera he placed in front of a sleeping body or a tall building or the upper body of a man being (we infer) fellated, in each case inviting us to contemplate not so much the content being watched as the very act of watching. The boredom that takes hold of me after, say, fifteen minutes of watching any of these films sends me away from the image on the screen and into an agitated bubble in my own head. The absence of anything much to look at displaces my attention to the process of looking itself.

'Just play it all on one level,' Warhol counsels in *The Philosophy*, and much of his art tacitly coerces us into assuming this stance. It gives us a glimpse of what the world would look like if we ceased to confer more importance on some things than on others, if we placed the contents of the external world and our inner lives on the one undifferentiated plane.

But remaining on this plane was another matter. At various points in his life, stirrings of desire, rage and pain would peek out from under the cover of his contrived neutrality, blotting the painstakingly cultivated surface of white-on-white.

Despite the carefully nurtured myth that Warhol had transcended sex, his aversion to desire was more a symptom of excess than the absence of bodily and emotional sensitivity. Thrust as a young man into the easy promiscuity of the 1950s New York gay scene, he preferred to draw than to touch the many cocks he encountered; soon enough he began sketching his friends Robert Fleisher and Ted Carey with various lovers, during which the arousal he sought to diffuse through his pencil was liable to get the better of him. His glassy aesthetic distance undone by sheer force of excitement, he would ask permission to sketch the lovers in his jockey shorts. 'When the action got too hot,' writes one of his biographers, Wayne Koestenbaum, 'he would scream, "I can't take it any more!"'

The scream plays at the edges of pleasure and trauma. The carapace of neutrality is breached by an uncontrollable surge of desire – the scream of the traumatized baby, smothered beneath the divine silence of the pastel cherub, suddenly audible.

This break was a recurring pattern of Warhol's many erotic and creative partnerships, expressed above all in his overwhelming physical inadequacy. His famous wigs and shades protected from the public gaze the face he considered irreparably scarred by his chronic childhood acne. The cold indifference he cultivated towards sex stemmed from a secret conviction of his undesirability.

During the 1950s he would develop serial crushes on beautiful, inaccessible young men, culminating in his decision in 1956 to undergo a painful procedure to have the red skin on his nose scraped away, only to decide it made him look worse. Measuring himself hopelessly against the ideals of male beauty everywhere surrounding him and conducting serial affairs that culminated in his painful rejection, he became morose and resentful.

Long periods of celibacy, during which Warhol proclaimed the virtues of abstention, alternated with bursts of fevered sexual activity. But in reaching for love, he seemed inevitably to overreach and court rejection. In 1954, he fell helplessly in love with

Charles Lisanby, a handsome socialite. Swept up in the glamour of Lisanby's charmed circle, populated by movie stars and society beauties, Warhol lavished gifts (a tendency to which love and insecurity made him especially prone) on the object of his affection.

Lisanby offered companionship but, despite Warhol's hankering, not sex. The impasse came to a head in 1956, when Lisanby accompanied him on a trip across the Far East. Opening his hotel door to Lisanby's knock and finding a beautiful young man standing by him, Warhol screamed in rage. The emotional eruption was the first and last Lisanby would see; the rest of the trip unfolded without the smallest ripple of tension.

Two decades later, Bockris notes, the trip would be alluded to in *The Philosophy* as the trigger for his subsequent indifference to all of life's vicissitudes, encapsulated in his favourite maxim: 'So what.' Heard in the broader context of Warhol's life, the phrase loses its happy flippancy and takes on a chilly inhumanity.

As he became increasingly famous, wealthy and influential, and as the anarchic creativity of the Factory community proliferated, a disturbing narrative arc seemed repeatedly to play itself out across a series of relationships. A new face would enter the Factory – a would-be lover, an ingénue, an emerging artist – and quickly assume a place at its centre. Each was subjected to the same sequence of rapid and intense bonding, which gave way to an equally rapid and violent unravelling, and finally to abjection, madness or death.

Fame and money interested Warhol much less than power, suggests Malanga: 'Andy, like Hitler, created the illusion of strength by surrounding himself with people who would do his bidding.' The comparison may be wildly overblown, if not downright offensive, but there are times when grotesque exaggeration conveys an atmosphere more effectively than exact description.

Many of Warhol's glib written and spoken pronouncements express the same impulse to turn live human suffering into an object of cool aesthetic interest. It is difficult to avoid seeing his relationships as exercises in this process of transformation.

The dancer Freddie Herko, a member of the circle around Warhol's studio designer and, eventually, right-hand man, Billy Linich (later better known as Billy Name), had become part of the Factory scene in 1964, appearing in various Warhol films and plunging zealously into its culture of narcotic excess and manically performed interpersonal rivalry.

On 27 October of that year, having for weeks promised a 'suicide performance', he put on Mozart's 'Coronation' Mass at a friend's Greenwich Village apartment and, high on LSD, danced naked out of a fifth-floor window to his death. On hearing the news, Warhol asked, '"Why didn't he tell me he was going to do it? Why didn't he tell me? We could have gone down there and filmed it!"'

For his detractors, the remark was confirmation of Warhol's horrifying callousness. The drag queen Ondine, his loyal and lifelong friend, offered a more ambiguous interpretation of the suicide as the fruit of an enigmatic creative collaboration. Warhol had facilitated and realized his counterpart's deepest ambition, 'so that Herko could actually die as he wanted to do all of his life'.

Either gloss points to the same aspiration on Warhol's part: to make a gratifying aesthetic spectacle of raw human suffering – to transform a traumatized scream into a flattened 'So what.' Warhol's startling imagination turns a lazy expression of generalized indifference into an audacious principle for the transformation of life into art. Seventy years earlier, Oscar Wilde had proposed the same transformation in terms of an elevation of beauty over ugliness. In stripping out all such noble aims from the process, Warhol effects a kind of demonic inversion of his predecessor's aesthetic idealism.

The nihilistic chaos of the Factory provided a reliable production line of self-destructive raw material. The most notorious of many such cases was Edie Sedgwick, the delicate and androgynous beauty, most famous of Warhol's superstars and lead actor in his most important films, including *Kitchen*, *Beauty #2* and *Girls in Prison*. Sedgwick arrived at the Factory in early 1965 with a substantial history of anorexia, drug dependency and psychiatric admissions. Relations among her old and wealthy Massachusetts family were at a baroque level of dysfunction; two of her brothers had committed suicide shortly before she met Warhol.

She was, in other words, intensely vulnerable to the oscillations between obsessive attention and humiliating neglect that she experienced during her two years at the Factory. In directing her film performances and choreographing her public appearances, Warhol created the template for the self-generating celebrity of today's social media stars, selling her swelling crowd of followers the dream of looking and being just like her.

Warhol evidently saw himself mirrored in Sedgwick's craving for love and attention, and her way of summoning an extravagant bravado to mask her intense fragility. If this identification initially expressed itself in an affectionate protectiveness, Sedgwick seems eventually to have drawn the contempt he felt for himself. The 'envy of every hip girl in town', in Bockris's estimation, descended inexorably into drug addiction under Warhol's mentorship.

The descent was captured in his films, which struck Sedgwick as an ever more abject public humiliation, exacerbated by Warhol's failure to pay her for any of her performances. Meeting him at the Russian Tea Room, she staged a plaintive confrontation, telling him, '"Everybody in New York is laughing at me! ... These movies are making a complete fool out of me! Everybody knows I just stand around in them doing nothing and you film it and what kind of talent is that? Try to imagine how I feel!'"

Four years after she drifted away from the Factory, Sedgwick died from an overdose of alcohol and barbiturates. With hindsight her tragic end was a result of her hopelessly low self-worth. 'Standing around doing nothing', once the unique basis of her creative achievement, had become a humiliating burden.

The writer Robert Heide, with whom Warhol collaborated on many films, described their walk through Greenwich Village one night in 1965, after saying goodbye to Sedgwick for the last time. Walking up Cornelia Street, Heide showed him the spot where Herko had leapt from the window. To which Warhol replied, "'I wonder if Edie will commit suicide. I hope she lets me know so I can film it.'"

In flatly observing and recording the unfolding catastrophes of Herko, Sedgwick and others (Danny Williams, Andrea Feldman, Jean-Michel Basquiat) after them, Warhol was taking vengeance on the very fact of feeling, on the flows of emotional and sexual desire that threatened the hard borders of his body and mind. With a handful of men, Warhol softened those borders, granting them admission into his home and his heart.

Soon after moving into a new Factory building on Union Square West in 1968, a shy and handsome young man appeared delivering a Western Union message, of which Paul Morrissey, Warhol's manager and collaborator on his later films, took delivery.

Jed Johnson had just arrived in New York from his home town of Minnesota with his twin brother, Jay, and had promptly been mugged, losing all his cash. The manager at the Western Union branch where he sent home word of his misfortune had taken pity on him, and offered him some delivery work to earn enough to

tide them over until funds arrived. The contagion of pity spread
to Morrissey, who offered Jed a job sweeping floors.

The nineteen-year-old Johnson would soon come to represent
the more elegant and respectable public face of Warhol's enter-
prises in later life. It took little time for Warhol to fall for him
and confer on him a special place in the new Factory set-up as an
editor and art director on his films.

Less than a year after Johnson appeared in Union Square,
Warhol was shot, near fatally, by Valerie Solanas, ensuring that
his new companion's role would be one of carer as well as lover.
'So what' was no longer an option.

Their relationship is remembered by the Warhol entourage
as unusually tender and respectful. "'Somehow,"' Malanga
remarked to Bockris, "'I felt that Andy might have actually got
somebody that he could love in Jed."' Johnson was his companion for twelve years. His most important role was the acquisition
and interior design of the Upper East Side town house for which
Warhol acquired a massive and extravagant collection of antiques.

The slow and painful breakdown of their relationship was
triggered by the critical and financial catastrophe of Warhol's last
film, *Bad*, a story of a criminal girl gang, in 1977. Wounded by the
failure, Johnson shifted his focus towards his interior design work,
his new-found independence arousing resentment in Warhol and
causing tension between them.

It was not until late 1980 that Johnson moved out of the house
they shared. Warhol reacted with his familiar flippancy, dismiss-
ing Johnson to shocked friends as "'just a kid who worked at the
Factory"'. But sustaining the impassive front proved much harder
this time. He began frequenting S&M bars with an English aristocrat where, according to a friend's recollection, "'they shit and
piss and it entertains you"'. He was drinking heavily through the
course of the day, the area around his bed strewn with vodka

bottles. He cried to his friends about his fears of ending his days alone.

Warhol eventually recovered his sobriety and flat composure, but the episode vividly intimates the horror of abandonment that fuelled his fantasy of becoming a machine.

Is it irony or destiny that a body obsessively imagined by its bearer as a site of danger and vulnerability should end up being shot by a stalker, whose intent above all was to attack the victim's bodily and psychic boundaries? The bullets Valerie Solanas fired into Warhol's chest on 3 June 1968 would destroy his last vestige of trust – in other human beings and in the integrity of his own body, which could now be restored only precariously and with the aid of an external device. 'Profoundly disembodied already,' remarks Koestenbaum, 'he became, after the assassination attempt, more radically severed from his body, now a canvas of wounds and scars – the apparatus of his torn and flayed flesh held in place, for the rest of his life, by tightly bound abdominal belts, corsets that Brigid Berlin dyed for him in optimistic pastels, like the colours of his silkscreens.'

Being shot confirmed for the author of *The Philosophy* that all experience, even and especially at its most traumatic edge, is essentially 'television': 'you don't feel anything.' It is the same philosophy that imagines an aesthetic utopia in which all paintings are the same size and colour, that enjoins us to play all relationships 'on one level' of genial indifference: 'very light, cool, off-hand, very American'. In a Warholian utopia, the excitations and agitations of desire, pain, frustration and even pleasure would be cancelled out in the name of nirvanic bliss.

The cultivation during the early Factory years of his trademark flat, affectless mode of speech and movement was the manifest expression of this inertial ideal. But here a striking paradox comes

into view: Warhol's investment of his whole self in doing, feeling and being nothing was also an expression of his prodigious
productivity.

The chapter on 'Work' in *The Philosophy* turns on the erosion
of any distinction between work and life: 'just being alive is so
much work at something you don't always want to do. Being
born is like being kidnapped. And then sold into slavery. People
are working every minute. The machinery is always going. Even
when you sleep.' We are ransomed to work for as long as we're
alive, slave labourers on a zero-hours contract, subject to the
flows, sometimes even, sometimes violently unstable, of ener-
getic input and output circulating through us. The machinery
is always going.

Perhaps, then, Andy got to the Factory early and worked so
unrelentingly because even if he were to stop doing and making,
he would still be stuck with the work of simply being. And so his
work and life were dedicated to the strange ideal of lifelessness.
'The negative message that emerged from the Warhol Factory
was really a memento mori,' remarked the critic Calvin Tomkins.
In his films the camera whirrs away, keeping a vigilant eye on
its objects for hours on end in the service of attaining a state of
absolute stillness and silence.

In July 1963, during the Death and Disaster period, Warhol
bought the Bolex 8-mm camera and made his first film, proposing to his lover John Giorno that he make him a movie star by
filming him sleeping. *Sleep* is a four-hour film which shows the
naked, sleeping Giorno, the camera lingering hypnotically on
smaller and larger fragments of his body from different angles
and perspectives: head, torso, buttocks, the full body seen from
the foot of the bed or sideways or above.

It is very difficult, as Koestenbaum suggests, to watch *Sleep*
without thinking of the corpse of Andrej Warhola from which

Andy had taken flight twenty-one years previously. 'At last,' he writes, 'Andy performs his filial vigil; *Sleep* is a wake.' The motionless paternal body the young Andy couldn't bring himself to look at was transmogrified into the lover's body he couldn't take his eyes off.

Staring at a sleeper is minimally yet decisively different from staring at a corpse. Motionless for long stretches, withdrawn into itself, the sleeping body is absent from the world, divested of the interests and desires of waking life. The evocation of death at certain points is irresistible; filmed on his back from the foot of the bed, Giorno's head and torso assume a leaden immobility that recalls an open coffin, or Frankenstein's monster awaiting his fatal animation.

But of course Giorno isn't dead. His face twitches, he turns on his side, his trunk hosts the rise and fall of his breath. He evokes deathliness only because we're seeing him in the most elemental state of life, bordering both the final and irreversible stillness to which we all succumb and the anticipation of his imminent awakening into life and desire.

Warhol's camera eye in *Sleep* is very far away from the anonymous gaze of the Death and Disaster series or the stony neutrality of the stationary camera placed years later in front of the Empire State Building. The camera switches angles, zooms in and out, taking up an intrusively curious relation to its oblivious object. There are interminable shots that home in on Giorno's body to the point where it becomes inhuman, an abstract composition of texture and shadow. But when the camera pulls back to reveal the curved line stretching across the base of the screen as the crack of his sculpted buttocks, the apparent formal objectivity of the previous shot takes on the creepiness of the stalker's obsession.

Sleep ties erotic desire, like aesthetic creativity, to the sleepy state in which we're suspended between life and non-life.

'Spying on motionlessness,' comments Koestenbaum, 'is a rather specialized erotic discipline.' Warhol works through the night, sacrificing his own sleep to capture his lover's. All his labour and creativity are invested in the state of total disinvestment. In contrast to his predecessors in the Surrealist movement, it is sleep rather than dreams that interests him – not the working part of the nocturnal psyche ('Dreams,' writes Freud, 'only show us the dreamer in so far as he is *not* sleeping'), but its non-working, inertial counterpart. His abundant reserves of creative and sexual energy are all put in the service of sleep and its various cognate states in waking life: apathy, emptiness, indifference.

'Machines have less problems,' Warhol famously told *Time* magazine in 1963. 'I'd like to be a machine, wouldn't you?'

And then, to the *Observer* in 1966: 'I've never been touched by a painting. I don't want to think. The world outside would be easier to live with if we were all machines. It's nothing in the end anyway. It doesn't matter what anyone does. My work won't last anyway. I was using cheap paint.'

The human as machine, the great serial motif in Warhol's life and work, is profoundly ambiguous. Its expresses a wish for the excision from life of pleasure and pain, love and hate, excitement and fear, and all the 'problems' deriving from them. As a machine, the self has the privilege of being behind its controls. It is freed from permanent enslavement to its desire and the frustration that follows in its wake. But this solution to the trauma of feeling threatens an obverse trauma, a kind of living death.

Nearly thirty years after his death Warhol remains for me something like the presiding spirit of our time, because he lays bare the contradiction which animates, and de-animates, our psychic and cultural condition. Through his life and work, we enter into the heart of consumer culture's hedonic, lurid glamour.

But no sooner are we inside it than we experience a pull towards inertia and indifference, as though at the centre of the affirmative logic of consumerism is a massive and irresistible negation of life.

The supremacy of American culture lay, for Warhol, in the radically equalizing effect of mass production and consumption. The mass proliferation of things, far from making demands on our desire, neutralizes it. Warhol's serial images, he claims, gesture towards an ideal future in which all paintings are the same size, shape and colour. In the words of *The Philosophy*, 'As soon as you have to decide and choose, it's wrong.'

So he makes and writes and speaks with the one incessant and unswerving aim of flattening the world, disclosing its underlying sameness, which is also its nothingness: 'Everything is nothing,' he declared more than once. Bockris: 'From making love to making art, he noted repeatedly, "the most exciting thing is not doing it".' Our Disney–Pixar world in which everyone is different and special in their own way is disclosed to us as one in which everyone and everything is the same, in which there is, as the title of Warhol's projected TV show had it, 'Nothing Special'.

The title amplifies his status as a Schopenhauer for the age of consumerism. For his German philosophical predecessor, existence was a fleeting and illusory blip in the original fundament of non-existence – a loan received from death, with sleep as daily interest. Warhol's iconography of glamour is a Trojan horse concealing a virus of indifference. And in our age of 24/7 flows of information, in which torture and genocide jostle for our attention alongside the surgical enhancements of our favourite celebrities, in which trauma wrapped in a pastel blandness is our cultural norm, who would dare claim the virus has spared them?

Chapter 2

The Slob

At some point on almost any given day, my mind and body stop working.

It usually happens at night as I'm slouched on the sofa, staring into an opaque TV screen, surrounded by the remnants of a wasted evening. My book lies face down, my shoes are kicked off; next to me are two remote controls, a bowl of peanuts and a half-empty beer bottle.

Impassive and unkempt, I am one more lifeless object in this melancholy tableau, as lumpen as the things around me. A nagging voice in my head urges me to 'Get up! Clear the floor!' But in this mute region of myself, the principles of action and purpose don't apply. The stuff on the floor radiates a repulsive force. The injunctions to clear up congeal into pure noise. If I shut my eyes, a viscous black ink submerges the things around me, then the room they're in, then the house, then the street, then finally the whole world beyond. No book or shoe or bottle will ever again encroach on my perfect peace, and I will never again be called upon to do anything or go anywhere. Raising myself from my lethargy to deal with this mess feels like a physical, even a metaphysical disturbance, a violation of cosmic justice.

We are rarely more likely to feel hate for someone we love as when they wake us out of a deep sleep. Our thrashing and snorting aren't expressions of personal animus towards them, but of the universal human horror of being wrenched out of the bliss of quiescence. In being woken up, we are forcibly returned to a world of passions, joys and sorrows for which we may feel profoundly unready. Whoever wakes us becomes in that moment a generalized representative of a world that wants too much from us.

The scattered objects around me are wordless personifications of the world's demand to be taken care of, at my expense. It isn't at all obvious to me why, in the war between me and things, things should always be expected to win.

But as I scan the mess, I concede that winning they are, that I can only hallucinate this stuff away for so long. With each passing second, my resolve weakens, my resignation sharpens and my protest is reduced to a stamping of my inner feet and a silent cry of 'Why should I?' In compliance with the laws of domestic realpolitik, I start picking up the mess.

Scenes like this are replicated daily in living rooms, offices and playrooms across the world. As with most of the events of ordinary life, their banality ensures that they are poorly perceived and little attended to, spoken of only in the most trivializing language: slobbing, vegging out, slacking.

I am as prone as anyone else to this kind of contempt. I deride my internal protest as the petulance of an inner toddler. I'm quick to set myself apart from the slob within, who a few moments ago wanted nothing more than to conk out amid the evening debris. Yet 'Why should I?' is a cogent question, its reach deeper and wider than the current dilemma as to whether or not I should pick my things up off the floor.

The nineteenth-century German philosopher Arthur Schopenhauer was philosophy's great misanthrope and took the question very seriously. Reflecting on the phenomenon of habit, he suggests that it is no more than lassitude in the cunning guise of diligence: 'Genuine *force of habit* ... really derives from the *inertia* which wants to spare the intellect and the will the labour, difficulty and sometimes the danger involved in making a fresh choice, and which therefore lets us do today what we did yesterday and a hundred times before that.'

Received wisdom would have it that picking up after oneself is the ingrained responsibility of an adult as against the lazy indulgence of a child. Schopenhauer instead points to the possibility that, in so far as it involves circumventing the 'labour, difficulty and sometimes the danger involved in making a fresh choice', it may be a lazier and more childishly compliant option than asking why you should do so.

Toddlers and adolescents alike challenge the dictates of domestic order. Ask a toddler to pick up his toys and he might object tearfully that he doesn't want to, *you* do it; ask the other to pick up her clothes and she'll tell you to just, like, *lay off*, you're so uptight. Both responses are contemptuous of our carefully ordered world. They mock our wish to clear the floor so we can breeze across it and get things done, so we can carry on doing today what we did yesterday, and a hundred or a thousand times before that. What's the point in that? Why should I?

Perhaps we laugh at the entitlement of small children and teens because it spares us the effort of taking them seriously. We discern in their anger only what they've yet to grow out of, not what we've failed to preserve. In becoming the guardians of an active, purposeful life, of aims, growth and development, we lose touch with an equally fundamental impulse in us towards inactivity and aimlessness.

Our alienation from this impulse is a clue as to why the slob, a figure so apparently harmless and easy-going, is so apt to be an object of fear and disgust. One of the great stand-offs of modern domestic life centres on the teenage bedroom, where unwashed clothes proliferate. Perhaps we fear opening the door onto some hated and long-renounced dimension of ourselves. The word's origin is instructive: 'slob' dates from the late eighteenth century and derives from the Irish word *slab*, meaning mud, or, in its Anglo-Irish variant, sludge or ooze.

An oft-repeated speculation of Freud's has it that in the evolution of our species, our heads were originally in close proximity to our anal and genital organs. In setting them at a distance, evolution encouraged us to disown our animal origins, to renounce our dog-like shamelessness with regard to excretion and sex. Straightening our backs and tilting our chins up towards the firmament, we freed our heads from the disgusting and arousing smells of our intimate bodily selves. Cleaving to the ground, we were slaves of chaotic and untameable matter; raised into the air, we acquired dignity and the order and discipline of form.

The slob disturbs us because he puts us in touch with that formless, muddy region of the self we thought we'd risen above. You feel it when you sink exhausted into the sofa, abandoning yourself to gravity's inexorable downward pull. You feel it when your mind yields to its own sludgy undertow of blank stupidity, when all your inner voice can do is hum moronic advertising jingles. How can you possibly pick things up when you are on the level of a thing yourself, as dumb, inert and useless as a bowl of peanuts?

Writing in France in 1929, with fascism and war looming on the European horizon, the writer and thinker Georges Bataille cast doubt on any notion of a benign order of nature. Humanity, he suggested, has long laboured under the comforting illusion of biological life as tending upwards: 'with their feet in mud but their heads more or less in light, men obstinately imagine a tide that will permanently elevate them.'

In moments of slobbishness, we are taunted with the possibility that the only way is down, that human dignity is a sentimental illusion. The slob shows us to ourselves not as a tree standing tall but as the plant which, writes Bataille, 'rises in the direction of the sun and then collapses in the direction of the ground'.

When we surrender to lassitude, it is as though the forms that bind and support the world fall away, exposing the void beneath. We are put in touch with a universe which is, in Bataille's word, 'formless', lacking shape or structure.

Bataille laments our investment in the idea of an ordered universe, which he sees as a projection outward of our ideal of ourselves. It is surprising how tenaciously such notions lurk in our minds, in spite of the conscious cynicism we may express towards them. It is difficult to have a career or an interest or a great love (requited or not) without some implicit faith, however inchoate, in the essentially meaningful and purposeful nature of life and the world.

Having myself enjoyed all these privileges, I may not seem the most convincing proponent of the idea of life as formless. I am easily mistaken, not least by myself, for a square who works hard, pays taxes and lives cleanly. These disclosures notwithstanding, I can claim a long and deep intimacy with lassitude and aimlessness.

My conscious sense of this intimacy dates from the year I turned four, when my family decamped temporarily to Jerusalem. Given the facility of small children to acquire languages quickly and effortlessly, it was a good age at which to be taken abroad. I was sent to a *gan* or nursery, which would soon have me speaking like a native. The litany of Hebrew songs and prayers I already knew would give me a head start.

Yet Hebrew for me was a language of sound rather than sense, its rhythms snapping like bubble gum, its word endings an inexhaustible trove of rhyme, the words themselves stuck like glue to lilting melodies. What any of it meant didn't trouble me at all.

The Hebrew spoken in the nursery's close, gloomy bungalow wasn't like the songs I'd learned. The words weren't, as in synagogue, flung in the air towards no one in particular, but directed from one person to another. That I was expected to understand these words, and to use them to communicate myself to others, was a shock for which I was quite unprepared. Sounds that in England had fallen lightly on my ears suddenly acquired the weight and density of mud.

In the nursery, at the tip of the oval of tiny chairs, sat the *ganenet* or head teacher, a thin and leathery woman with big glasses and a long, tasselled black linen skirt. She would greet me fulsomely each morning, turning to me with an opened-mouth smile and saying my Hebrew name, inducing a triumphant flash of recognition that would then be swept away by a stream of clipped and guttural nonsense: *ef-fo-ba-ha-ti-lo-mi-en-do-ke-ze-ya-nu-sha-BA! Ve-ku-za-ni-lo?!* The kids joined the chorus, their voices melding to conjure a thick ambient cloud round my head: *NNGAAAAAAAA!*

The accumulating confusion plunged me deeper into despondency with each passing day, until one morning I tried to respond urgently in my own language in the hope of dispersing the cloud. Instead, my voice just disappeared into it.

What happened next is unclear. In my own unreliable version of events, I see the *ganenet* squatting, face level with mine, rubbing my arm and cooing soothingly, failing to notice that the words intended to salve my rage were inflaming it. Family folklore, fed by eyewitness reports, has it that I dissolved in tears before making an unconvincing attempt to beat her up.

The scene that follows has an unsettling certainty. I am alone in the sandpit, the shady street before me, the long flat hut behind me, the harmonies of children's play now a soundtrack to my disgrace. My body falls floppily over my legs, giving me the feel of a morose ragdoll. I am picking up handfuls of sand and letting them sift through my fingers. Dry-eyed and numb, I am the emblem of defeat.

I'd spend much of that year alone in the sandpit. Back at home, sat at the kitchen table, I'd listen in stony pique to my elder brother's easy chatter with his native Israeli classmate. How had he adapted himself so effortlessly to the world? How did everyone know all these words and tunes and rules? Where had I been when they were learning all this? I felt myself to be slow, more in the literal than the euphemistic sense; skinny and nimble, I nonetheless dragged my body through the world as if tethered to some heavy, slobbish doppelgänger. 'Why should I?' might have been my catchphrase.

Back in London, my recovery of language brought me relief but did nothing to abate the slowness. Primary school only entrenched it. To kids and teachers alike, I was comically dull-witted, my oblivion a reliable staple of classroom hilarity. There was the Year 1 class teacher who, having checked over my exercise book and sent me back to my place, stage-whispered 'So *dopey*!' to my back as I wended my way through lines of desks. There was the Year 2 teacher – and I am sufficiently disconcerted at this to wonder whether it could actually have happened – who called on me to answer a question in class and, on my responding that I didn't know, scrunched up her face and repeated, '*I don' knnnoooow*', complete with the low flat drone and lolling tongue used by kids in those days to mimic a 'spastic'.

The apotheosis of this running gag came about five years later, when a maths teacher, enjoining me in a falsetto sing-song to 'Concentr*ate*!', kicked me hard on the shin, hitting me with the precision of an unorthodox pedagogic experiment: let's see if the bisection of a line can be effectively demonstrated through the medium of random violence!

As I rode the wave of pain, a question forced its way to the front of my mind: why me? At first a cry of self-pity, it came to be imbued with genuine curiosity. What was it about me that had so long provoked these outbursts of casual cruelty from grown women and men? 'Who am I bothering?' I wanted to protest. '*I'm not doing anything!*'

The narrator of 'Bartleby, the Scrivener' once again helps to make sense of the conundrum. The attorney prides himself on managing the ill-temper and incompetence of his employees. But in the face of Bartleby's immobility and silence, all his negotiating skills dissolve in bewilderment.

Like the attorney, my maths teacher knew how to handle openly disruptive elements – when to win them over, when to put them down. But the challenge of a pupil not doing anything is more elusive. '"Nothing so aggravates an earnest person,"' says the attorney sagely, '"as a passive resistance."' An active resistance – clowning, insolence, defiance – can be heard, understood and if necessary counteracted; but passivity offers nothing to hear or understand. To be passive isn't so much to challenge the rules of the game as to refuse to participate in it at all.

For the 'earnest person' – that is, for anyone who sees the world as a serious place in which to conduct oneself seriously – 'I'm not doing anything' is the most intolerable of provocations. It hints that life could be lived without any discernible aim or desire. What is often said exasperatedly of slobs or wasters is also said of ghosts: they seem to be there but they're not.

In his doctrine of 'immaterialism', the eighteenth-century Irish philosopher Bishop George Berkeley posits that the worldly things we consider solid and real are mere illusions of our perception. When Boswell asked Dr Johnson how he would refute this argument, the latter famously kicked a stone and declared, 'I refute it *thus*!' I wonder if my maths teacher had something similar in mind, an urgent need to kick reality into me, to reassure himself that I was there and not a ghost.

That, as they say, is what a slob really needs: a good kicking.

The human species, claims Freud in his 1930 book *Civilization and Its Discontents*, is founded on two basic tendencies: 'the compulsion to work' and 'the power of love'. These are the forces ensuring the expansion, development and progress of civilization. Freud named the energy feeding work and love 'libido' (a Latin word meaning wish or desire), a term that has since passed into popular parlance to denote an individual's sex drive. This casual use captures one important aspect of the word as Freud used it; unlike Jung, who defined it as a generalized mental life force, he saw libido as a specifically sexual energy.

But Freud's term connotes much more than physical appetite for sex. Libido is a sexual energy, but human beings have the unique capacity to 'desexualize' it – that is, to put in the service of non-sexual aims such as creative work, play and intellectual enquiry. Libido is the intensity or passion we invest in any object, enterprise or person we care about. Understood in this way, it starts to sound like a kind of motor fuel for life, powering our journey through the world.

But this turns out to be too simplistic. While libido impels our expansion and integration into the 'ever larger unities' of individuals, families, races and, finally, humankind, it can equally hold us back and put a spoke in the wheels of personal and collective progress. We see this tendency, Freud observes, when two people fall in love. We might expect the couple to be in a hurry to celebrate their love by producing a child and enlarging the stock of humanity; this, after all, is how things tend to go among other animals. But as anyone who's found themselves stuck on a sofa next to a newly formed couple can attest, 'when a love relationship is at its height there is no room left for any interest in the environment; a pair of lovers are sufficient to themselves.'

New lovers, in other words, are liable to a kind of complacent satisfaction in one another, a lazy unwillingness to look for interest anywhere else. Freud speaks of the lovers' blissful contentment as a form of 'fixation' – somewhat disconcertingly, given he first coined the term to describe the logic of sexual perversion. For Freud, a perversion expresses an individual's stubborn persistence in staying where they are, something the infatuated lover and the pervert have in common.

In the context of the apparently liberated sexuality of our time, it might seem odd to think of the pervert as set in his ways. Sadomasochism or fetishism tends to be celebrated today as adventurous and transgressive, the expression of a desire to escape the restrictions of normative sexuality. Freud sees in them instead a tendency to fixate on one element or stage of sexual desire at the expense of its full experience – for example, to be aroused only by a single part (such as the foot) rather than the whole of the lover's body, or by a single sensation (such as pain) rather than a range of them.

We may be wary of the moralizing connotations of the word perversion these days, especially in reference to consenting activity. But in seeing perversion in terms of fixation, of our 'disinclination to give up an old position for a new one', Freud points us away from an understanding of perversion in terms of pathology or depravity and shows us its continuity with the broader spectrum of human behaviour. All our desires and passions, he observes, are liable to get stuck in a groove, to become maladaptive, regressive, resistant to change or challenge – in other words, perverse.

In fact, once we notice the universality of this tendency, the examples quickly proliferate: think of the child who, having discovered spaghetti or fish fingers, cannot be persuaded to try anything else; or the celebrity fan who follows the minutest utterance and movement of their idol to the exclusion of all other interests; or the rejected lover who spends life pining inconsolably for the one they've lost, refusing to 'move on'. These very different phenomena share the same profound resistance to movement and change. They are underwritten by what Freud calls 'the inertia of the libido', a kind of tenacious adhesion to the person or place or thing we have chosen, as well as anxiety and resentment in the face of any pressure to leave them behind.

We are so used to thinking of our passions as active and purposeful, we fail to notice how lazy and complacent they can become. We picture libido as a fuel coursing abundantly, speedily and without resistance through a roaring engine, not as a sludge sliding slowly and heavily down a fuel pipe, blocking the carburettor and causing the engine to sputter out. We are alive to the dynamism of the libido, but much less so to 'the sluggishness of the libido'.

Passion and desire have become inextricably bound up in our minds with doing, so that the notion of a passion for inactivity or slowness, for 'preferring not to', is barely intelligible to us. The idea of a sluggishness built into the libido offers a radical challenge to our received notions of human life and selfhood, one with urgent relevance to our culture of frenetic scheduling, hyperactivity and permanent distraction. In conceiving of ourselves so narrowly as creatures of action and purpose, in insisting we put all our time to work, we are declaring war on an essential dimension of ourselves, depriving ourselves of what the British psychoanalyst D. W. Winnicott calls 'the simplest of all experiences, the experience of *being*'.

Winnicott uses this simple yet enigmatic word to describe the inner life of a baby who hasn't yet differentiated herself from her mother. It is from this diffuse, unorganized experience of being that our sense of selfhood eventually emerges. But as we come to identify ourselves (or confuse ourselves) with the psychologically developed self who consciously thinks and acts (with a creature, in Winnicott's language, of 'doing'), this original layer of psychic life becomes increasingly inaccessible to us.

As the American psychoanalyst Jonathan Lear points out, in his tendency to ascribe functions and purposes to all activities of the mind, however incomprehensible they may seem, Freud seems implicitly to endorse the conception of the human being as a creature of doing rather than being. This is true even where we appear to act in ways that damage us or undermine our own interests – however self-defeating such behaviour might appear on the surface, Freud insists, there is always some motivation for it. Underlying this insistence on the rationality of our most extreme psychic and behavioural tendencies is an implicit 'teleology' of the mind, a conviction that whatever we do has a purpose, however concealed from us it may be.

What is missed by Freud's thinking is the possibility that, as Lear puts it, 'some mental activity occurs without a purpose'. We may contain within us, alongside our drive to act and fulfil our worldly ambitions, a discreet but equally powerful tendency to refuse action and ambition, to let ourselves simply *be*. Recognizing such a tendency has profoundly political as well as psychological implications.

Once again, I stake a claim to a special intimacy with this inborn antipathy to action. Like most children, I was fed the virtues of hard work, perseverance and determination, and like some, I was chastised for being lazy, dreamy and dopey, descriptions I didn't contest because they were basically true and, in any case, I couldn't be bothered to argue.

Being lazy or (as a school report put it) 'lacking in any sense of urgency' was for me never the expression of intentional defiance or opposition. I felt it more as a fact of being, so that the repeated demand to wake up, step on it, get my act together made no more sense than asking a sugar-fuelled child to calm down.

Like Bartleby, I never actively refused or even objected to work. Unlike Bartleby, I actually did it, in spite of my preference not to. I waded through lessons and games and homework like so many pools of molasses because nothing else occurred to me. And if it had, scheming to avoid work would have seemed too much like work. I didn't try to be passive, I just was. To complete the tasks assigned to me, without grace or pride, was the path of least resistance. I was a brilliant attestation to Schopenhauer's insight that the profoundest inertia conceals itself behind the bushel of habit.

Nor, for the same reasons, could you have called me a malingerer. I had nothing but priggish disdain for the classmates who kept themselves off school with fake ailments. All forms of truancy involved conscious effort, which I disliked, and guile, which I lacked.

This meant I was off school only on the rare days I was genuinely ill. The bouts of stomach flu still live in my skin's memory, the slightest movement like the poke of a cold finger.

But the purgatory of the first day off sick was redeemed by the paradise of the second, a cautionary convalescence the school insisted on, to ensure against contagion and restore my modest reserves of strength. These days of sanctioned inactivity were a true coming home, not only to my bed but to myself. I could finally do what I wanted – nothing – and with impunity. Alone in the stupor that follows illness, I felt more properly myself than at any other time.

There were in those days no satellite channels beaming streams of anaemic, laboratory-made kids' TV. Instead there were low-budget soaps in which women in satin blouses and blue eyeshadow sat long-faced at kitchen tables, instructional programmes about household budgets and gardening, and 1950s comedies in Day-Glo colours featuring ungainly men and horse racing.

The content of this stream of tripe was irrelevant. I was in search not of diversion or stimulation but of pure inaction. The murmur of the TV's empty sounds and images was my ally in this quest, as were the plump velvet sofa cushions and the warmth of the nearby radiator. This was life reduced to the most elemental bodily gratifications, a retreat from the world in which things happened, in which one was called on to play a part, do things.

My convalescent idyll was transient, shot through with the nostalgia that was already spoiling and sweetening its perfection, the same nostalgia I'd feel for it tomorrow as I stared into the busy scrawls on the blackboard. Around the edges of my oasis of contentment, that prowling tiger of reality.

We are witness today to an investment in the conception of the human being as above all, and in all senses, a *working* being. If there exists in us a resistance to perpetual activity, it is denied across politics, commerce and culture. Working, understood as both labour and functionality, is now the imperative of our time, as evidenced by policies on welfare, education, retirement and disability by liberal democratic governments across the world.

Running in concert with this political drive to ensure that we are all hard at work is a culture of permanent distraction. No sooner is a child born today than her nervous system is engulfed by an unremitting stream of stimuli beaming from an array of electronic devices. The same devices will often absorb the attention of her siblings and parents, pulling them into another universe even as they appear to be occupying this one.

The space for inactivity and stillness, for time spent without immediate purpose, is being closed down. In the words of cultural theorist Jonathan Crary, 'nothing is ever fundamentally "off" and there is never an actual state of rest.' Every moment of a given day, every phase of a given life, must be accounted for. Idle time, time without content, provokes fear and contempt.

Ours is not the first culture to repudiate idleness. From the Bible's reproaches and warnings to the sluggard, to our tabloids' bilious rages against economic migrants and benefit cheats, idleness has always been a source of dire prophecy and invective. In the popular imagination, the shiftless slob provides a lightning rod for our resentment towards those who would live easier lives at our expense.

Nor is such ire the exclusive preserve of the political Right. Not to be outdone by his capitalist counterparts in the zeal for productivity, Lenin regularly bemoaned the Russian malaise of *Oblomovschina* – 'Oblomovism' or 'Oblomovitis', an allusion to the protagonist of Ivan Goncharov's classic 1859 novel, *Oblomov*.

At the start of the novel, Oblomov is subject to a state of permanent inner agitation, exacerbated daily by proliferating financial demands, administrative tasks and social visits, and retreats into the cocoon of his stale bedsheets, fending off the regular exhortations of his tireless friend Stolz to get up and embrace life. But Stolz's reproaches and encouragements, the narrator implies, miss the mark; Oblomov's recumbence is a matter of neither necessity nor pleasure, but 'his normal condition'.

It turns out that this condition was made normal by a childhood of unstinting indulgence on his family's bucolic estate. The novel's famous dream sequence is closer to a soft-focus memoir. Oblomovka is a refuge of perfect calm and contentment, where a child's wishes merge seamlessly with reality. It is also a feudal estate manned by a retinue of servants quietly ensuring that the child is spared any perception of the work involved in sustaining this illusion, so that the adult Oblomov finds that 'the fairy-tale had become mixed up with real life in his mind'.

In his cobwebbed, dust-covered Petersburg apartment, Oblomov finds himself disturbed by the 'fuss' made by his cantankerous manservant Zakhar when cleaning his rooms. Zakhar's fussing forces him to see what the staff of Oblomovka spared him, that his horizontal existence is maintained by the vertical labour of others: 'Oblomov would have liked to have his rooms clean, but he could not help wishing that it would all happen somehow of itself, without any fuss.'

I recognize my own late-night sofa reverie in this infantile yearning for the abolition of all traces of work from the world, for the room to clean itself because I want it to. The novel seems to hint that, left to himself, the human being would seek an idyllically workless life. If there is no parent or teacher to induct the child into the burdens of necessity, this fairy tale is liable to 'become mixed up with real life'.

For most of us, childhood is an awakening, variously gentle and rude, from this reverie; for Oblomov it is its realization. His dubious gift is to have been spared the intrusion of the external world for so long that he cannot take its existence seriously. This is why he, like every slob, induces so much envy, cruelty and rage in those around him. We want to tell the slob that we too would spend the day lying down if we could, our every need met 'somehow of itself', but we've had to grow up and renounce this wish, to acknowledge the chasm between ourselves and the centre of the world. Why can't you?

And so we outwardly scorn what we secretly desire. The slob may be the object of our mockery and disgust, but he is equally a source of admiration and envy. A gallery of drunken louts (Trimalchio, Chaucer's Miller, Falstaff), spacey fantasists (Quixote, Snoopy), hopeless slackers (Oblomov, Lebowski) and entitled slobs (Diderot's Rameau, Homer Simpson) attest to the enduring heroic status of the slothful in the history of Western culture.

It is no coincidence that all these figures are fictional characters. The slob we have sought to banish from the real world returns to haunt us in imaginary form. The likes of Dr Johnson, Lord Byron, H. D. Thoreau, Walt Whitman, G. K. Chesterton and Bertrand Russell may have extolled the virtues and pleasures of laziness, but as real historical individuals they are all caught in the paradox of having harnessed their idle impulses in the service of major cultural achievements.

In turning the idle life into a project, a life's work, and so becoming names in the annals of civilization, these self-proclaimed idlers couldn't help betraying themselves. The true slob can only aim to be forgotten, to leave nothing of themselves to be preserved or admired. Fictional characters, on the other hand, license us to indulge the fantasy of a total, uncompensated waste of both time and self, to admire the irresponsibility, profligacy and shiftlessness our education and culture teach us to hold in contempt.

So how is it that a civilization so devoted to the ideal of work could be so enchanted by these figures of pure indolence? The answer is that the opposing impulses are each allied to one of 'two principles of mental functioning' (the title of a famous 1911 essay by Freud). The first of these, the 'pleasure principle', is geared towards the elimination of tension, which is achieved only when we get what we want. If we are hungry, for example, or sexually aroused, we discharge the onrush of libido, and the excitement that accompanies it, by having a meal or an orgasm.

Pleasure, in other words, resides not in the stimulus itself, but in the even state induced when it's discharged, got rid of. But if we managed all flows of libido in this way, we'd be stuck in a permanent alternation of excitement and exhaustion, making it very difficult to get anything done. We need to keep some of our energy in reserve in order to manage the many tasks of living.

This is where the second of the two principles, the 'reality principle', comes in. In gradually internalizing this principle, the mind comes to benefit from the pragmatic gains of delaying gratification. The more strongly the reality principle can entrench itself in us, the higher the degree of mastery we can exert over ourselves and the world.

Freud saw the scientist – in the broadest sense, the dispassionate seeker after truth – as the person in whom the reality principle is most fully developed. Science demands the discipline of waiting patiently, of doing without the gratifications of certainty and reality. Science is hard work because it operates in reality, and in reality there are no short cuts.

Freud's adherence to the superiority of the scientific orientation to the world places him squarely in the Enlightenment tradition of rationality and moral self-discipline. But he equally rejects the Enlightenment's conception of the human being as given inherently to reason and virtue. On the contrary, in the deepest cells of our inner selves, he suggests, we are servants of the pleasure principle, seeking the most easeful and untroubled path through life possible. In the first instance, we are all slobs. It is only gradually and unwillingly that we learn to accommodate ourselves to reality and the limitations it imposes on us.

The great thinkers of the Enlightenment spent much time engaged in a war against this infantile, pleasure-oriented self. Our selves, they posited, like our civilization, may undergo an infancy defined by dependence, ignorance and irrationality, but the arc of the human story is one of progressive movement towards autonomy, knowledge and reason. The true aim and destiny of the Enlightenment self was to bring reality under the rule of the intellect, rather than surrender to the dim, childish urgings of pleasure.

The slob and waster, as the critic Pierre Saint-Amand has recently shown, were for this reason the Enlightenment's mortal enemies. The seventeenth-century moralist Antoine de Courtin's *Traité de la paresse* ('Treatise on Laziness') condemned laziness as 'a numbness, a despondency, a desolation, a weight that depletes courage and instils a repugnance for all good deeds'. Laziness undoes the autonomy and responsibility that underwrite manhood (in the eyes of Enlightenment thinkers, the slob is distinctly unmanly) by undermining what Saint-Amand calls 'the necessity of *doing*'.

The slob's shiftlessness, moral laxity and hedonism are living refutations of the Enlightenment's cherished piety. That, at least, is the theory. In practice, many writers and thinkers of this period had a much more ambiguous and complex relationship to the idle type, an oscillation between disgust and fascination brought to life memorably in Denis Diderot's fictionalized dialogue *Rameau's Nephew*.

Diderot is an undisputed giant of the French Enlightenment. The author of an eclectic range of essays and fictions, he is famed above all as the editor of the first great modern encyclopedia, comprising seventeen written volumes and including substantial contributions by the most celebrated thinkers and writers of the day, including Voltaire, Montesquieu, D'Alembert and Rousseau, as well as Diderot himself. The *Encyclopédie* is a monument to the grand project of accumulating and disseminating knowledge.

Diderot's life and work attest to an unswerving dedication to moral and rational progress. Yet he is also the author of *Jacques the Fatalist*, a novel comprised of a rambling dialogue between a valet (Jacques) and his nameless master, one of literature's great homages to the joys of aimless chatter and a sustained joke about the idea of rational progress.

And perhaps his greatest literary creation is an epic slob and waster. Like many of Plato's dialogues, *Rameau's Nephew* begins with a chance encounter that leads to an extended disputation on how to live, delivered to the author, Diderot, who becomes a character in his own book. Unlike in Plato, the leading voice in the dialogue speaks in the name not of wisdom and virtue but of dishonesty and vice. Rameau is a music tutor and 'one of the weirdest characters in this land of ours where God has not been sparing of them'.

Diderot meets him in an idle moment of his own, taking shelter from the cold and rain in the Café de la Régence, watching a game of chess. Their talk turns to Rameau's difficulties. He lives by sponging off rich households, into which he insinuates himself by means of flattery and deceit, and from which he's inevitably ejected for overstepping the mark. Diderot listens to his defence of his amoral, self-indulgent, dependent and thoroughly useless life with both outward disgust and surreptitious amusement, even admiration. There is a knowingly perfunctory quality to Diderot's objections, a sense that he's enjoying his interlocutor's perverse self-justifications too much to spoil them with serious counter-arguments.

In any case, there is nothing Diderot can say about Rameau that Rameau hasn't already said about himself. Diderot calls him 'an idler, greedy, cowardly and with a soul of dirt', to which Rameau replies, with the shamelessness peculiar to the slob, 'I believe I've told you that already.' Forever ducking and diving, he fantasizes about a future in which he will squander untold riches on women and drink while paying back all the humiliations he's suffered at the hands of his aristocratic paymasters. Diderot lavishes ironic praise on this 'worthy use you would make of wealth ... You would ... be most useful to your fellow citizens and most glorious for yourself.'

But Rameau is immune to irony. The virtues of honour, seriousness and usefulness with which Diderot reproaches him are for Rameau mere vanities, empty words hiding under the pretentious cover of universal laws. In a brazen travesty of Solomon's wisdom, he commends Diderot to 'drink good wine, blow yourself out with luscious food, have a tumble with lovely women, lie on soft beds. Apart from that the rest is vanity.'

Rameau is a bombastic spokesman for the supremacy of the pleasure principle. The sensual pleasures of good wine, luscious food and lovely women are mere way stations on the journey to a soft bed, the blissful annulment of all mental and physical effort. The ultimate end of pleasure, at least as Rameau and Freud see it, is not arousal but peace.

The problem with the virtuous life which Diderot defends is that it refuses to leave you in peace. It requires self-denial, discipline, a vigilant attention to the intentions and effects of your own thoughts and actions. It is a persecutory voice, insistently calling you out for your irresponsibility and selfishness. Not only are you ignorant of the virtuous life, Diderot chides, 'you ... are not even capable of learning'. 'All the better,' replies Rameau. 'It'd make me peg out through hunger, boredom and remorse.' To train oneself to bear a life poor in food and amusement and rich in self-reproach, says Rameau, is entirely self-defeating. It means embracing rather than minimizing privations, wilfully denying yourself what you want.

The dialogue suspends us between repulsion and attraction. Rameau's prescription for life, to give nothing and demand everything, is morally and logically outrageous. Yet it's hard not to be taken in by the cheek and exuberance with which he defends the indefensible, or to surrender to the finally unanswerable logic that says a difficult life is not preferable to an easy one. In ventriloquizing him so seductively, Diderot brings us into contact with the Rameau concealed in us all, the big, entitled baby who rails against the obstacles reality puts in the way of his contentment, who doesn't see why he should be asked to wait, to work, to be responsible.

Rameau appeals to me because he dares to give voice to the entitled slob that lives a shamed and furtive existence in myself. Having the good fortune to do rewarding and involving work over long days and long weeks, to claim to be lazy would be a disingenuous pose. My different claim is that my apparently solid and reliable dedication is wrested from a fierce gravitational pull towards a degree zero of work.

'Whatever produces the phenomenon of the world,' writes Schopenhauer, 'must be capable of not doing so and consequently remaining inactive.' I frequently feel this insight reverberating in my gut – less in substantive activities and more in the intervals that punctuate them, those workaday tasks that cumulatively 'produce the phenomenon of the world'. Clearing the table, climbing the stairs, walking to the station, I can find myself overwhelmed by the possibility of not doing these things 'and consequently remaining inactive'. My interior voice, speaking mostly in the embarrassed tones of Oblomov, occasionally in the shameless tones of Rameau, furiously protests the unremitting rules of activity, responsibility, purpose. I do not want to work and produce and participate and contribute. I would rather other people did that so I don't have to. Perhaps this goes some way to explain my infatuation with the Rameau of our own day, our

living homage to sloth, waste, irresponsibility and infantile gratification: Homer Simpson.

Snoopy, Garfield, Homer – why should cartoons be such a
fertile breeding ground for iconic slobs and wasters? The large
chunk of childhood I squandered reading and watching cartoons
showed me the secret affinity between the two. Slobs are stock
figures in cartoons because cartoons, for all the painstaking work
involved in their production, are the fruit of the most slobbish
region of our imagination.

This may seem a counter-intuitive claim. The creations of Tex
Avery and Hanna-Barbera are alive with manic energy, every
frame a frenzied overspill of noise, violence and joy. But this is
exactly what makes watching them such a blissfully sedentary
activity. Bugs, Daffy, Tom and Jerry live in a world from which
the tiresome constraints of reality – physical laws, morality,
death – have been conveniently expunged.

Maurice Blanchot notes that the closest approximation in our
experience to a world freed from the impositions of reality is
the world of artistic creation. The artist, he writes, 'seems to be
subjected to a state of inactivity because he is the master of the
imaginary ... The truth is that he ruins action, not because he
deals with what is unreal but because he makes *all* reality available
to us.' Blanchot's point is that in the realm of the imaginary one
can do and undo anything – and no art form brings this home to
us more vividly and insistently than cartoon animation.

Real life is hard work because so much gets in the way of
what we would like to do. Cartoon life removes the obstacles of
reality – the limitations of our bodies and minds, as well as of the
physical and social worlds – inviting us into a world where we
can create or destroy anything without effort, where Rameau's
bugbears of hunger, boredom and remorse have evaporated. Cats
and ducks and people can be sliced, inflated, stretched, exploded,

burned and beaten with ease and impunity, unimpeded by the joyless finger-wagging of conscience or logic.

This is how Homer's slobbery can happily coexist with a manic excess of activity. He can become an astronaut, rock star, hobo or Mafioso without any of the annoying prerequisites of training or experience. Homer embodies the fundamental affinity between the slob and the cartoon – the fantasy that you can do anything without having to do anything.

Episodes of *The Simpsons* often centre on Homer's shameless craving for inactivity, and the comically circuitous roads he travels to achieve it. He becomes morbidly obese in order to gain eligibility for disability benefits, turning his life into one long renunciation of reason and purpose. In a *Treehouse of Horror* segment, following his ingestion of intergalactic goo, he morphs into a voracious cannibalistic blob, an embodiment of pure consumption.

Homer is something like a pop cultural incarnation of the Sovereign Man envisioned by Georges Bataille. The Sovereign Man is the embodiment of a new economy of 'pure expenditure', driven by a refusal of the delayed gratifications of the 'reality principle' in favour of the immediate discharge of desire. The will to produce is swallowed whole by the will to consume. The lurid, faintly urinal glow of warm colours suffusing the characters of *The Simpsons* is a kind of atmospheric analogue to the nirvana of inanity bestowed by a bottomless abundance of Duff Beer and Lard Lad Donuts. These are the colours of contented suburban decadence, the landscape of easy gratification and casual waste.

Perhaps this explains why the show is so enamoured of apocalyptic environmental events, usually triggered by Homer. In one of the most uncompromisingly nihilistic episodes, Homer's aversion to disposing of his own garbage spurs him to stand successfully for election as Springfield's Sanitation

Commissioner, winning over town hall meetings with the slogan 'Can't Someone Else Do It?' (a canny riff on 'Why should I?'). Homer's laxity and wastefulness spread contagiously through the townsfolk, whose sanitation service now eliminates not only garbage but any need for self-care. In an inspired fantasy of collective civic slobbery, men in epauletted sailor suits appear from nowhere to wipe sauce off the front of shirts and dispose discreetly of old porn stashes.

Homer's solution only proliferates the waste he was elected to contain. He blows his office's full annual budget in a month and resolves the crisis by leasing the town's disused mines as an outsourced landfill for cities across America. The whole of Springfield becomes a putrid dump, its parks, golf courses and eventually the town hall itself gushing waste from geysers of backed-up trash. The town is left with no choice but to transport itself wholesale five miles down the road.

The episode presents Homer as the harbinger of the world's return to a state of chaotic formlessness. His campaign mimics the conventional rhetoric of can-do politics geared towards ful-filling efficient goals, but conceals an underlying nihilism and irrationality that threaten to crumble the structures holding up the world.

Homer shows us why the slob is simultaneously venerated and resented. Confronted by the imperative to face reality as it is, he yells, 'Why should I?' and sinks ever more defiantly into the life of aimless sloth the rest of us have been forced, resentfully, to renounce.

Unlike the burnout, whose enjoyment of lassitude is spoiled by nervous agitation, shame and guilt, the scandalous courage of the slob embraces the inertial state, and rejects openly the diligence and responsibility that confer full social legitimacy in a culture defined by work and productivity.

~

Chris didn't sit down, he crashed. Having lumbered into the room, he seemed ready to execute the automatic series of movements we call sitting down – bending his knees, gently lowering himself onto the seat, shuffling into his preferred posture and angle. Instead, he simply let his knees give out, succumbing to the force of gravity and landing with a muffled violence that shook the chair, and me.

It seems to me now that in that split second his unconscious found a way to communicate the bewildering shock of his story, the sudden downward crash reverberating in his mind and body. Pulling at his matted hair and oversized sportswear, he told me I'd probably be surprised to hear this, but not long ago he was working ninety-hour weeks in an investment bank in the City of London. He wasn't wrong – of all the images I could conjure, few seemed more incongruous than the shambling figure before me gliding down the corridors of some glassy corporate palace.

Chris had been plucked by the bank from an elite graduate finance programme in Paris and plunged into its overdriven working culture. For the next two years, he acquired and merged companies with the same easy mastery he'd once brought to the accumulation of his dazzling academic and sporting achievements.

Until one morning when his 5.30 a.m. alarm failed to trigger the usual reflexive bound out of bed. Instead he switched it off and lay there, staring into the wall ahead, certain only that he wasn't going to work. After six hours of drifting between dreamless sleep and blank wakefulness, he pulled on a tracksuit to go to Starbucks and the local Tesco Metro, piling his basket with the boxed doughnuts and ready meals that had since become his diet, largely consumed during box-set binges. 'That's how I got this,' he said with a disarmingly sweet smile, tenderly rubbing the slack mound of flesh under his top. Shoulders, chest, stomach – his whole body seemed to have collapsed in solidarity with his soul.

About three months had since passed. He'd lost his job and morphed with startling speed from thrusting go-getter into the heap slumped opposite me. He did nothing and saw no one. Contact from curious or concerned colleagues had tailed off, until he received notice of the termination of his contract in a win-dowed manila envelope. He was intrigued to find it didn't bother him. He spoke to his parents in America only as often as was necessary to put them off the scent. They both knew the hours he'd been working, so neither expected to hear from him all that much, and he never told them anything important anyway.

Three months had passed in a solitary haze of TV and saturated fat. 'I was a jock, if you can believe it. Now I'm a professional slob.' He was amazed by his own appetite. Just yesterday, by around 11.30 a.m., he'd consumed his recommended daily calo-rie allowance in breakfast cereal alone. 'I am in baaad shape,' he drawled gleefully. I said he seemed to be willing himself to lose his shape, in more ways than one. 'Well,' he said with the slightest shade of defiance, 'maybe I never wanted to *be* that shape.'

Chris had grown up an only child in an affluent suburb of St Louis. He recalled his parents, now divorced, channelling the frustrations of their loveless marriage into the ferocious cultiva-tion of their son's achievements. The straight-A grades, baseball team captaincy and Ivy League scholarship he'd eventually won had, as he saw it, been ordained pretty much from the moment he was born.

With no prompting from me, he recalled going to an old-fashioned downtown barbershop with his father at the age of fourteen and watching in the mirror as Dad instructed the barber in clipper numbers, tracing a line round his son's head with his finger. 'I told him, "But Dad, I hate that cut." I wanted to look like a rock star, not some fucking marine. He didn't shout or change expression, he just looked straight at me and said, "This is the cut you have." And that was kind of it, from that moment on. That was the cut.'

'Your shape,' I said.

'My shape.'

When the barber had finished, Chris noted his father's approving smile in the mirror and resolved to cling for all time to the path of least resistance. In his mind's eye, one or other of them was forever hovering behind him, ready to radiate the same glow of approval in the mirror. The weird thing about this was how much you could achieve through sheer compliance. The marine look had been no coincidence. 'A marine gets an order to advance or to fire, he doesn't stand around stroking his chin, wondering if he wants to or if he should. He doesn't wonder at all, he just does it.'

He came to approach all of life's tasks with the same unquestioning focus, never once pausing to ask if he took any pleasure or interest in what he was doing. He knew what was wanted of him, and that was enough to suspend indefinitely the question of what he wanted for himself.

There were moments nonetheless when neither he nor the world around him felt right. When he received the Dartmouth scholarship letter he felt the strangest twinge of panic as he stared at it and had the feeling it wasn't intended for him at all. 'Perhaps you were right,' I suggested. 'You might have felt that for all the endless hard work, it didn't have much to do with you.' He sighed. 'Maybe. It wasn't so clear at the time. My father seemed to spend his life being angry, my mother being sad. That had something to do with me. I thought the letter would change something for them. And he reads it and claps my shoulder and she reads it and squeezes my hand, and they say, "That's great, son", "That's so incredible, baby", and go straight back to their bubbles of unhappiness.'

In the years that followed, he plunged himself ever more single-mindedly into the progressive accumulation of achievements. But the spectral presence of his parents seemed to dissipate. He was clocking up degrees, promotions, bonuses, driven by some inexorable desire that had never really been his but now no longer seemed to be anyone else's. He was blind, compulsive, unstoppable.

Until one day at the bank, he became aware of how much time he was spending sunk in strange reveries at his workstation, yearning to go back to his place and sleep. When the phone or the sound of his name sprang him out of his dreamy retreat, he would be gripped by a terrible panic. 'One time this guy asked me if I was OK, like he was really weirded out. So I looked down and my shirt was drenched in sweat. It was around three weeks later that I stopped going to work.'

What had triggered this small apocalypse of the soul? We turned over this question, session after session, seeming always to arrive at the same formulation: 'All I know is that I needed to stop.' 'I needed to stop' – with every repetition, that sentence became more enigmatic to me. 'Stopping' somehow lost its purely negative sense of bringing to a halt. In Chris's experience it acquired the quality of a real activity, untried and mysterious.

Winnicott suggests that the self is inhabited by the two primary elements of 'being' and 'doing'. The sense of being, he writes, 'forms the only basis for self-discovery and a sense of existing'. A psychic disorder sets in when the element of doing is promoted, with the corresponding impoverishment of being. Chris's nervous compulsion to do had substituted for as long as he could remember for a sense of his own existence. His increasingly frequent intervals of catatonic absence at work, the sudden revelation that he wasn't going to leave his bed, the insatiable consumption of comfort food: these were expressions of protest against a lifelong tyranny of action, and of a wish to recover himself as a creature that breathed and tired and hungered, that simply *is*.

Limbs loose and eyes shut, he lay on the couch speaking at times in a languid drawl, at others in spurts of seeming urgency. How long could he go on filling his days with sleep and food like some goddamn baby? Starbucks, Tesco, here – that was as far as he'd got for months now. When does this become an emergency? When do I decide I need to do something?

I wondered if it hadn't occurred to him that the emergency had already happened, that the thing he really needed to do was what he was now doing. He bristled: 'Are you serious? What I'm doing? What am I *doing*? I'm doing NOTHING!'

I said nothing in response, and we remained in silence. As the session came to an end, I thought I saw him smile.

Two days later he told me he'd gone further than the supermarket for the first time in months. The plan had been to go to the local running track and start getting back into shape. But suddenly aware of the perfectly crisp January sun, he started walking, and couldn't seem to stop. He walked through Haggerston, Highbury, Bloomsbury, through Camden, Tufnell Park and across the Heath. He just walked and walked until he finally slumped onto a bench in contented exhaustion and watched the sun go down.

'And then I laughed to myself. I am twenty-nine years old. I ran track for high school and college. I've covered thousands of miles. And yesterday, for the first time in my entire goddamn life, I took a walk without knowing where I was going.'

'THIS HUGE HILL OF FLESH': ORSON WELLES

At the age of fifty-eight, during one of his increasingly frequent chat show appearances, Orson Welles told host Merv Griffin that he had spent his youth 'trying to be old'; now was the time 'to start pretending to be young. But never middle-aged. I'm leaping nimbly out of it.'

Most of us experience ageing as a linear process, with one stage of life giving way to the next. Welles saw it instead as a series of elective inner states; youth can follow age as much as precede it, while the unwanted passage between them can simply be leap-frogged. We could be tempted to dismiss this peculiar undoing of life's chronology as so much glib TV sofa chat if it didn't capture so strikingly the trajectory of Welles's own life.

Having turned up, age sixteen, on the doorstep of Dublin's Gate Theatre and been swiftly cast in major roles, he had by his early twenties become the most celebrated figure in American theatre and radio. At twenty-five, he was the recipient of an unprecedented and much envied Hollywood contract conferring creative carte blanche to make his first film, *Citizen Kane*, which since the 1950s has persistently topped critics' surveys of all-time-greatest movies.

Barely out of adolescence, Welles had attained the kind of status usually reserved for revered grandees in their twilight years. Yet by the time of his appearance on *The Merv Griffin Show*, he had long been an involuntary practitioner of the precarious DIY approach to film financing and production, these days more read-ily associated with hungry aspirant film-makers in their twenties.

The crowning glories of late life give way to the gritty strug-gles of the Young Turk. Welles was on the mark in his late essay film, *F for Fake*, when he quipped that he'd started at the top and worked his way down. What is missing from the quick-burning arc of his life and career is a period of middle age, of steady and sustained consolidation of his established reputation. He may have passed through his forties and fifties, but, true to his word, he was never middle-aged. He continued to make films but could not adapt himself to the efficient churn of Hollywood product; he married serially and sired children, but could never settle down to conventional family life.

It's difficult to learn and write about Welles's life and work without feeling oneself cast in its gigantic shadow. I contemplate his creative risks, financial profligacy, insatiable wanderlust, his excessive consumption of drink, sex and food, from the heart of my own middle age and feel oddly shamed by the uneventfulness of my own life. The early mornings, the reliable sequence of precisely timed sessions, the sedentary stillness of the analytic chair, the commitment to think rather than act, all the rituals and attitudes that comprise the everyday experience of the psychoanalyst, can seem very small in the face of a life so large.

At the age I am now, Welles was making *The Trial* on the fly in the cavernous ruins of the Gare d'Orsay. Two years later he was directing his own poignantly elegiac performance as Falstaff in *Chimes at Midnight*, the artistry of which lies in a profound spiritual and physical identification with his character, conveyed even in still photographs. The lank hair and unkempt beard, the folds of the black cloak spread over his six foot three frame, now burdened by over 300 pounds of flesh, all register the force with which life had branded Falstaff and Welles alike.

John Gielgud, his Henry IV, noted that an outbreak of eczema prevented Welles from washing his hands during the period of filming. He was also suffering a gall bladder condition resulting from his insupportable girth. Welles had nothing but contempt for method actors, but *Chimes at Midnight* made him one by default – the ravages of Falstaff's hard living had become indistinguishable from his own.

In the third volume of his definitive biography, Simon Callow touches on Welles's fierce impatience with those who failed to absorb his direction quickly enough: 'The one thing Welles could never tolerate was slowness.'

Isn't 'slowness' a kind of synonym for middle age? In middle age our lives and characters become more predictable, more entrenched in their habits and set in their ways. This makes us less available to surprise, to the sudden eruptive bursts of creative energy and inspiration that powered Welles's work as a director. To be slow in response to a Welles suggestion is to take a moment or two to listen, process, think through the options. The problem with this approach is that by the time the other person has got to where Welles is, the moment has passed. Slowness intrudes a break in his flow, disturbing the seamless continuity of the creative process.

Youth, on the other hand, is spontaneous, excitable, reckless. It lets itself be carried on the wave of the moment, to discharge impulses rather than ponder them. In this sense, Welles never surrendered his youth. He may, as he says, have spent his early years 'trying to be old', but then what could be more youthful than that? What distinguished Welles from almost every other young person was that his mad wish to be old came true; at twenty-five, his CV was sufficiently full and expansive for a wildly ambitious man twice, if not three times, his age.

A flame as ferociously bright as Welles's doesn't let itself be tamed and harnessed as fuel for an even, moderate life. It will not be reduced to the mild flicker of jadedness, lost ideals and shabby compromise we sometimes call middle age. It becomes instead more ferociously intent on consuming all before it, until flesh and soul take on the dimensions of a Falstaff: bloated, exhausted, slobbish.

*

Welles's flame evidently burned bright from the very first. His prodigiousness was established as soon as, if not before, he came into the world. His mother, Beatrice, tireless patron of the arts and chair of the Kenosha Board of Education, immediately recognized and assiduously nurtured her infant child's astonishing precocity, reading him Shakespeare before he could speak, immersing him in an ether of poetry, music and high-flown chatter.

When Beatrice died from a long and painful bout of jaundice, which was then a fatal disease, the nine-year-old Orson felt himself to be charged with fulfilling the special destiny she had set out for him. It is difficult to imagine the state of permanent and unrelenting pressure that would have lodged in him from this point on. As long as she was alive, he could seek to modify or challenge, or even reject the ideal she projected onto him. But her death made this punishing ideal a permanent feature of his internal reality; he was consigned forever to the shame of never having done, or been, quite enough. Warhol responded to this predicament by cutting off desire; Welles preferred to pursue it relentlessly, until finally he was insupportably jaded and heavy.

The bombastic confidence and authority he projected outwards were shadowed by an intense vulnerability, manifest not only in periodic bouts of depressive breakdown but in somatic afflictions, most painfully the chronic asthma and eczema that would accompany him through life. Skin and breath are the membranes separating inside from outside; in Welles they were desperately thin. Neither his brilliance nor his ferocity, his superhuman levels of activity or his imposing and rapidly expanding frame could finally conceal the weeping wounds beneath.

It didn't help that the young Orson was denied the protective boundaries of paternal discipline. His father, Dick, was an absent heel, an inventor and functioning alcoholic playboy from whom his mother separated when Welles was four. As ineffectual as he was affectionate, Dick could not interpose the layer of sober realism that might at least partially have shielded Orson from his mother's intense idealization. Nor was there a robust sibling rivalry to divert the attentions of mother and child from one another; his brother, Richard Jr, ten years his senior and hard to discipline, had been packed off to boarding school while Orson was still a baby. Once out of his mother's sight, he seems to have stayed largely out of her mind, ceding its resources wholesale to his younger brother.

From birth, Welles had been recruited by his mother into her all-consuming project to make him great. The prologue of his second film, *The Magnificent Ambersons* (1942), hints at his internal atmosphere of entitlement and lawlessness that this peculiar mode of child-rearing might have engendered. Having terrorized the townsfolk in a horse carriage and assaulted the father of a local boy, little George Minafer, scion of the great Amberson clan, sporting long, coiffured golden curls, ruffled velvet doublet, kilt and cane in some egregious parental fantasy of Scottish aristocracy, stands haughtily tall, back to his elders in a show of grand indifference to their half-hearted scolding.

It is a strangely distressing image of the child cultivated as the exception, exempt from boundaries and limits. It also has an unmistakable hint of self-portraiture: 'Any form of limitation, obligation, responsibility or enforced duty,' writes Callow, 'was intolerable to him and made him claustrophobic and destructive.' The adult George Minafer is scandalized by his would-be bride's insistence that he earn his own living; the leisured life he intends, he tells her, is infinitely more 'honourable' than 'scrubbing dishes, selling potatoes or trying law cases'.

In one respect, the comparison with Welles is well off the mark. While young George cannot be persuaded to work, young

Orson, spreading himself frenetically between stage, radio and cinema, could not be persuaded to stop working. But the contrast conceals a deeper and more subtle affinity. What the two share is a profound sense of entitlement: a properly aristocratic contempt for middle-aged graft, for steady, diligent movement towards middle-class goals – solvency, stability and respectability.

Welles's young adulthood coincided with the emergence of consumer society and the increasing ubiquity of what I've called the slogan of the ego ideal: 'We can!' The slogan radiated everywhere, from parenting manuals to pop psychology, advertising to schoolroom. While it tends, as we've seen, to arouse deep feelings of inadequacy and shame, it can equally provoke a sense of entitlement, for it encourages us to view with contempt all limits on ambitions, desires and capacities. 'Good wine', 'luscious food', 'lovely women' – like Rameau, Welles bristled at any interference in his pursuit of pleasure.

Welles seems to have been the beneficiary and victim of a particularly outsize ego ideal. It was the spur to his boundless creative achievement, but also the source of his immense emotional and physical vulnerability. The bombastic inflation of his public self was separated by a hair's breadth from the catastrophic deflation of his private self.

Believing in the limitlessness of one's own powers begets a very particular relationship to reality, brought into sharp relief by Marlowe's *The Tragical History of Doctor Faustus*, a play staged by Welles for the Federal Theater Project on Broadway in 1937, with himself in the title role. Like Faustus, Welles was a keen magician – in the strict sense of the magic act he performed at various points in his life to enraptured audiences and in the looser sense of conducting both life and art as so many conjuring tricks.

The conjuror emits an oddly beguiling a sense of entitlement.

Like God, it is enough for him to state his wish for it to come true. Things inexplicably appear and disappear on his say-so. He performs for us perhaps the most fundamental of all childhood fantasies, to do away with the tiresome dictates of reality. One of the most basic tasks of education is to instil respect for these dictates and demonstrate to the child the futility of seeking to defy them. The joy aroused by the conjuror lies in his blithe defiance of this spiteful lesson, the subversive assurance that reality need not get in our way.

This is the fantasy realized by the Faust myth. In Marlowe's version, Faustus's incantations conjure Mephistophilis, whose first words are, 'Now, Faustus, what would'st thou have me to do?' The Devil's servant announces himself by inviting his conjuror to speak his desire without constraint. Faustus replies:

> I charge thee wait upon me whilst I live,
> To do whatever Faustus shall command,
> Be it to make the moon drop from her sphere,
> Or the ocean to overwhelm the world.

The fantasy of a world freed from the confines of physics and morality is both demonically depraved and childishly innocent, the universal wish of daydreaming children down the ages.

Welles's young life seems to speak of what happens when this wish becomes reality. Like Faustus, he was possessed of a wild and dangerous energy which he channelled into the acquisition of various kinds of magical knowledge. And like Faustus, the young Welles gives the impression that all his frenzied efforts are a smokescreen to hide the fact that everything falls into his lap for the simple reason that he wants it to. No sooner had he appeared in Dublin at the age of sixteen than he was playing on one of its most famous stages. No sooner had he broadcast an overblown radio adaptation of H. G. Wells's *The War of the Worlds* than the science fiction hokum of alien invasion became a terrifying reality for tens of thousands of listeners. The passage from our wishes to their realization, so bitterly difficult and uncertain for most of us, seemed the smallest trifle for the young Welles.

It may be worth recalling that Faustus's defiance of God's cosmic order sends him straight to the fires of hell. The most poignant moment in the play occurs when Mephistophilis, incarnation of evil, is moved to pity by Faustus's journey to damnation and appeals to him to pull back from the brink:

> O Faustus! leave these frivolous demands,
> Which strike a terror to my fainting soul.

Reading the story of Welles's life, it is tempting to make the same futile appeal to him not to sell his soul, and not only because of the increasing number of disasters he came to inflict on himself. This may seem presumptuous and wrong-headed counsel to a man whose name is a byword for the refusal to capitulate to commercialism. Welles never compromised his artistic integrity (at least not as a director, his real vocation; as an actor, he appeared in some unforgivably bad films), but he may have sold his soul in the subtler sense of exchanging a rich inner life for a crowd-pleasing performance of his selfhood.

There are few modern public figures whose bearing, gestures and vocal tone are more unmistakable, more stubbornly themselves. But his uniqueness was cultivated not in the service of his self-development, but in a desperate and insatiable hunger for the applause and acclaim of others. As the cultural critic Peter Conrad suggests, growing up was painful for Welles, for it meant giving up on the 'unanimous adoration' of adults. Critics were at once dazzled by and suspicious of the spectacular virtuosity of his stagecraft, his startling composition of cinematic shots and hypnotic use of sound, perpetually wondering if such ostentatious mastery masked some irremediable thinness of substance.

Intriguingly, this suspicion reared its head most prominently in response to *Citizen Kane*, his most fully realized and universally celebrated work. In his lesser-known guise as a film critic, the great Argentinian writer Jorge Luis Borges castigated the film for being 'too gigantic, pedantic, tedious' in a brief and notoriously waspish review. Borges focuses on Welles's fractured mode of storytelling. The film 'overwhelmingly, endlessly' presents fragments of the media mogul Charles Foster Kane's life, 'and invites us to combine them and reconstruct him'.

What results is a portrait of Kane as 'a simulacrum, a chaos of appearances'. In a phrase (borrowed from the writer G. K. Chesterton) that has become famous, he calls the film 'a labyrinth with no centre'. The review's plaintive tone may issue from Borges's discomfort at the striking affinity between the experience of seeing the film and that of reading his own stories, but it has become a kind of compressed statement of the most insistent criticism of *Citizen Kane* and of Welles more generally: that he was an empty vessel, identified with Kane above all in appearing to exist only through the fantasies of others rather than in his own right. He too is a mosaic of disorganized fragments his public were invited to combine and reconstruct.

When Faustus conjures Alexander the Great from the dead so that the Imperial court can watch him slay his great foe Darius, he cautions the emperor not to get carried away by appearances. For all their uncanny resemblance to living beings, they are 'but shadows, not substantial'. Welles never ceased invoking the conjuror as a model for the artist, the one like the other spiriting weightless illusions from nothing and nowhere to fool their credulous audiences. Both use up immense reserves of discipline and method in conjuring these insubstantial shadows, and in appearing to do so with casual ease.

The artist, in other words, is a figure who can do anything, who possesses the divine capacity to make his own reality, and who at the same time does nothing, leaving untouched the reality of everyone else. His imaginative productivity looks like a waste of time and resources from the perspective of the active world; his manic energy in making art an indulgent sloth.

Howard Teichmann, Welles's stage manager for the Mercury Theatre's production of *Julius Caesar* in 1937 (already a major theatrical celebrity, he was still only twenty-one) offers a vivid image of this duality. Welles, he says, would sit at a table in the theatre's centre aisle whispering directions into a microphone. This work table would double as a dining table: 'When he was hungry, he would send people out and they would bring in the steaks and the French fries and the ice cream and pots of coffee a foot and a half high, which he would consume with great relish.'

Rehearsals would run to the rhythm of his still-adolescent body clock, which often meant starting late at night and finishing in the early hours of the morning. Indeed, Welles's early adulthood unfolded like a realization of the most excitable male adolescent fantasies. The voracious appetites of young men for power, food, sex, fame, limitless creative freedom, ordinarily gratified only in their solitary bedroom reveries, met with real-world consummation for Welles. And so his adulthood assumed the ambiguously charmed atmosphere of his childhood – a vast magician's playground in which his wishes were the world's command.

As he conquered swathes of the American cultural terrain – theatre, radio, cinema and eventually political journalism and oratory – his capacity to sustain his imposing presence in each of them simultaneously seemed like the most audacious trick of all. 'On a purely quantitative level,' comments Callow, 'his productivity is almost impossible to grasp.' During one period of frenzied simultaneous activity, a reporter tracked Welles's various commitments while staging his Verne-inspired musical extravaganza, *Around the World*, at Broadway's Adelphi Theatre in 1946. During this run, in addition to directing and starring in the show, Welles premiered a nightclub act at the Copacabana, where he performed in the early evening, which required writing himself out of *Around the World*'s early scenes. After one set at the club, he would run to the Adelphi, perform his various parts, 'then hustle back to the Copa for his two late shows'. He arranged to perform *King Lear* on those afternoons on which there was no matinée of *Around the World*, and set in train plans for a revival of *Five Kings*, his epic condensation of Shakespeare's history plays. In between rehearsals and performances, he found the hours to devise and cast the script for his Friday night half-hour radio drama and to write his Sunday radio lecture.

What can this ungovernable excess of activity mean? While many of Welles's innumerable commitments were taken on to pay off the colossal debts he accumulated, through both personal investments in creative projects and profligate daily spending, this only begs the question of how he got caught in this cycle of uncontrolled expenditure and equally uncontrolled overextension.

Both forms of excess had an inflationary effect on Welles's self-image. He overspent in the hope of realizing his expansive creative ambitions, or to feed the popular myths of his unbound recklessness. In overextending himself, he proliferated different versions of himself, both behind the scenes and before his public. In taking on so many different projects, he carved out ever larger expanses of space on stage and screen, on the airwaves, in the newspapers, all of which needed to be filled, in a striking externalization of what he did with the empty space in himself.

Frustrated by the insistent questioning of his 1962 interviewer Jean Clay, Welles compared himself to the Oriental and Christian mystics who think of the self as 'a kind of enemy'. His work, he continued, 'is precisely what enables me to come out of myself'. He crystallized this thought in a simple and provocative formulation: 'I like what I do, not what I am.'

Is what he 'does', conjuring countless iterations of himself on and off stage and screen, an extravagant way of evading the encounter with what, or who, he is? 'Asking me questions is death to me,' Welles elaborated. 'I'm fanatically against psychoanalysis. Freud kills the poet in man. He kills the contradictions – and they're essential to him.'

These contradictions were embodied in his many performances of himself and others. They interposed a dazzling and busy screen of images in front of the empty space of 'what I am'. In seeking to know himself through what he did rather than was, he consigned himself to being the object of a permanent outside gaze, to experiencing himself only via the gazes and fantasies projected onto him by countless others. Draw back the veil of these performances and what remained, beyond a terrifying void where his self might have been? Perhaps praise and notoriety became Welles's only means of affirming his own existence.

A psychoanalyst might be expected to warn of the deleterious consequences of self-evasion to an individual's creative life. But Welles, like many artists, alerts us to the absence of any easy correlation between a healthy creativity and a robust sense of self. In fact *F for Fake*, his last full-length film and one of his most under-appreciated, goes about cheerfully dismantling any such correlation.

F for Fake is an essay film orbiting around the idea that art and selfhood alike are illusions, frauds, forgeries. It opens on a train station platform with Welles performing magic tricks for enraptured little boys under the gaze of a young woman watching from the train window. 'Up to your old tricks again!' she calls to Welles with a dazzling smile. The woman in question is Oja Kodar, the young Hungarian artist who became the companion of Welles's last years. The hinted relationship between the massive, ageing Welles and the ostentatiously beautiful young woman three decades his junior proves the first of many moments begging the question always posed to the conjuror: how on earth did you do that?

The question echoes as the film draws us into a labyrinth of deceptions laid by the real-life flamboyant Hungarian art forger Elmyr de Hory and his biographer, the rakish American art writer Clifford Irving. De Hory is in legal exile on Ibiza, living with one of the many art dealers to have become rich off his eerily exact modern art forgeries. Irving, also based on the island, is introduced as the author of *Fake!*, a biography of de Hory, only to be revealed soon afterwards as also the author of a hoax biography of Howard Hughes based on forged primary documents. But Hughes himself turns out to have been something of a con artist who frequently fooled his public by sending hired doubles into the media glare to pose as himself.

This vertiginous proliferation of fictions sets in train Welles's meditation on the place of fakery in his own career, from blagging parts at Dublin's Gate Theatre on the back of a claim to be a famous New York actor (a lie that would soon enough morph into a truth), to the notorious *War of the Worlds* radio hoax that convinced thousands of credulous listeners of the real-time invasion of America by hostile extraterrestrials, to the blurring of the real and fictional lives of, respectively, William Randolph Hearst and Charles Foster Kane. Spinning the web still further, Welles reveals that the original inspiration for the *Citizen Kane* tycoon was not Hearst but Howard Hughes.

Welles, as the director, is established from the first as a trickster, the unreliable narrator of a tale of a pair of unreliable narrators. The effect of this intricate tangle of tricks is to sap personal identity, art and life itself of all substance. 'The art world,' remarks Welles at one point, 'is a large confidence trick.' So-called experts can be called upon to authenticate fake artworks confidently and to cast doubt on the provenance of authentic ones; experts, laughs Welles, are 'God's own fakers'.

With its playful skewering of expertise and its dizzying demonstration of events and people that fake themselves, *F for Fake* has become a startlingly resonant film in the age of Brexit, Trump and 'fake news'. It presages those events' sudden and radical dissolution of all the political and cultural norms we had complacently fooled ourselves into thinking of as permanent and durable.

The film's final sequence is an elaborate camera trick in which Welles levitates an elderly man posing as the corpse of Kodar's grandfather to head height and wraps him in a winding sheet, which he then removes with a magician's flourish, to reveal ... nothing.

In this moment Welles is unveiling the void of art and of his own self. But instead of engendering horror, this revelation of the essential emptiness of the artist is transformed by its artfulness into a moment of enchanted lightness. De Hory, a French tabloid headline declaims at one point in the film, 'sold his soul to the Devil'. In line with Faustus, the forger turns objects of substance, masterpieces heavy with cultural status and financial value, into 'shadows, not substantial'. But this alchemy sends the conjuror not down to a Faustian hell but up to a Wellesian heaven.

*

The exuberant lightness on display in *F for Fake* hardly tells the whole story. Conjuring is a precarious model for art. One small slip in the intricate mechanism of a trick and the effect of effortless airiness gives way to awkward gravitational slump. For all Welles's ability to entrance his audience, Faust himself couldn't have sustained the sheer volume of his creative output without occasionally falling prey to error and worse.

As his reputation for overspending his budget, exceeding his schedule and alienating his producers grew, so did his difficulty in financing his own film and stage projects. His life increasingly resembled an anxious and exhausting juggling routine, one and then another of the filming, writing, radio broadcasting, acting and hustling balls threatening to crash to the ground at any moment. Running out of money in the middle of a shoot, he would repeatedly be forced to interrupt production to travel to one European film set or another and perform bit parts in garish epics for extravagant fees.

Engulfed by desperate and unsustainable creative and financial demands, Welles was prone to feelings of inadequacy, a tormenting suspicion that he should be achieving more and better, leading to episodes of depressive collapse. Such moments show us something of the abject state of shame and self-disgust he sought to escape through manic overactivity. Perhaps Welles couldn't abide slowness because it would give him the time to be with and contemplate himself.

In 1938, his staging of the William Gillette farce *Too Much Johnson*, which had pioneered the integration of film into stagecraft, was cancelled after performances so shambolic as to provoke disgruntled audiences into hurling objects at the stage. Here was the ultimate confirmation of the agonizing doubt that had accompanied the enraptured adulation he'd known since childhood. A few days had been enough to turn the indomitable wunderkind of New York theatre into a laughing stock.

In *Run-Through*, a memoir of his years as Welles's theatrical partner, John Houseman described Welles's reaction to the debacle of *Too Much Johnson*: 'he retired into his air-conditioned room at the St Regis, where he lay in darkness for a week surrounded by 25,000 feet of film ... convinced that he was going to die, racked by asthma and fear and despair.' Other figures in Welles's circle spoke of the unrelenting attacks of self-loathing to which he subjected himself during such crises. It was at these points that his asthma came most virulently to the surface, as though his breath had become an expression and instrument of the hatred he harboured towards himself.

The health problems arising from his rapidly expanding girth were numerous and chronic by the time Welles had reached the age of forty. His joints and feet were in constant pain, while to his severe asthma were added frequent bouts of tonsillitis. The pattern of punishing periods of frenetic activity interspersed with odd retreats to his bed became more entrenched – 'the real explanation,' writes Callow, 'of many of his mysterious absences'.

There is something oddly poignant about these abrupt disappearances, some intimation of an entropic collapse lurking behind his tireless creative bombast and self-inflation. Welles's visible grandiosity was twinned with a concealed inadequacy, an ambiguity especially marked in his work as a stage actor. He augmented the direction of each production with overall creative control over design, lighting and sound, ensuring that his attention was occupied by multiple conceptual and practical demands at every moment of rehearsal.

Diffusing himself in this way left little time to rehearse his own role, so that he would work for the first time with his fellow actors only in the final stages of rehearsal, a predicament that cannot have been less than terrifying for either of them. Given that he would be playing the likes of Othello or Lear, this meant that the entire play had been staged around an absence; another actor might speak his lines, but this could give no indication of Welles's own eventual timing, tone or movement.

For what possible reason would an actor wilfully put himself and his cast at such a parlous disadvantage in performance? Welles's daredevil bravura could only have been a cover for his self-doubt and shame. His limitless capacity for self-display on and off stage masked profound insecurities about his acting. Writing as a distinguished actor as well as a biographer, Callow remarks that Welles's acting was liable to be caught between rhetorical and sentimental modes, both of which 'deny real feeling; seeking rather to impress the spectator than reveal an inner truth. They are external applications, designed to mask the absence of emotion.'

Just as Iago and Desdemona were made to act around an absent Welles, Welles could only act around his absent self. Perhaps he deferred rehearsing with his cast for fear of exposing this absence to those with the emotional acuity and perceptiveness to see through to it. The film-maker Richard Fleischer's account of directing Welles in *Compulsion*, the 1959 dramatization of the Leopold and Loeb case which cast him as the defence attorney, gives some ballast to this speculation.

Welles would insist on filming close-up and reverse shots with the other actor off camera. 'He played the entire scene just as though the actor were there,' writes Callow, 'reacting to non-existent dialogue, responding with his own interrupting, overlapping, laughing, growing angry, exactly as though there were someone there speaking to him.' Where he couldn't help acting with another actor, he avoided eye contact, forgetting his lines if it was made inadvertently. In shooting the courtroom sequences, he was forced to ask E. G. Marshall, the actor to whom he delivered his speeches, to close his eyes, a request which then spread to all the actors playing assistant DAs sitting alongside Marshall. "'There they were",' Callow quotes Fleischer, "'all lined up, listening intently, with their eyes closed.'"

These anxieties appear the more striking given that there is no evidence Welles suffered from stage fright or anything similar. On the contrary, he had placed himself from a very young age before audiences of hundreds, thousands and eventually millions, often in under-rehearsed or improvisatory performances, without the slightest hint of fear or fragile confidence. The fright struck him, it seems, only before an audience of one. Large audiences, watching from a safe distance, could be spellbound by his conjuror's illusions. It is the single, emotionally attuned individual who threatens to see past the tricks.

Welles over-consumed as wildly as he overproduced, and likely for some of the same reasons. He drank, ate and fornicated to excess and freely spent his own and others' money, accumulating massive debts for both parties. The staging of *Around the World* in 1946 cost his backers $300,000, 'at a time when a big musical generally cost $100,000'. Reviewing the show, the critic Wolcott Gibbs noted that the technical complexity and huge cast 'make the cost of *Around the World* literally prohibitive', going on to suggest that 'an enterprise that can't possibly make money would, of course, have an almost irresistible charm for that rich, unusual mind'.

Gibbs's speculation may be casual, but it taps acutely into the ways creativity and destructiveness seem so often to shade into one another across Welles's career. To claim that his creative achievements were ruined by his self-destructive tendencies misses the more ambiguous and complex relationship between the two: Welles was evidently fascinated by the creative potential of destructiveness, and vice versa.

Broadway and Hollywood each demand a certain responsibility of art and the artist. Crudely speaking, he or she should not offend popular morality or standards of taste, nor stray too far from narrative and generic conventions. These moral and aesthetic responsibilities are allied to the fiscal responsibility not to overspend one's allocated budget. The artist is producing an object for consumption according to a basic economic principle: it should make more money than it costs. The backers should see a return on their investment.

This is the responsible, 'middle-aged' notion of popular art which Welles defied compulsively. It is rooted in the basic capitalist principle of investment for growth and expansion, or, as we say, a healthy return. Cast in this light, Gibbs's apparently whimsical notion of a show designed to lose money begins to look distinctly dangerous. It evokes Georges Bataille's notion of a 'general economy'; where, in the conventional or 'restricted' economy, investments return enlarged to facilitate further investment and further growth, in the general economy there are neither investments nor returns, only pure, unbound expenditure and waste.

To suggest a neat alignment between Welles and Bataille is stretching the point. But it is hard to miss the echo of Bataille in Welles's persistent offences against the middle-aged economy of healthy returns. Such offences, already an occupational hazard during the early years of the Mercury Theatre, became a way of life from the point Welles left Hollywood for Brazil in 1942, on a commission from the Office of Inter-American Affairs to make a film promoting pan-American unity. The planned compendium film, *It's All True*, was to be the cultural centrepiece of a broader diplomatic project to boost relations with South America. Its chronically overrunning budget and schedule secured its place as the pre-eminent disaster of Welles's career, and the first chapter in his drawn-out but inexorable decline.

By the time the project's financing was pulled, Welles had irremediably alienated both his American location crew and the producers back home. None of the film's four segments, two of them comprising endless hours of raw, shapeless documentary footage, was completed. To compound his self-inflicted injury, he had left Hollywood as post-production on his second film, *The Magnificent Ambersons*, had just begun, in the unfounded hope that he could edit it from South America. After many bitter long-distance exchanges, the final cut (or better, given the loss of a full hour of the original, the final mutilation) was edited and scored against his express wishes, and released while he was still in Brazil, on an inauspicious double bill with *Mexican Spitfire Sees a Ghost*.

The hapless predicaments and reckless self-sabotage of this period – abandoning his exquisitely styled film to the studio wolves in one place, while squandering the budget for the next film in another – recurred reliably through the remainder of Welles's life. The most distressing aspect of this repeated scenario was that it always centred on post-production, the transformative and intricate processes of editing and scoring he considered to be the creative heart of film-making, and the primary means by which he imprinted his singular signature.

One film after another yields a different variation on the same story, in which Welles loses creative control at the point most damaging to its aesthetic and narrative integrity. If he wasn't trying once more to edit the film by remote control, he had ceded the right of final cut in his contract, fallen out with his studio backers over budget or schedule or, perhaps worst of all, wilfully walked off to the next project before the current one was finished.

Projects conceived in passion, invested with abundant aesthetic intuition and technical knowledge through the course of their execution, were left to collapse before they could be gathered together, ruined by alien hands with little understanding of or appreciation for his original vision. It was as though the first moment of creative elevation was only ever a prelude to a fateful inertial collapse.

I wonder if this movement of rise and fall doesn't also describe the grim fate of Welles's body. The imposing frame of his youth began as the engine of his voracious ambition. The round-the-clock consumption of steak dinners, ice cream and brandy seems entirely of a piece with the gigantism of his creative vision and character. But the difficulty of keeping in check the effects of such compulsive eating eventually dragged him downward physically and psychically. Georges Bataille might have written a sketch of Welles's body, noting its unerring demonstration of the logic of nature. Like the plant as envisioned by Bataille, over the course of time Welles's frame 'rises in the direction of the sun and then collapses in the direction of the ground'.

Peter Conrad writes of the destructive rampages that accompanied Welles's fits of temper: in one episode he trashed all the rooms on the floor of the New York Ritz-Carlton; in another he set fire to the curtains at Chasen's restaurant in Hollywood after throwing dish heaters at Houseman. Such rages, writes Conrad, 'were a complaint against the stubborn, resistant nature of reality. They allowed Welles to return to that malleable state before anything was fixed, before forms and rules were imposed on us ...'

This state, commonly known as chaos, is the condition towards which Welles's life and work are always gravitating. It is the dissolution of all the structures we thought solid and reliable, the inexorable movement of souls and bodies towards their own collapse. In middle age, most of us seek to suspend this movement for a while, to establish some sense of our own durability in the universe, however fleetingly. Welles preferred to 'leap nimbly out of it' – at times, at least in his art, to float above it, but more often submitting to the fall of gravity, until his final crash to earth.

In his masterly portrayal of Hank Quinlan, the demonically corrupt cop of his 1958 Mexican border thriller, *Touch of Evil*, Welles comports and shoots his body as a kind of uncontainable mass that overspills the boundaries of the screen, as though the texture of evil resides in excess flesh. For the role of Quinlan, he augmented his already considerable upper body with a huge layer of prosthetic padding, conferring a quality of sublime terror on the character's corpulence.

The grotesque excess of Quinlan's body contrasts with the vulnerably slack, ageing flesh of his Sir John Falstaff, the enchanting, entitled, self-interested, mendacious, slobbish and profoundly chaotic clown. More than one commentator has hinted at Welles's deep identification with the character, lending his performance an inner fullness and substance lacking in any of his other Shakespeare leads. The Falstaff of *Chimes at Midnight* is not the anarchic party animal of so many other productions, but a man ravaged by physical and emotional decay, wearied of the role in which life has cast him. His smile is tired, haunted by an irremediable sadness, disappointed by what he and his life have come to.

In Falstaff's implausible stories of his own heroics, there is a hint of Welles, the relentless self-mythologizer, spinner of many, mutually contradictory yarns of his youth, on all those TV talk shows. Peter Conrad writes that by 1950, at still only thirty-five, Welles felt 'he had squandered his youth and forfeited its promise'. That self-reproach is discernible behind Falstaff's tired eyes throughout *Chimes at Midnight*, but most poignantly in the pivotal scene that sets in train his slow humiliation and eventual demise.

The scene sees Hal and Poins goading Falstaff into fantastical inflations of his heroics during the highway robbery at Gadshill, before finally revealing they are on to him; they, after all, were the masked men who had set upon him and his hapless companions in crime, 'and, with a word, outfaced you from your prize'. Having brought him low, Hal asks 'this huge hill of flesh': 'What trick, what device, what starting-hole, canst thou now find out to hide thee from this open and apparent shame?'

It is a question Welles had found himself confronted by with increasing frequency as he stumbled into one and then another self-made disaster: which of your old tricks can you come up with this time?

In Shakespeare's *Henry IV*, Falstaff, true to form, delivers a new lie to cancel out his previous lies: he was in on the joke all along! 'By the Lord, I knew ye as well as him that made ye.' The film turns this sly get-out into a moment of unbearable poignancy. It shoots Falstaff from below, sat behind his tavern table, wearing a hearty grin until the penny drops; in one brief moment, the master of the scene has become its humiliated victim. Stung into silence, he holds the grin frozen for the second it takes him to find his comeback line.

That second's frozen grin, the image of a man clinging desperately to the wreckage of his long lost dignity, is one of Welles's most startling magic tricks. In a mere, barely perceptible stiffening of his facial muscles, he renders visible the broken remnants of a man's inner world. Atop his sagging, slobbish trunk, his face resembles a medieval emblem for the vanity of pleasure. In that one moment, it seems to me, all the humiliations of his life are revealed and redeemed at once.

PART TWO

Antigravity

Chapter 3

The Daydreamer

Looking at my family's old photo albums, I am unsettled by the boy who stares dreamily back at me. I always expect to see the hapless dope I remember from within, not this fine-boned imp.

He may look lost in a poetic reverie, but I feel my younger self lumbering through the world with the gait of a fat old man, pushing myself forward in resentment of the fact of physical existence. Thoughts travelled through my head at the same pace, as though in mimicry of my sluggish limbs. Mathematical and historical facts crawled into my ears, only to expire on their way to the banks of cognition and memory. My childhood was a drag.

Even so, life had its gratifications: reading or making up stories and poems or songs, looking at or drawing pictures and cartoons. Only in activities requiring more enthusiasm and spontaneity than real effort could I break free from the tiresome bounds of myself and find ways to be anywhere but where I was, anyone but who I was.

I seemed to have no aptitude for anything else. I would lag behind the task at hand, barely processing instructions before everyone else had executed them. Cross-country runs would be won before I was 200 metres in, shots on goal would glide blithely through my legs, easy catches brushed the tips of my fingers as they fell to the ground. Major cities were mapped, major events dated, major organs labelled before I was at all aware of where or when I was supposed to be.

In science, the one concept I could relate to was gravity. Gravity was my element and I was its living proof. That the cosmos conspired to pull you down – that wasn't physics, that was life. I would return compulsively to those final frames in the serial *Peanuts* strip: Lucy pulling the ball away from Charlie Brown at the last moment; the precarious diagonal of Charlie Brown's body, the violent rise and fall of his 'AAUGH!', his aerial suspension amplifying the 'WUMP!' of his fall to earth.

I hadn't read Bataille then. But when I did many years later, and discovered his description of the flower 'that rises in the direction of the sun and then collapses in the direction of the ground', his vision of formless collapse as a cosmic destiny, I was startled by the force of recognition. Charlie Brown had long taught me that the soaring body or spirit already contains its own fall.

In my daydreams, I hovered above the clouds; in rare periods of wakefulness, I struggled to get an inch off the ground. I was a wantonly bad pianist. Even now, decades after giving up, I occasionally feel that same sharp stab of guilt at my failure to practise. Because I didn't practise, I didn't improve; because I didn't improve, I couldn't bear to practise. The predicament was a prison of shame from which I could never break out. Yes, I *could* practise, but who could endure that repetitious crunch of botched chords, those dissonant reminders of the permanent disharmony between my fingers and eyes?

Every week I'd spend an hour sweating under the withering gaze of my piano teacher, my fingers falling into the cracks between the keys. I could sympathize with his mirthless response to my ineptitude. Any time I dared a surreptitious glance upward, I could hear the silent protest on his face. 'I play Liszt at the Wigmore Hall,' it said. 'Surely no one needs cash this badly?'

'Why always in the clouds?' teachers would ask in equal measures of bemusement and exasperation. The answer even then
seemed obvious – it was nice up there, and crap down below.
Up there the ball was never pulled away and my foot fired it into
the next galaxy. The encumbrances of my earthly body – weed-
iness, clumsiness, slowness – fell away, revealing a creature of
heroic strength, grace and wit, James Bond in the body of a small
boy, or maybe the other way around. Life on the ground was an
unending series of obstacles between me and whatever I might
want. Physical, intellectual and creative tasks imposed daunting
requirements, levels of dexterity, rigour and application I knew I
couldn't meet, inducing a permanent state of morose resignation.
'I can understand someone finding it hard, I just can't understand
someone who doesn't try,' a PE teacher remonstrated sadly during
a session of circuit training I was dragging myself through. I
myself didn't and still don't find it that hard to understand the disinclination to make an effort at something you hate and do poorly.
Nor is it yet clear to me if that's my problem or the PE teacher's.

My PE teacher, much like all the other adults I encountered,
could see only docile defeat in me, along with a sluggard's aversion to the real effort of self-improvement. They didn't see, and
weren't much interested in, the perpetual and miraculous transformations I was effecting all the time, in the small and infinite
space behind my forehead.

Why always in the clouds? Why not? Can you honestly claim to
have something better to offer? Like every daydreamer, I doubted
it. As I experienced it, worldly reality made you work like a slave
for very little reward. Why not create your reality elsewhere?

On odd occasions, my spacey inner life found favour on the
ground. One afternoon during my eleventh year, our sprightly
old music teacher gathered us on a long bench in the gym,

announced an expansion into drama and called on volunteers to improvise a scene solo, playing all parts. In a neat inversion of the usual tableau, mine was the one arm to shoot up.

I glided across the room and launched without pause into a skit featuring a highly strung father leading his children into the picnic area of a park and unravelling helplessly as they wreak havoc around him. I channelled the tones and gestures of the pitiful man, delinquent kids and enraged passer-by, my voice and face morphing from the malevolent sweetness of a pigtailed little girl into the hoarse protests of a retired colonel. At the edges of my classmates' laughter, I could discern their incredulity at my being intentionally rather than accidentally funny.

I doubt this performance would have stayed with me if not for the magical sensation of lightness it aroused. My tongue and limbs, unburdened of the weight they seemed to have borne forever, discovered a nimbleness and wit they'd hitherto known only in daydreams. Here I was, hovering gracefully above the ground rather than dragging myself across it.

The school play – Shakespeare, Shaw, Dylan Thomas, Wilde – went on to pull me through the grinding days and terms of secondary school. But whatever the variations in the size or nature of the parts I played, the source of my delight remained the same it had been that day in the prep school gym: the stage licensed me to be an assassin, ghost, butler or seductress without the unpleasant graft required to be any of those things.

Acting itself, of course, requires a great deal of graft, and makes demands on talent, effort and technique as prodigious as any of the arts. But as in all the arts, the graft is in the service of imaginary rather than real life, of a world without weight or substance, in which no kings are actually stabbed, no hapless men actually duped, other than in the willed and shared illusion of players and audience.

From this perspective, there's a ticklish irony about the use of the term 'acting' to designate dramatic performance. The Latin source word, *actus*, after *agere*, to do or drive or make happen, denotes a thing done, an event having occurred. But acting in a play makes nothing happen. If you murder a king, you're clapped and encouraged to do the same the following evening. Acting is a way of being someone else while remaining oneself, of doing something without doing anything.

Isn't this an essential lure of art? Art ushers us into the imaginary world, where the rules and logic and facts governing life in the real world are abolished at a stroke. Doing things in the realm of reality is hard work, for reality allows us to operate only in a small corner of the world, where it intrudes endless obstacles – the limited capacities of our bodies and minds, the iron laws of the physical and social worlds. But the white page, blank canvas or bare stage invites us to bend, break, remake and unmake the world at will, to inhabit infinite selves, places and times beyond our own.

Artists never seem to be able to escape the world's suspicion of their essential idleness, even when obsessively disciplined and prolific. This may seem like a contradiction, but it makes perfect sense to anyone who's been labelled a daydreamer or space cadet. In the classroom, my head was a busy hive of frenetic and intricately conceived stories and characters and speculations. But if it wasn't engaged with the trigonometry problem or Latin noun declension on the board, the teacher in question saw me as lazy. And he was basically right; withdrawing into the fantastical realm of my own head was infinitely less demanding than learning, retaining and working with the difficult and resistant stuff of the world around me.

From the perspective of the real world, the artist's imaginary world is essentially inactive, however frenetic it may seem;

indeed, as Maurice Blanchot observes, it 'ruins action'. If you engage an enemy soldier in a real battle, you risk being wounded or killed yourself; but in the war in my head, I take no such risks. I can shoot whomever I wish with perfect accuracy and impunity, or be shot myself, get up and dust myself off. This was what I liked so much about stage acting – it released me from the mean-spirited life which limited me to being this person in this time and place. The realm of action is constrained; the realm of acting is unlimited.

I continued to audition and rehearse and perform through secondary school and into the first year of university, where my ambition was crowned by the title role in *Doctor Faustus*, performed to a few dozen in the round on a set-less, prop-less floor that rendered invisible Faustus's Satanic conjurations.

If the irony of playing Faustus was lost on me then, it isn't now. In the play, Faustus forsakes the modest satisfactions of earthly life, in which you work hard and without guarantee to try and get something you desire, for the infinite pleasures of an alchemical life in which you can attain your desire merely by declaring it. Faustus was a self-portrait, a mirror to my fantasy of being or having whatever I wanted without needing to do anything much in the process.

Lurking within Faustus the obsessive scholar, assiduously conquering one field of knowledge after the next, is an entitled brat whose fantasy is to institute a universe of instant gratification and minimal effort, in which all impediments between desires and their fulfilment have been removed.

The resonance of that fantasy, its unnerving fidelity to the entitled brat I carried in me, powered my performance, which was probably overexcited as a result. I retain some hazy images of my impassioned climactic address to the hallucinatory Helen of Troy, of my subsequent horrified swoon when she was revealed as the bearded Mephistophilis. But far more vivid to me now is the silence that followed as the lights went down, the fleeting eternity in which I passed from the corpse of Faustus back to myself and heard myself say, inside the sealed box of my head, *'I'm giving up acting.'*

The sheer clarity of the internal announcement was at once shocking and reassuring. I was as good as my silent word and, other than in the dubious guise of myself, haven't appeared on stage since. It remains one of the rare instances in my life of unquestioned and decisive action, albeit in the negative, triumphing over thought. I'm not sure that even now I understand that resolution and the iron certainty that came with it. Perhaps it wasn't unlike Faustus's sudden realization that Helen is a hallucination; I'd peeked behind the confident façade of my ambition and seen it was gossamer thin, that nothing was holding it up.

It dawned on me I didn't want to be an actor, only to perform and be praised. The difference between the two came into focus with a rare lucidity. I realized that coaxing applause from paying audiences not largely made up of people I knew would mean learning tap dance, stage fighting, mime, verse speaking – and rejection – and perhaps reckoning with the sudden intuition that I wasn't even that good.

Returning to this moment so many years later, the irony seems to turn neatly around itself. I thought I'd found in acting what Faustus thought he'd found in alchemy: a short cut to instantaneous happiness, bypassing the hardship and frustration that come of doing things properly. But as the Chorus encircled my corpse, exhorting the audience to regard my 'hellish fall', I came to the same horrifying insight as Faustus, albeit in a version more farcical than tragic: there are no short cuts to fulfilment.

I took my bow, breathing sweet relief.

*

When, on the set of *Marathon Man*, Dustin Hoffman told Laurence Oliver that he'd stayed awake for seventy-two hours to achieve his character's state of exhaustion, Olivier is said to have asked him why he didn't 'just try acting'?

Acting may withdraw the actor from the rigours of real-world activity, but the dramatized activity it performs instead is rarely less demanding. This is as much the case for the physical and formal disciplines of Japanese Noh theatre or silent-film acting as for the method actor's uncanny facsimiles of everyday behaviours and emotions.

I must have had some sense of the reality of these exertions as I lay spread-eagled on the floor in those dying seconds of *Doctor Faustus*, hardly less drained in body and soul than the corpse I was impersonating. For close to three hours I'd been reciting Elizabethan verse while lurching between ecstasy and misery, horseplay and madness. I had been at the centre of an action-packed performance, which was quite something for someone who hated action.

It was around this time, perhaps not coincidentally, that I'd sat in a seminar discussing 'The Critic as Artist', Oscar Wilde's 1891 essay in dialogue form. It hadn't taken long for a consensus of disgust to form around the essay's central contention, that action is essentially vulgar. 'Don't talk about action,' the critic Gilbert, dripping with aristocratic disdain, enjoins his interlocutor Ernest. 'It is a blind thing ... incomplete in its essence, because limited by accident, and ignorant of its direction, being always at variance with its aim. Its basis is the lack of imagination.' The tutor read this to us and nodded with un-Wildean earnestness as the accusations piled up. Wilde was 'elitist', 'arrogant' and didn't even make sense – 'I mean, what would happen to the world if people just *stopped* taking action?'

I wasn't ordinarily shy of an argument, but in the face of so much righteous hostility, I couldn't marshal the guts to take Wilde's part. I'd wanted to tell my fellow participants that their chronically humourless and literal-minded responses were doing more than I ever could to prove Wilde's point, but was endowed with enough cowardice to keep quiet.

Arty types are traditionally dismissed as dreamy escapists, *Luftmenschen* or 'air-people' in the appealing German phrase. But in one of his scandalous inversions of received wisdom, Wilde suggests that it's the so-called practical men and women of the world rather than artists who warrant that label. Frenetic activity tends cunningly to disguise its own emptiness. Action, in his glorious formulation, 'is the refuge of people who have nothing whatsoever to do'.

As often as not, we do things only because we can't bear to have nothing to do. This describes nicely the predicament of the obsessive. As Wilde was publishing his essay, Freud was speculating that the obsessive's blind compulsion to act might be a way of fending off the terror our thoughts would inflict if we were left alone with them. 'To do nothing,' says Wilde, 'is the most difficult thing in the world', because it deprives us of the easy evasions of busyness and purpose. Should we doubt this claim, we need only take a glance around the average café, tube carriage or family dinner table and observe the reflexive escape of the eyes and hands around us into the anxious demands and distractions of email, streamed box sets and Candy Crush.

It felt as though acting had released me from the kind of blind activity so disdained by Wilde. Stepping onto the stage, I could leave the sordid mundanity of the real world and take up residence in the ether of the imaginary.

This seems to be how Wilde himself understood the power and appeal of the actor. When Dorian Gray falls in love with the actor Sibyl Vane, he falls not for the woman behind the masks but for her miraculous power to transform herself. 'I loved you,' he tells her, 'because . . . you realised the dreams of great poets and gave shape and substance to the shadows of art.' But her metamorphic gift deserts her as soon as she realizes she loves Dorian more than the theatre, reducing herself in his eyes to a pretty mediocrity: 'Without your art, you are nothing.' The one person he doesn't want his beloved to be, in other words, is herself.

In his ruthless valuation of the weightless shadows of art as worth infinitely more than the cumbersome reality of living people, Dorian is very much Wilde's child. Only in so far as it doesn't dirty its hands with real people and things, they both suggest, does art attain something like meaning and permanence.

Acting had been a vehicle for my own wariness of action. For as long as I was acting, I wasn't in too much danger of getting caught up in real-world commitments. I was happy to pretend to be an engineer or doctor, and leave it to others to build real bridges or cure real cancer. Next to such serious activities, acting clearly wasn't doing much.

I didn't abandon the idea of acting for something closer to worldly reality but to pursue an academic career in American Literature. Academia, of course, is a career like any other, requiring qualifications, interviews, committee meetings and administration – activities (as any academic today will tell you) with an unhappy resemblance to real work and all its attendant stresses. In the face of today's academic culture of metrics, league tables, citation counts, of student-consumers 'rating' their teachers online while challenging poor grades, of quantitative demands for research output and 'impact' on the wider world, the stock figure of the begowned don ensconced in his study with a leather-bound Milton contemplating the medieval perfection of the quad through his window no longer exists anywhere beyond the tabloid imagination.

In the mid-1990s, I knew this was looming before me. But exercising my talent for conjuring away the things I preferred not to see, I saw instead only the chance to spend most of my days reading. And there are few more crystalline images of withdrawal from the world of action and purpose than a person reading.

It is one thing to read a novel or watch a play or even read a poem as a rewarding distraction from the day's demands. As a leisure activity, confined to the odd spare hour, reading serves as a palliative to the rigours of work. It is a turning away from the world that enables us to turn back towards it. But spending the lion's share of one's days with stories and characters and ideas made from the airy, insubstantial matter of words is liable to turn into something else, a preference for unreality, a refusal to respond to the world's call to participate in and contribute to its development and progress.

Many people would object that this need not be the case, and in one way I can see they're right. I've seen often enough how art can disturb the calcified terms of our daily reality, open up new futures, new vistas of personal and political possibility. But is it not equally true that we create worlds that don't exist because the world that does exist is so perpetually painful and disappointing?

I'm not alone in my doubts. The idea that it's worth forsaking the one real world for the infinity of imaginary worlds has an impressive pedigree. Take Xavier de Maistre, a French aristocrat and officer who, in 1790, was placed under house arrest in Turin for forty-two days for duelling with a Piedmontese officer. He whiled away the hours of solitude by writing a journal of his confinement, *Voyage autour de ma chambre* ('Voyage Around My Room'), in which we are invited to accompany him across the walls and floor of his bedroom, taking in the visible objects along the way.

The book begins by anticipating the new craze it might spark for travel into the interior of the self. This is a radically democratic mass tourism, requiring nothing in the way of disposable income or gratuitous effort. 'Let all the wretched, the sick, and the bored follow me –' enjoins de Maistre, 'let all the lazy people of the world rise *en masse* – and you ... who in your boudoir are contemplating renouncing the world *in order to live* ...' (the emphasis is his).

But rise where, and to do what? Surely if lazy people were to rise, they'd join the ranks of the active and purposeful and cease to be lazy? The answer is that they should rise not from their beds but *in* their beds, where the imagination can cross infinite spaces without the body having to move an inch, without a person taking the slightest action. De Maistre claims that the lazy renunciation of the external world is emphatically not a renunciation of life. On the contrary, one stays in bed '*in order to live*', to release the imagination from the chains of workaday worldly life.

The paradox of de Maistre's house arrest is that it was a genuine liberation, releasing him to a territory more expansive and beguiling than the city outside. 'Today,' he wrote on the day of his release, 'is the day that certain people, upon whom my fate depends, presume to give me back my freedom – as if they had taken it away from me! ... They may have forbidden me to travel through a city, one place, but they left me the entire universe: infinity and eternity are at my command.'

I found it impossible to read de Maistre's words without hearing the echo of my childhood self. I was forever being told by the adults around me, in tones of exasperated good humour, to come out of the clouds, to return to, and get on with, life on earth. My chastened meekness at such moments concealed the same arrogance you can discern in de Maistre. I may be inept in sports and slow on the uptake in the classroom, I secretly told them, but what do I care? While the other kids were slaves to the classroom, hemmed in by blackboards, exercise books and football fields, I was roaming freely around a universe at my command, without having to move from my chair.

De Maistre's bedroom voyage seals the link between idleness and imaginative life. But in so doing, it draws on a long tradition of questioning the privileged place of reality and necessity in our culture. Nearly 300 years earlier, a Dutch Catholic theologian, Desiderius Erasmus, a leading figure of the emerging humanism of the day, published *The Praise of Folly*, a lengthy mock-sermon delivered by the figure of Folly, personified as a woman in a jester's suit.

Folly employs every known rhetorical trick to persuade her listeners of the superiority of the foolish orientation of life. She recounts her origins as the child of Plutus, god of riches, and Neotes or Youth, the fairest of all nymphs. She comes into being on the Isles of the Blest, a land of unimagined luxuriance and ease where 'there is no work, no old age, no disease', suckled by the nymphs Methe (Drunkenness) and Apaedia (Stupidity) and attended by others, among them Lethe (Forgetfulness), Misoponia (Laziness), Hedone (Pleasure), Tryphe (Luxury) and Negreton Hypnon (Sweet Sleep).

Folly, in other words, is a creature cultivated by different personifications of psychic oblivion, in an atmosphere of sheer indolence. From this soil grows a model for the easiest mode of life, an eschewal of seriousness and truth in favour of folly and illusion. Folly enjoins us to forsake the severities of Truth for our preferred fictions and self-deceptions. Live this way, she assures us, and even in old age you will find yourself immune to the *taedium vitae* (weariness of life) that afflicts even the most youthful wise man.

Are the lives of the duped and deluded less happy than those of the clear-sighted? Are those so-called fools who look on their 'extraordinarily ugly' spouses and see Venus or Adonis any less gratified than those whose spouses are genuinely beautiful? The work of seeing, judging and thinking clearly and precisely is always demanding and usually deflating. Illusion is our only effective antidote against weariness, an antigravitational counterforce to the heavy burdens of wisdom.

The other end of the same century sees the birth of Folly's most illustrious disciple in the guise of a Spanish gentleman farmer who calls himself Don Quixote, Knight of the Sorry Face. With *Don Quixote*, Miguel de Cervantes invented the novel as the great pastime of all the lazy fools (Cervantes opens the novel by addressing his 'Idle Reader') for whom the infinitely elastic logic of the imagination is always preferable to the rigid laws of reality.

If *Don Quixote* invited us to laugh at its hero's madness from the Olympian height of our sanity and reason, it would long have been forgotten. Instead, it draws the thinnest of lines between Quixote's delusions – windmills as monsters, shaving bowls as knightly helmets, wineskins as giants' heads – and ours. The supposedly sane gentlemen, cads and distressed damsels that Quixote encounters on his travels are no less compulsively enmeshed than him in imaginary worlds. The difference is simply that they're able to harmonize their illusions with reality, while Quixote's delusions are on a perpetual collision course with it.

Does the transformation of the young nobleman Don Fernando from treacherous friend and seducer to courtly man of honour in the space of a few preposterous seconds stretch credibility any further than Quixote's metamorphosis from farmer to knight-errant? Fernando remains despicable in reality, just as Quixote remains a farmer in reality; but where it suits Fernando's companions to buy into the illusion of his moral transformation, it suits no one to believe that a windmill is really a monster, or that the psychopathic criminals Quixote unchains are really tragic victims of injustice. We are not Quixote only because we're not mad enough to demand that others take our delusions for truth; instead, like Fernando and his friends, we quietly maintain our illusions while reassuring ourselves and others that we don't have any.

Cervantes reminds us just how little separates us from Quixote, how readily we make our home in illusions. We are all 'idle readers', compulsive consumers of stories, prone to prefer the short cuts of the imagination to the hard pathways carved by reality. The sight of the dishes in the sink or the collapsed shelf in the under-stairs cupboard never fails to remind me I have a novel I want to read.

Perhaps this starts to sound too much like the truism that stories are an escapist refuge from a reality that's too painful, difficult or boring, which while not altogether untrue is too simplistic. What de Maistre, Erasmus, Cervantes, Marlowe and Wilde show us is that the world isn't reducible to the narrow sphere in which we live our active and purposeful lives. In the words of Picasso, 'Everything you can imagine is real.' The texture of the world is layered, complicated and enriched by the stories we tell and listen to.

The slob resists the world's demands by succumbing to the downward pull of gravity, the daydreamer by refusing it, by floating airily above his daily reality. Daydreaming is a refusal to equate life with quotidian existence.

But the imagination is hardly the exclusive preserve of daydreamers. Achievements in engineering, medicine or computing, or any other activities aimed at intervening in and transforming the external world, are as much acts of the imagination as those realized in books, paintings or operas. But the daydreamer, unlike the person of action, doesn't want his imagination corralled into the service of the world.

*

Reality needs the imagination if it is to grow and transform. But this dependence doesn't prevent them from coming into conflict. Daydreamers display a stubborn resistance to reality's claims and demands, resist submitting to the imperatives of social and economic utility. This turns them into objects of contempt and exasperation. Plato famously taught that no state oriented to right living could make room for artists of any kind, that a carpenter who builds a bed is in a higher relation to truth than the artist who paints one. In Plato's eyes, the seductive appeal of Homer and the tragedians only underscored how ruinous love of art is for our morality and humanity.

Art and artists, says Socrates, are dangerous because they seduce us into falsehood, stoking our fascination for the shadows of the world below at the expense of the true world above. A more modern and less metaphysical version of this argument might be that when the real world is afflicted by hunger, torture, oppression, disease and neglect, as well as by ordinary human misery, the investment of time and love in unreal characters, stories and images is wicked as well as idle.

It seems that these days only religious fanatics and furious self-declared taxpayers are willing to profess open hostility to art and artists. In our permissive culture, talk of art as idle and corrupting is unlikely to be met with more than dismissive laughter, which I'm as quick as anyone else to join in with.

Yet I'm also aware of something defensive in my position, a suppression of the involuntary shudder of shame I can feel when I look up from the pages of the novel or painting I'm absorbed in and recall that at this very moment a fellow human being is being starved or tortured or killed. Perhaps the appeal to the sublime pleasures and depths of art provides me with a shield against the embarrassment of giving over so much of myself to unreality, when reality cries out so desperately to be noticed.

The French philosopher Emmanuel Levinas is unusual among modern thinkers in his willingness to take seriously the case against art. Art, he observes in a 1948 essay, 'Reality and Its Shadow', isn't real action but its inversion. In action, 'we maintain a real relationship with a real object'; whereas art, formed not of real objects but of their shadowy, insubstantial reflections, 'neutralizes this real relationship'. There is, suggests Levinas, something 'inhuman and monstrous' about this world of shadows, and presumably about our fascination for it. Wilde, who argued so uncompromisingly for the superiority of this shadow world over the mundanity of the real one, also saw its inhumanity and monstrousness. Dorian Gray's pursuit of beauty is also a renunciation of morality, love and human solidarity.

I am, it's safe to say, no Dorian Gray. I fled into daydreams and stories and performance not, or at least not in the first instance, because I felt superior to reality but because I felt inadequate to it. But I eventually became aware of a more ambiguous motivation for these flights, a secret pleasure in my imaginative life as a vehicle for revenge on reality and everyone in it. I turned to the imaginary world in part because there I could be far better, instead of mostly worse, than everyone else.

Freud suggests that this is how creative writers are made. In turning away from the burdensome demands of reality, he says in his tellingly titled 1908 essay 'Creative Writers and Daydreaming', they immerse themselves in the weightless atmosphere of their daydreams and fantasies, shaping them into characters and stories, providing pleasurable diversions for those idle intervals in the busy lives of real people. This dedication to fantasy is what separates artists from scientists, those supreme realists with whom Freud readily identified himself.

There is, no doubt, a gratingly patronizing quality to this view of literature as a harmless bit of regression, 'a continuation of, and a substitute for, what was once the play of childhood', that provokes me into wanting to defend the seriousness of art.

But perhaps this defensive rush obstructs a receptivity to the important sense in which Freud's right. Whatever seriousness art can lay claim to, it isn't the seriousness of science. In science, even the most speculative theory is ultimately concerned with the real world, whereas in art, even objects as concrete as a urinal or an unmade bed belong to the imaginary world.

The used tissues strewn around Tracey Emin's bed are radically different from the ones mouldering in your pocket, however much they might seem indistinguishable. For all their soiling by stale bodily fluids, Emin's tissues are weightless and shadowy. This is what makes them so expensive. The collector is paying millions not for the disgusting tissues, but for the imperceptible element that turns them into the imaginary object we call a work of art.

My Bed is a representation of the depressive force of gravity. Through its pile-up of abject detritus, we glimpse a soul sinking downwards, into the chaos of pure matter. But in presenting this emotional and physical mess as a work of art, the scene is alchemically imbued with a curious lightness. Like saintly relics, the stained sheets and used tissues acquire an airy and enigmatic abstractness that lifts their lowly status as real things.

It is precisely this capacity of art to distinguish itself from ordinary reality that led Freud to conclude that while art may be fascinating, it cannot be serious in the way science is. Much as he admired and even revered art, he couldn't be persuaded of its capacity to intervene in and transform the world around us.

I'm reminded once more of Martin Creed's lovely formulation, 'the whole world + the work = the whole world', projected by him spectrally onto the fascias and walls of various public buildings. Our reverence for works of art is bound up with their lack of instrumental value, their inability to act. Precisely because of their weightlessness, the equation implies, they add nothing to the world – but neither can they be subtracted from it. The imagined world is as much the air we breathe as the real one.

Seven years into an academic job, my life took another surprising turn when I decided to train as a psychoanalyst. If Freud is correct in his conception of the psychoanalytic vocation, this should have been a definitive renunciation of daydreaming in the pursuit of scientific truth. Surely listening to the inner life of another person is an occupation more oriented to reality than is reading and writing about novels and poems? A person is a living, fleshy being subject to growth and change as well as regression and illness, where a work of art is a phantom object that seems suspended for all time in the same state. To recall Levinas, 'Eternally, the smile of the Mona Lisa about to broaden will not broaden.'

Freud insisted that, as a science, psychoanalysis belongs to the domain of the reality principle. Like any science, it demands the discipline of waiting patiently, of doing without the gratifications of certainty. Science is hard work because it operates in a reality that offers no short cuts.

But psychoanalytic practice appealed to me, and still does, more for its challenge to the tyranny of action. There are few psychoanalytic patients who will not at some point exclaim in frustration, as they turn over some life dilemma, 'Yes, all right, but what do I *do* about it?' And when the analyst declines to answer, opting instead to sit with the frustration, he's likely to be taken to task for just sitting there, staring gormlessly while the patient flails in uncertainty.

To some, and to me at times, my choice to train as an analyst might look less like a conversion to the scientific spirit and more like the culmination of my quest to do as little as possible. An analytic session, after all, consists of fifty minutes' open-ended, undirected conversation conducted quietly, with minimal possible intrusion from the world outside. The patient usually lies down, at times talking freely, at others falling into silent reverie. If a session has an aim, it is to put all aims in question, to nurture a certain suspicion of the question 'What should I do?'

Action, Wilde suggests, is 'limited and relative'. In its exclusive concern with the here and now, it suffocates our imaginative possibilities. 'The vision of him who sits at ease and watches', in contrast, is 'unlimited and absolute'. In liberating the self from the pressure to act, psychoanalysis radically enlarges the scope of what we can think and feel. One of the most understated yet important qualities of psychoanalytic speech, or 'free association', is the capacity it encourages in the speaker to follow the trail of his mind in the absence of any clue as to where it might be going.

This means, of course, that I in turn am following the trail of his trail, a man wandering tentatively behind a man wandering tentatively. Film and TV shrinks are so often represented as cunning trackers, hunting avidly for clues in their patients' material; there isn't so much dramatic promise in the real-world therapist's more common state of perplexity. Like Wilde's ideal artist, the analyst 'sits at ease and watches', and this confers on his vision, as on the artist's, an 'unlimited and absolute' scope. Instead of counselling his patient to do something or other, the analyst tries to expand and enhance her imaginative possibilities.

Doing without the anchor of practical counsel doesn't always feel liberating, however; it can seem like more being dumped without map, compass or GPS in the middle of a desert or forest. The joint work of analyst and patient is difficult because it's denied the hasty resolution of action.

From one perspective, psychoanalysis is barely work at all; strangers and friends alike will needle me for not doing anything, just sitting there, grunting and mouthing the odd platitude in an understanding tone. Others are wide-eyed at the effort of concentration and memory involved in retaining the details of many different lives, in making connections across each person's long and complex past and present.

Both are right; the analyst doesn't do anything and it is intensely demanding work. Early on in my training, as an honorary psychotherapist in a hospital psychiatry department, a patient in serious distress asked me for a hug. When I didn't respond, he screamed furiously, boring his eyes into mine, 'Why won't you give me a *fucking* hug, you heartless fucking so-called professional! Did I say professional?! I'm *sorry*, I meant DEAD-EYED CUNT!' There couldn't have been many more efficient ways to be taught that doing nothing at all is the most difficult thing in the world. What could have been more congenial to my easy-going nice-guy instincts than to just give him the hug? Far more difficult was to keep still, take the blows and wait. A hug would have fleetingly appeased his sadness and rage. Inaction, in contrast, kept him in contact with those feelings, and so with the chronic emotional deprivation and neglect he'd endured since childhood and had spent so much of his life trying to forget and deny.

In his 1912 paper 'Recommendations to Physicians Practising Psycho-Analysis', Freud describes the listening of the psychoanalyst, which he calls 'evenly-suspended attention', as a kind of sustained practice of inaction. It is a state of undirected alertness, a curiosity and openness unconstrained by prejudices and expectations.

Authentic openness requires the analyst to switch off his ordinary, purposive mode of listening – to stop listening, that is, *for* something – and make himself available to whatever comes. As soon as he tries to steer a specific path through the patient's speech, 'he begins to select from the material before him', which is 'precisely what must not be done'. To listen selectively is to lose all availability to surprise: 'if he follows his expectations, he is in danger of never finding anything but what he already knows.'

In this wariness of the already known we hear a teaching about creativity in the much broader sense. Nothing inhibits creativity more reliably than the habit of trying too hard. Our effortful, conscientious modes of looking, listening and thinking rarely lead us anywhere we don't already know. When ears, eyes and other receptive organs lose their availability to surprise, they become leaden and clumsy: the painter becomes a mediocre copyist of photographs, the screenwriter's characters speak in clichés.

The predicament is hardly exclusive to artistic creativity. The harried GP scribbling a prescription, barely pausing to look up from her chair, cannot read the expression or hear the tone that might reveal more from her patient than a sore throat; the beleaguered primary school teacher focused on eliminating noise from the classroom misses a child's urgent distress or inspiration.

For the psychoanalyst, this attunement to the other person's unconscious is an explicit requirement. The analyst, says Freud, must open his unconscious 'like a receptive organ' to the communications of the patient's unconscious. But it is also an implicit requirement in any zone of creative life – work, sport, domesticity, friendship, sex – in which we enter into relationships, with others or ourselves.

Overwork, overstimulation, perpetual communication, anxiety, insomnia: the social and material conditions of our everyday lives are profoundly inhospitable to the kind of receptive, inactive patience which sustains all forms of creative life. Physical and mental busyness are ways of entrenching a kind of inertial sameness, into which the unknown and unexpected cannot intrude. Being is the essential antidote to the non-stop inertia of doing, a way of resisting the gravity that drags us downwards.

~

During our short first consultation, Grace sat straight-backed at the edge of the chair, as though preparing for a quick getaway. But her upright posture was in contrast to the downward cast of her eyes, which seemed to be sinking slowly into quicksand.

I caught little bursts of fizziness bubbling under the stagnant surface of her depression. As she spoke of the childhood emergence of her musical talent, a smile played at the corners of her eyes and lips, the tiniest glint in the cloud of darkness that had settled over her. At twenty-four, anything that complicated the rudimentary functionality of her daily life – art, sex, friendship, ideas – had been ruthlessly excised.

How had it come to this? She was carrying the burden of a traumatized childhood, most devastatingly the death of her sister in one of the bombing raids that ravaged her country of birth. During school, she seemed to have found ways through the fog, a cunning and defiance to cut through the grinding sadness of home and the wall of hostility at school – manically inventive dances choreographed in her bedroom mirror, a talent for mimicry. But the threat of collapse under the weight of her near-permanent anxiety never abated.

Music – singing, drumming and eventually composing – had been her lifeline, a way of at once remembering and transcending the brutal war from which she'd fled with her family at the age of six. It took her to music college, where she threw herself headlong into its crucible of fevered passions, fuelled by rivalrous and precarious triangular friendships and creative alliances. She made evanescent compositions lasting seconds or hours, collages of sustained top notes, classical fragments, dead air, samples, wordless and violent testimonies to the horrors she'd narrowly escaped.

She topped her final-year group and left college hungry to

write and play. At the same time, she was enduring night after night of troubled sleep broken by extravagantly brutal dreams, most often visions of the menacing approach of her dead younger sister, her face a mess of bloody accusation.

A few months after graduation, she conducted 'The Sky', a new piece she'd composed for brass, strings and voice that articulated her daydreams of soaring above the blood and fear in which her young life had been soaked. A critical audience of modern music aficionados liked it. There was talk of contracts and commissions.

Four years had passed between that evening and her first consultation with me, during which she had neither played nor written a note of music. Far from encouraging her, the applause that greeted the work was felt by her as an insupportable weight on her nerves, leaving her barely able to move or speak to anyone for days.

It is difficult, reflecting on this episode now, not to think of Icarus, the emblem of the overreaching Romantic artist, soaring majestically towards the sun, heedless of his father's dire warnings. Bataille writes of how the myth splits the sun in two – 'the one that was shining at the moment of Icarus's elevation, and the one that melted the wax, causing failure and a screaming fall when Icarus got too close'.

Grace reached for a transcendent sun of aesthetic and spiritual illumination, only to be burned by the heat of a worldly sun that sent her crashing into a bottomless sea. Unlike Icarus, she surfaced and resolved to float to survival, retreating to the even, lifeless life she now felt to be the only one she could live. She would be free of the ambition, erotic desire and creative excitements that had so long defined her. She did bar work, a little private tuition, read the paper.

She could no longer bear to hear music, her own or anyone else's. She could fall into a pleasant enough reverie imagining herself cosied underneath the arm of some loving companion, but the prospect of a real erotic encounter reduced her to speechless paralysis. For every rise in internal excitement, there was a pitiless counteraction.

Imaginative life had become traumatically dangerous. It was liable to make her hyperventilate, freeze, cry, or to tip her over the edge of madness. Sleep, stillness, a life of quiet if grim uneventfulness would be better. Or it would have been, if she could just attain it, if her mind could let her alone. Instead her dreams, anxieties and longings persisted at the highest pitch. This was why she'd come to me: aliveness felt impossible, but deadness was unbearable. She had somehow been reduced to the stark options of a fevered and exhausting imaginative life and an indifferent, lifeless reality.

Winnicott describes a patient who from childhood had diverted all her creative and emotional energy into her daydreams, to the point that 'the main part of her existence was taking place when she was doing nothing whatever'.

The patient, he writes, had sought to fill her daily life with 'futile activities' like 'compulsive smoking and various boring and obsessive games'. The effect of all this was only 'to fill the gap, and this gap was an essential state of doing nothing while she was doing everything'. The moment I read this passage I felt an immense inner kinship with this woman, perhaps the same kinship that had enabled me to attune myself quickly to Grace's resigned inertia. 'Doing nothing while doing everything' perfectly captures the peculiar, inert busyness of the daydreamer. Daydreams can be a rich creative resource only if the daydreamer can facilitate a passage from the inside of her head to some receptive surface in the external world – paper or canvas or lab or sporting field.

Winnicott tells of his patient becoming frightened during her analysis, realizing how easily she could have ended up 'lying all her life in a bed in a mental hospital, incontinent, inactive and immobile', while remaining the omnipotent author of 'wonderful things' in the sealed-off privacy of her own mind. Her predicament is her unwillingness to traverse that passage between her head and the world outside it, no doubt because this inevitably involves some disappointment. Creative activity is so often painful because what you create will almost always fall short of the 'wonderful things' you'd imagined creating.

But renouncing creativity, not writing, painting, building or playing, is no remedy for this disappointment. As Winnicott points out, under these conditions, the brilliance of the daydream is in inverse proportion to the impoverishment of reality. This is certainly what had happened to Grace. In the silence of her mind, music was being composed and played perpetually; but getting it onto music paper or into a performance venue, sharing it with other ears, submitting it to the envy, criticism, admiration and rivalry of her peers – she didn't see how she could bear the anxieties aroused by all that. There was a fantastical world of creative fulfilment and recognition, kept assiduously apart from the real world of flat, resentful survival.

Our work together, every weekday for close to a decade, turned on the struggle to bring those two worlds back into contact, to render her imaginative life bearable and usable for her real one. This meant first a loosening of the tight protective fencing around her dreams and fantasies, which frequently featured scenarios of cold sexual manipulation and violence, in which I came increasingly to appear, at times as victim, at times as aggressor.

In the course of Grace's analysis, the baroque surface of those dreams began to reveal themselves as screens for a yet more terrifying scenario of total abandonment, a vision of herself as a lone dot in an endless and void expanse. The destructive orgies had been the mask of a more terrifying nothingness, a world in which her body and soul were left unseen and untouched.

Analysis provided her with a receptacle for these oscillating fears of excess and emptiness, a place in which they could be heard and talked about. This was an unprecedented experience for her, the child to a father who had derided her vulnerability and a mother whose own traumatic history had deprived her of the capacity to listen to and hold her daughter's terrors. Mad with grief at their little daughter's death, her parents were bereft of the inner resources to recognize and console Grace's loss of a sister. That process could finally begin in this room.

The anarchy and madness of her unconscious life didn't disappear; but they found words and shapes and sounds that made her dreams and fantasies thinkable, available as creative resources rather than cut off as hostile internal forces. The unconscious could never become an unambiguous ally, but it ceased to be an enemy. From being the helpless victim of her psychic life, she became, with me alongside her, its curious interlocutor.

This was hardly easy. Repeated encounters with the most feared and hated elements of her inner life induced deep misery and rage, not infrequently directed against me. As a child, her father would terrorize her by demanding immediate answers to deliberately confusing questions. During adolescence, her mother would excoriate her apparent passivity and lassitude, demanding that she *did* something. It took a long time for Grace to conceive that I could listen or speak any differently.

But she falteringly came to recognize analysis as offering her a daily interlocutor who demanded neither answers nor actions. Her speech could drift into minute details of work gossip, daily snacks, intrigues in her new house-share. The dangers of her own mind remained vivid, but they ceased to overwhelm her, to shut down her curiosity about herself.

As we ventured into the different regions of her unconscious life, a parallel process took hold outside the consulting room. It began on the bus home from a session, with a few notes, musical and verbal, scribbled on the back of a gas bill envelope. The notes accumulated and with trepidation were transferred to a password-protected file on her laptop. Five years into the analysis, these had coalesced into the portfolio she submitted for her successful application for a master's in Composition.

There was a good deal more turbulence in the years that followed, inside and outside the sessions. But this turbulence now belonged not to a fearfully enclosed mind but to the fullness of a real life. The psychoanalytic response to Grace's inertial collapse hadn't been to coax her into action but to undo its persecutory hold on her, to create the conditions for a free return to the world. This world was simultaneously the same as and different from the one she'd previously inhabited, encompassing both her creative and her workaday selves and enabling contact between them.

At the end of our last session, she handed me a wrapped package. After she left, I took a long breath and opened it to find a note of thanks and a CD. Written in black marker on its surface: 'BETWEEN SKY AND SEA'.

'I Dwell in Possibility': Emily Dickinson

On 11 March 1884, Otis Phillips Lord, a retired Massachusetts Superior Court judge and state politician, suffered a stroke from which he died two days later, aged seventy-one.

Shortly after the death of his wife seven years earlier, Lord had declared his love to the daughter of his late lifelong friend and colleague Edward Dickinson. She was an enigmatic recluse of forty-seven living in Amherst. He could have had no inkling that the coming century would establish her as one of if not the greatest of American poets.

Their correspondence is the only unambiguous evidence we have from Emily Dickinson's life of a passion returned and a shared life contemplated. Lord had been pressing marriage on her until the moment of his death. If she never assented, it wasn't because she didn't love him. Her devotion to him is captured in a vignette from an account of her funeral written by her mentor Thomas Wentworth Higginson: '... the sister Vinnie put in [the coffin] two heliotropes by her hand "to take to Judge Lord".'

Dickinson's side of the correspondence with Lord overflows with open and tender passion. Writing in 1878, she tells him, 'I have done with guises', hinting at the dissimulations and evasions that marked her former relations with men. 'I confess that I love him –' she continues. 'I rejoice that I love him – I thank the maker of Heaven and Earth – that gave him me to love – the exultation floods me.'

But the pitch of her ardour begs an unavoidable question: why did they continue to live apart? Why had she fended off the successive proposals not only of marital but of sexual union? Some measure of an answer can be found in a letter to him that year, in which she told him, 'Don't you know you are happiest when I withhold and not confer—dont [sic] you know that No is the wildest word we consign to Language? ... you ask the divine Crust that would doom the Bread.' Two years later she wrote, 'It is strange that I miss you at night so much when I was never with you –'.

The ardent suitor, the withholding maid; what makes these letters more than a rehearsal of tired caricatures of gender and sexuality is their unexpected and disconcerting eroticizing of renunciation. 'No' expresses sexual wildness rather than morality. Her bed is more torridly charged for his never having been anywhere near it. Permanent separation, prohibition and privation preserve the 'Bread' of passion that the 'Crust' of consummation would 'doom'.

Four years later, in 1882, following her mother's death, Dickinson lovingly entertained Lord's proposals to come to Salem as his wife. Referring to the teasing sobriquet of 'Jumbo' he'd conferred on her after she gained a little weight, she declares, 'Emily "Jumbo"' to be 'Sweetest name, but I know a sweeter – Emily Jumbo Lord. Have I your approval?' For years, real-world obstacles prevented their union – on his side, the implacable hostility of a niece who had been made chief beneficiary of his will; on her side the obligation to care for her ailing mother. But, despite her avowals, her mother's death brought her no closer to Salem. She remained in Amherst, continuing to dodge his appeals until, a little more than a year later, his stroke brought them to an end.

Throughout her life, Dickinson's letters had been thick with intimations of passion. They conveyed passing crushes, tender affections and erotic longings to friends, to mentors, to anonymous and perhaps imaginary lovers, alternating between tones of vulnerability, boldness and coyness.

The letters leave us with at least one intractable ambiguity.

'We have met with little but bafflement as to the specifics of Emily Dickinson's affairs of the heart,' writes Richard B. Sewall, Dickinson's most authoritative biographer. Between 1858 and 1862, she wrote three letters as 'Daisy' to an addressee she called 'Master', burning with an ardour at once playful, wrenchingly vulnerable and imploring. Scholars and critics have spilt much ink speculating over the identity of the unnamed addressee. But there is no evidence the letters were ever sent, no indication whether the feelings they expressed were reciprocated, or even whether the man in question really existed. In other words, we don't know if the infatuation was declared or mutual or real, if the letters were intended as avowals of love, literary creations or some uncertain hybrid of the two.

Perhaps Dickinson was simply more interested in verbal than in corporeal forms of love. And yet her love letters – and poems – were hardly empty exercises in literary style. It's hard to imagine anyone reading them without being struck by their exuberant, tortured, often violent erotic intensity.

The durable popular version of Dickinson is that of the New England spinster recluse, scratching away daily at her modest table, diverting her disappointed passions into verse, as though poetry were the consolation prize for women who had missed out on the real one. But the unconsummated affair with Lord suggests that, even when offered the exemplary happy ending, Dickinson preferred to miss out. Perhaps the retreat into uncompromising reclusion was the consequence not of pitiable romantic disappointment but of a bid for radical personal and literary independence and imaginative freedom.

Her refusal brings to mind French psychoanalyst Piera Aulagnier's notion of a primal drive in the psyche towards what she calls 'desire for non-desire', the paradoxical passion for the annulment of passion. This is the passion Dickinson hints at with her enigmatic insistence on 'No' as 'the wildest word we consign to Language'.

None of Dickinson's biographers can avoid her life's sheer une-ventfulness. 'It would be difficult to cite an American author of commensurate power whose life offers less in the way of striking occurrence,' says Cynthia Griffin Wolff. 'Other all-time poets have counselled invisibility as the condition of truth,' writes Lyndall Gordon. '... None pursued invisibility as strictly as Dickinson.'

The poems repeatedly affirm her invisibility. In a lyric self-portrait of 1862 (no. 486), the speaker is seen in terms of the modesty of the space she occupies, both in her house and in the minds of others. She begins:

> I was the slightest in the House –
> I took the smallest room ...
> I never spoke – unless addressed –
> And then, 'twas brief and low –

The poem concludes, with a hint of bathos more Dickens than Dickinson, 'I had often thought/How noteless – I could die –'. And yet the mood of wistful self-pity, the poem's intimations of shame at taking up even this tiny corner of the world, are belied by its declarative tone. The speaker is oddly self-assertive about her self-effacement.

Disappearance, confinement, radical solitude ... The more ruthlessly Dickinson embraced these conditions, the more she cut off her route to the sanctioned cultural expressions of nineteenth-century womanhood: marriage, motherhood, service to the local community, perhaps even fleeting fame as an author of the kind of popular sentimental poetry and fiction women were licensed to write and read.

Dickinson's life challenges fundamental and universally shared assumptions, implicit precepts so entrenched in us that we barely know how to question them. It is obvious to us that it's better to go out and live in the world than to sit in a room and daydream about it, that it's better to experience real love with another person than to imagine love in solitude. But are these axioms quite as obvious or unquestionable as we tend unthinkingly to presume? Should a daydreaming life, a life in which the imagined world takes pride of place over the real one, always be seen through the lens of pathology? Winnicott suggested as much in his account of the highly dissociated patient who retreated into daydreams to fend off the risks and agitations of living. He describes the blank, languid reveries in which she wandered into a private fantasy world as 'an essential state of doing nothing while she was doing everything'.

Dickinson forswore the boundless expanses of the world for the boundless confines of her room and head. 'The Brain –', as one of her most famous first lines declares, 'is wider than the Sky –' (no. 632). Her niece Martha, who had grown up in the house next door, wrote of her aunt sitting in her bedroom, holding up an invisible key and miming the locking of the door, saying, 'Matty: Here's freedom.' In the eyes of the world she was 'doing nothing', while in her own mind she was 'doing everything', travelling fearlessly to the furthest extremities of possible experience – sexual ecstasy, traumatic pain, madness and death.

Yet Dickinson's prolific creativity, dazzling as it is, does nothing to alter the most insistent theme of her life and work – the renunciation of the external world for the solitary realm of the imagination. The renunciation is the very condition of both the poet and the poetry – it enables her to be a poet and is the substance of the poems.

The British psychoanalyst Gregorio Kohon questions the

tendency of some of his colleagues to assume that the tendency to internal withdrawal (what his fellow analyst John Steiner calls 'psychic retreat') is always and necessarily pathological. It only becomes so, he suggests, when its form is 'intensely rigid' – that is, when it cuts itself off from any creative impulse.

Winnicott himself recognized how much our creativity depends on maintaining contact with the 'still, silent spot' at the heart of the psyche. Few artists bear out this insight more potently than Emily Dickinson. To adapt an aphorism of Sartre's, Dickinson may have been a compulsive daydreamer, but not every compulsive daydreamer is Emily Dickinson. There is no more definitive proof of this observation than the 1,775 poems she bequeathed the world. Who could read these and still claim she 'did nothing'?

Withdrawal into the solitude of a bedroom has been a recurring motif of this book: for Tracey Emin, a descent into the apocalyptic depths of her own depression; for the young *hikikomori*, a rejection of work, society and the pressures of an attainment society; for Xavier de Maistre, an enforced but unexpectedly joyous discovery of the infinitude to be found within the tightest restrictions. Withdrawal signifies a refusal of the limits and constrictions we impose upon ourselves as soon as we commit to this or that project or institution – a country, a profession, a marriage. Live here and we cannot live there, do one job and we cannot do another, marry one person and forsake not only all others but independence. For Dickinson to go to her Lord in Salem would mean an expansion of her place in the world, but a constriction of her imaginative life. No nineteenth-century bride, however gentle and undemanding her groom, could expect to maintain the permanent and sovereign freedom of a locked room.

And so she made excuses, postponing their union into a receding future, making an erotic virtue of abstinence, until his death rescued her from the dilemma. Her frustrated suitor, who seems to have known little of her poetry, might have spared himself the frustration of being fobbed off had he read just this one, written in 1862, sixteen years before they declared themselves:

> I dwell in Possibility –
> A fairer House than Prose –
> More numerous of Windows –
> Superior – for Doors –
>
> Of Chambers as the Cedars –
> Impregnable of Eye –
> And for an Everlasting Roof
> The Gambrels of the Sky –
>
> Of Visitors – the fairest –
> For Occupation – This –
> The spreading wide my narrow Hands
> To gather Paradise –

(no. 657)

'Prose' is Dickinson's quietly disparaging term for worldly life. She opposes it not to 'Poetry' but to a bold synonym for it: 'Possibility'. To write poetry is to inhabit the house of possibility, its numerous windows opening in all directions onto different vistas. Equally integral to the house's architecture are its impregnably sealed rooms, closed off to prying eyes and a roof made of none other than the sky itself. Her visitors are not friends or suitors intruding on her vocation, but the Muses inspiring it, expanding her poetic hands wide enough to encompass Paradise in verbal form.

As she grew older and more reclusive, Dickinson became as

allergic to earthly visitors as she was receptive to imaginary ones, despite often craving their presence. When she became intimate in correspondence with the newspaper editor and writer Samuel Bowles – identified by some commentators as one of a series of objects of consuming and unrequited love – she would implore him to visit her in Amherst, only to remain in her bedroom or away from the house when he did. 'Perhaps you thought I didn't care,' she wrote to him in 1862. '... I *did* care, Mr Bowles ... but something troubled me – and I knew you needed light – and air – so I didn't come.'

Later that year, after a seven-month convalescence in Europe, he visited the family again. Dickinson stayed upstairs and sent down a note beginning, 'I cannot see you.' Similar incidents recurred intermittently over the years that followed. When he visited in 1877 and was again told she could not see him, he is said to have shouted upstairs, 'Emily, you damned wretch! No more of this nonsense! I've travelled all the way from Springfield to see you. Come down at once.' According to her later editor and biographer Thomas Johnson, 'She is said to have complied and never have been more witty.' With Bowles as with Lord, she withheld her presence not because she didn't want to see him but because she did.

Mabel Loomis Todd, whose long affair with Dickinson's brother, Austin, would eventually shatter the family unity, and who later became the most significant of the posthumous editors of Dickinson's unpublished poetry and correspondence, wrote in her diary of her disconcerting first encounters with the poet in 1882: 'She always wears white, & has her hair arranged as was the fashion fifteen years ago when she went into retirement. She wanted me to come and sing to her, but she would not see me. She has frequently sent me flowers & poems, & we have a very pleasant friendship in that way.'

Despite Todd's regular and extended trysts with Austin in the parlour beneath Dickinson's bedroom, the two would never meet face to face. Todd would occasionally see her receding back or hear her footfall, but no conversation ever took place in person. The air of dramatic contrivance conveyed by Todd's account is telling. By communicating with Todd in silent, portentous gestures while denying her an encounter in person, Dickinson nurtured a relationship in absentia. With Bowles and Todd as with Lord, Dickinson sought to maintain relationships that lived off the airy nourishment of words rather than fleshly presence.

Dickinson was not quite an absence to Judge Lord. He had known her since she was a child and visited her frequently after he was widowed. As the horrified testimony of her sister-in-law, Susan, informs us, their strange, indefinitely suspended court-ship, while evidently unconsummated, included many breathless embraces in the downstairs parlour.

Long before his proposals, Dickinson had warned him obliquely that nothing could induce her to surrender the Edenic freedom of a locked room. The poignant irony here is that it may have been just this quality of otherworldliness that drew Lord to Dickinson. In support of this speculation, Sewall points us to an eulogy Lord had delivered in 1871 for Asahel Huntington, District Attorney for Essex County and 'a much-beloved local dignitary'.

It is striking to note which among the many virtues of the departed Lord paid the most impassioned tribute to. Huntington was, he said, 'a man of more than usual inertia', meaning not listlessness or apathy but 'a quiet repose of mind – an indisposition to obtrude his own reflections upon others – an apparent inattention . . .'

If these are qualities he deemed most worthy of love and respect, it is not difficult to see how Dickinson might have cast a spell on him. In Lord's eulogy, withholding becomes a noble quality of spirit. We tend to complain when our interlocutor seems to be 'elsewhere', and feel disconcerted when they give no clue as to what they're thinking or feeling. 'More than usual inertia' in another person signals an absence, even a haughty remove, from reality.

Around four decades after Lord's eulogy, Freud would describe psychoanalytic listening in strikingly similar ways. To pick up on the patient's unconscious communications, he says, the psychoanalyst must assume a mental state 'free of any presuppositions', an ear undistorted by her own 'expectations and inclinations' and a mode of 'evenly suspended attention' (compare Lord's 'apparent inattention'). For both Lord and Freud, the state of distraction creates the space for an unusual internal sensitivity and receptivity. The psychoanalyst, in this view, is a person of 'more than unusual inertia'. So too is the poet. Withdrawn into the quiet repose of her locked room, 'doing nothing', she can venture infinitely further than a woman bounded by the obligations and conventions of marriage.

Dickinson's life and poetry were shaped by a series of confinements – geographical, physical and emotional. Aside from a ten-month stint in 1847, aged sixteen, at Mount Holyoke Female Seminary, ten miles south of her home in Amherst, and a series of extended stays in Boston in 1864 for the treatment of unspecified medical problems, she lived her entire life in the same house, the Homestead, now the Emily Dickinson Museum. By the late 1860s, she left the house only when necessary, remaining in her room when visitors came.

The scope of her personal relations was equally constricted, comprised for most of her daily life of her mother, Emily, her sister, Lavinia, and her brother, Austin, who after his marriage in 1856 lived in the adjoining house with his wife, Susan, an intimate (sometimes turbulent) friend of Dickinson's and the first and most substantial 'secret sharer' of her poetry. For months at a time during her childhood and adolescence, her father, Edward, a lawyer and career Whig party politician, was absent, first in Boston as an elected member of, successively, the Massachusetts House of Representatives and Senate, and later in Washington as a member of Congress.

While there were visits and correspondence with her mother's family, their residence twenty miles away in Monson meant the paternal family legacy was a more palpable presence in her childhood home. Growing up in Amherst, Dickinson could never avoid the shadow of the paternal line, specifically the long and imposing shadow of her grandfather. Scion of a venerable Amherst family, Samuel Fowler Dickinson was raised in the ways of Trinitarian conservatism, encapsulated in the latter-day Puritan teachings of Jonathan Edwards. Amherst was a Trinitarian bulwark against the rising tide of Unitarian liberalism across New England, and Samuel had become a zealous devotee after recovering from a life-threatening illness at the age of twenty-one.

His religious passion found expression in a visionary educational project. After founding the Amherst Academy school in 1814 (attended by Emily and her siblings three decades later), he set his mind to the project of creating of a Trinitarian college to provide an elite education to a new generation of the Christian ministry. Initially enthusiastically pursued, the Amherst College project began to founder under the weight of its fundraising difficulties, as well as the entrenched opposition of both Boston Unitarians and rival Trinitarian colleges. Gripped by an obsessional and reckless zeal to realize his scheme, Samuel Dickinson neglected his legal practice, while sinking all his financial resources into building the college, eventually losing the family home, bankrupting himself and ruining his professional reputation.

The impetuous passion of the father ensured that his eldest son, Edward, was prematurely schooled in the demands of adult responsibility. Tasked from boyhood with restoring family honour, Edward repeatedly interrupted his college education to help the family finances, going on to build a successful legal practice and political career. He placed Amherst College on a sound financial footing and bought back the lost family home.

It may sound like an uplifting story of filial redemption, but the obligation to repair the damages done by his father took its toll on the son. Where Samuel possessed the charisma of the visionary, Edward's burdens rendered him an austere and rather joyless character. 'Nothing in Edward's life,' writes Wolff, 'could match the emotional and spiritual vitality of Samuel Fowler Dickinson's original vision.'

Nowhere was Edward more demonstrably a stranger to passion than in his pinched courtship of Emily Norcross. Their correspondence reveals his uncomprehending bewilderment and frustration in the face of her evasions, long periods of silence and frequent demurrals at his requests. His tone is fraught with barely concealed irritation; but at no point do we hear him assume the tones of the solicitous or ardent lover. His torrent of agitated reasonableness seems only further to entrench her resentful passivity. This complex emotional legacy would be passed on to Dickinson and her siblings. The spectre of a grandiose and inspirational religiosity loomed, but was reduced in her father's house to a spiritually empty husk of convention.

Dickinson's mother brought a further layer of emotional tension into the family home. In a letter to Thomas Higginson from 1874, Emily Dickinson wrote, 'I always ran Home to Awe when a child, if anything befell me. He was an awful Mother, but I liked him better than none.' Higginson also recalled her saying to him in person, 'I never had a mother. I suppose a mother is one to whom you hurry when you are troubled.'

Dickinson's mother, she implies, was both there and not there, physically present but lacking the open ear and mind that would give a child the feeling of their each substantially existing in the other's mind. Her apparent emotional unavailability to Dickinson's 'troubled' child self renders her a blank in the memory of Dickinson's older self, a non-existence in corporeal form.

In a seminal paper, the French psychoanalyst André Green coined the term 'dead mother' to convey this internal experience of maternal absence. A child raised in intimate proximity to a mother's extended mourning or depression, he suggests, may form an indelible internal picture of that mother as 'a distant figure, toneless and practically inanimate . . . a mother who remains alive but who is, so to speak, psychically dead in the eyes of the young child in her care'. This description is similar to Dickinson's recollection of the mother she 'never had'. But what underlay the depressive and lethargic moods of the senior Emily Dickinson? The resentful passivity she displayed during her long and tortuous courtship suggests an inchoate resistance to her future marriage. Perhaps because she had no wish to marry Edward Dickinson, or because she sensed no real ardour from him, she seems to have entered marriage in a mood of reluctant compliance rather than of enthusiastic desire. Once married, she was left alone with her young children for months on end as her husband pursued his political career in Boston and Washington. She was the bewildered protagonist of a life she had neither chosen nor especially wanted, having never had the chance to discover the life she did want.

This might account for her reaction to the crowning moment in her husband's long and arduous mission to restore his father's name: the repurchasing of the Brick House (later Homestead) his father had lost, and which the Dickinsons returned to in 1855. According to Wolff, far from celebrating with her husband, she fell at this time into some 'nameless, disabling apathy'. The affliction was a long-lived and immobilizing melancholy, as puzzling in Dickinson's eyes as it was intractable. 'Mother lies upon the lounge, or sits in her easy chair,' she wrote to her older friend Elizabeth Holland at the time. 'I don't know what her sickness is.'

It is impossible to know why the recovery of the old Dickinson house should have induced such a catastrophic reaction in Emily Norcross Dickinson; but it matches up with her disconnectedness from the life in which she found herself, her inability or unwillingness to identify with the place assigned her by the name of her husband. The apparently solid and reliable world around her became a river whose course she could neither control nor resist, bearing her helplessly downstream. Her chronic lethargy was the visible expression of an aimless and terrifying internal drift.

It isn't surprising, then, that the course of life chosen by her daughter should have been an exact inversion of her own. Resisting the siren calls of marriage and polite society, holding fiercely to her autonomy and seclusion, Emily Dickinson ensured that, if nothing else, she would direct the current of her own life's river.

Dickinson may have eschewed her mother's hapless destiny, but she showed an impressive capacity to inhabit it imaginatively. An existential lassitude haunts many of her poems, such as this one, again from 1862:

There is a Languor of the Life
More imminent than Pain –
'Tis Pain's Successor – When the Soul
Has suffered all it can –

A Drowsiness – diffuses –
A Dimness like a Fog
Envelops Consciousness –
As Mists – obliterate a Crag.

The Surgeon – does not blanch – at pain –
His Habit – is severe –
But tell him that it ceased to feel –
The Creature lying there –

And he will tell you – skill is late –
A Mightier than He –
Has ministered before Him –
There's no Vitality.

(no. 396)

'Langour' takes over where suffering stops. The heightened agitation of the nerves burns them out, to be succeeded by a zero degree of 'Vitality', a lethargy of the life drive beyond the reach of any surgical skills.

Many of Dickinson's most famous poems make an impossible venture to the threshold of death, or even its aftermath. This one takes us instead to the barest, most elemental level of life, a region of mist and fog, where consciousness is deprived of all awareness of itself. It evokes the atmosphere of acedia, a numbing of feeling and depletion of meaning, which seemed to hover around her mother. Its vision of an inner life shrouded in grey fog anticipates the exhausted, hollowed-out external landscapes of later dystopian visions – Samuel Beckett's *Endgame*, Cormac McCarthy's *The Road*.

Another poem from the same year (no. 305) consists of two quatrains differentiating 'Despair' from 'Fear'. The latter is the feeling accompanying 'the instant of a Wreck –', the former the moment 'the Wreck has been –'. In the moment of despair:

> The mind is smooth – no Motion –
> Contented as the Eye
> Upon the Forehead of a Bust –
> That knows – it cannot see –

Despair becomes frighteningly indistinguishable from contentment. The vision of the wreck has so traumatized its viewer as to induce a catatonic blindness that looks and even feels strangely like nirvanic bliss, a mental smoothness and immobility that brings an end to all the disturbances our vitality engenders.

The speaker of a poem from the following year (no. 786) addresses herself directly to the departed object of an unassuageable grief. Rather than sink into the blank lethargy of the earlier poems, she elects 'To fill the awful Vacuum/Your life had left behind –' by plunging into frenetic activity:

> I strove to weary Brain and Bone –
> To harass to fatigue
> The glittering Retinue of nerves –
> Vitality to clog

The aim of this punishing overwork is not to revive the spirit but to induce exhaustion, clogging her capacity to feel the painful weight of her loss. But the poem's startlingly bleak conclusion disabuses us of this illusion:

No Drug for Consciousness – can be –
Alternative to die
Is Nature's only Pharmacy
For Being's Malady –

The malady of every conscious person, in other words, is that none of their efforts to evade the pain and agitation of feeling, however strenuous, can succeed. More than a century later, Warhol would find a less elevated language to say the same thing: 'Just being alive is so much work at something you don't always want to do.' We are creatures consigned to the burden of gravity, forced to bear the strain of being conscious. Perhaps nowhere did Dickinson find this truth writ larger than in the daily sight of her mother's faraway gaze.

The paradox of Dickinson's poems of languor and weariness is that they render these states so vividly. The long dashes intruded into the middle as well as at the end of lines break up their metrical flow ('The Surgeon – does not blanch – at pain –/His Habit – is severe –'); but in disturbing the line's fluency, they also mime the breathy enervation and shock brought on by imagining such states. The deadened body and soul are infused by a live if horrified fascination.

Dickinson's ventures to the furthest edges of inner experience evoke the kind of visionary delirium we associate with religious ecstasy. If her mother's languor haunts the poems, so does her grandfather's passion. But there is none of Samuel Dickinson's evangelical certainty in Dickinson's relationship to the cosmic mysteries. Where her grandfather saw a benign and just God directing the course of the world, she perceived a primordial confusion and obscurity. In many of her poems, immortality is conceived not as the blissful reward of the righteous but as the soul's condemnation to an obscure and malignant endlessness.

In poetry, Dickinson found a different path of inspiration. Where her grandfather embraced the cumbersome responsibility to perform God's work on earth, she sought transcendence in the airiness and ethereality of words. Her most insistent metaphor for poetic language is *snow*, the whitest and most evanescent substance, dissolved the instant we try to take hold of it. Poetry cannot be grasped and weighed down; it is the primary medium of antigravity.

The riches of poetry are in this respect the opposite of those we pursue in profane life. The glory of the poet isn't that of fame, wealth or any other of the solid external signs of worldly success, but of a kind of poverty, as a short poem of 1877 intimates:

> Who never wanted – maddest Joy
> Remains to him unknown –
> The Banquet of Abstemiousness
> Defaces that of Wine –
>
> Within its reach, though yet ungrasped
> Desire's perfect Goal –
> No nearer – lest the Actual –
> Should disenthrall thy soul –

(no. 1430)

In these lines is a striking anticipation of that strange love letter she would send to Judge Lord the following year. 'Maddest Joy' is experienced not in attaining 'Desire's perfect Goal' but in *wanting* it. To realize desire is to betray it – the true banquet is exalted not by wine but by 'Abstemiousness'.

Dickinson's abstemiousness, however, was not the tranquil release from desire sought in Buddhist practice. It was a fevered heightening of desire with a view to its ultimate denial. This may well sound to us like a serviceable definition of torture. Yet Dickinson came to see it as the most ecstatic state we can aspire to. She located the true substance of life in the pure space of the imagination, unsullied by the inevitable compromises and corruptions of worldly reality. We should not doubt her when she tells Lord how much she wants to marry him. Her unrealized passion for him is not some prolonged, sadistic deception, but the expression of her belief in the emotional and spiritual superiority of wanting over having.

To be a poet is to commit to a strange contract with oneself: to amass untold riches in the realm of 'Possibility' in order to renounce them in the realm of 'Prose' or external reality. This retreat into a more private and invisible glory shouldn't be mistaken for modesty. It is a kind of defiance of gravity, a rising above the laws and conventions that govern life on earth. Daydreaming for Dickinson was not a retreat into listless inactivity, but the basis of the highest vocation.

For Wolff, this stance is not only very far from the tired legend of the quiet and unassuming spinster but also the boldest blasphemy, pitting the snowy, weightless creations of the poet against the oppressively solid and unpliable creations of God: 'In the poet God discovers a creature of His own making who can sing and dance as He cannot.' The challenge isn't quite Satanic, however, for the poet does not and cannot seek to outdo God in power and force.

Her only power is a kind of willed impotency. The corollary of her infinite power in the realm of 'Possibility' is her inability to make anything happen in the realm of action and change, or what we more commonly call reality. Another poem from 1862 reads as a kind of manifesto for this conception of the poet:

This was a Poet – It is That
Distills amazing sense
From ordinary Meanings –
And Attar so immense

From the familiar species
That perished by the Door –
We wonder it was not Ourselves
Arrested it – before –

Of Pictures, the Discloser –
The Poet – it is He –
Entitles Us – by Contrast –
To ceaseless Poverty –

Of Portion – so unconscious –
The Robbing – could not harm –
Himself – to Him – a Fortune –
Exterior – to Time –

                                                    (no. 448)

The 'familiar species' of flora lying forlornly outside our front door, like the 'ordinary Meanings' of our everyday speech, is dried up, lifeless. The poet's alchemy involves extracting 'sense' – or 'scents' – from flowers that had seemed to us bereft of either perfume or significance. How does she achieve this? Not by creating a picture intrinsically inaccessible to the rest of us, but by 'disclosing' some latent scent we hadn't yet perceived. What we smell when the poet's words release the flower's dormant perfume seems to us at that moment so indisputably present, we find ourselves wondering why 'it was not Ourselves/Arrested it – before –'.

The poet is a kind of convenience device, saving us time and effort. Her abundant gift of disclosure, enabling us to see endless pictures concealed in and around us, 'Entitles Us – by Contrast –/To ceaseless Poverty –'; in other words, she does it so we don't have to. Her imaginative wealth bestows on us the right to a kind of imaginative laziness. We can endlessly 'rob' her of her pictures, or read her poems, while leaving her none the poorer.

We can steal so freely from her because we aren't really taking anything. Her store of images is a 'Portion – so unconscious –', 'a Fortune –/Exterior – to Time –'. This is a wonderfully precise evocation *avant la lettre* of Freud's definition of the unconscious as 'timeless'. Nor is the comparison merely impressionistic. The contents of the unconscious, like the contents of the poem, do not exist as objects in our time-bound world. Where money and fame are finite commodities whose loss we cannot always restore, the poetic imagination and the unconscious are infinite resources; we can take from them in the knowledge there's always more where they came from.

There is a clue here to another of Dickinson's great renunciations. In addition to marriage and social status, Dickinson refused publication, which would have validated her as a poet in the eyes of the world. Her attitude to publication was rather more ambivalent than her most trenchant pronouncements on the subject suggest. She made initial contact with potential mentors like Bowles and Higginson to sound out their responses to her poetry, and Bowles published six of her poems in his Springfield *Republican* with her consent. Only five further poems were published during her lifetime.

There are strong hints in the correspondence with Higginson that she was seeking his encouragement to publish. In her first letter, from 1862, she implored him 'to say if my Verse is alive?'

But when he expressed doubts about how such a dark and obscure poetry would be received by a reading public, suggesting she delay publication, she retorted that the aspiration was 'foreign to my thought, as Firmament to Fin –'. In the same letter, she responds wittily and rather witheringly to his critical remarks: 'You think my gait "spasmodic" – I am in danger – Sir –/You think me "uncontrolled" – I have no Tribunal.'

The note of proud pique is undeniable, but perhaps Higginson's appeal for a more tempered and regular poetic diction will only have confirmed Dickinson's doubts about the compromises imposed by publication. It is these doubts that might have spurred her creation, between 1858 and 1865, of forty 'fascicles' or 'packets' containing around 800 poems, posthumously discovered by her astonished sister.

Each fascicle consisted of twenty poems handwritten on four or five folded sheets, carefully bound and threaded together with string. Commentators have argued and puzzled over whether these painstakingly handcrafted artefacts constitute proof of a final renunciation of conventional publication or, on the contrary, a means of ensuring it.

Perhaps the puzzle is a false one. Having invested so much in the presentation and preservation of her poetic legacy, Dickinson kept it hidden while she lived. But she also allowed it to be found after she died, as though she were splitting off the act of publication from any personal striving after fame and fortune. Dickinson wanted the world to recognize her poetry, but wanted equally to ensure that recognition would not be sullied by worldly ambitions and desires. Becoming a celebrity poet in her own lifetime would in her mind have been the most egregious instance of sacrificing the bread for its crust.

Dickinson's fascicles are a bold gambit from this perspective, for in secretly preparing the way for a posthumous publication she

would not live to witness, she shows quiet conviction in the vin-
dication of her poetry's greatness by posterity. In this way, poetic
and personal glory were kept safely distinct from one another.
Her most celebrated poetic broadside against publication, from
1863, turns on just this distinction:

> Publication – is the Auction
> Of the Mind of Man –
> Poverty – be justifying
> For so foul a thing
>
> Possibly – but We – would rather
> From Our Garret go
> White – Unto the White Creator –
> Than invest – Our Snow –
>
> Thought belong to Him who gave it –
> Then – to Him Who bear
> Its Corporeal illustration – Sell
> The Royal Air –
>
> In the Parcel – Be the Merchant
> Of the Heavenly Grace –
> But reduce no Human Spirit
> To Disgrace of Price –

(no. 709)

To invest 'Our Snow' is to make a discrete, saleable commodity
out of the incorporeal substance of poetic language. The fascicles
assured the transmission of the poems to succeeding generations
while keeping the poet's spirit clean of any 'Disgrace of Price'.

*

Dickinson was the inheritor of her grandfather's visionary extravagance, but his seer's sensibility had to pass through the intervening generation before it came to her — that is, through the disenchanted austerity of her father and the anxious lethargy of her mother. The divine creation that shone so brilliantly in the eyes of Samuel Dickinson becomes a far more ambiguous force under Dickinson's gaze. Heaven and earth, life and death, are alike haunted by obscurity and chaos.

Some basic articles of religious faith remained, but in radically altered form. The famous poem 501 of 1862, for example, opens with a confident assertion of the existence of an afterlife: 'This World is not Conclusion.' But the world beyond imagined by the poem is hardly the Celestial City of *The Pilgrim's Progress*. Contemplating it begets not inspired visions of Paradise, but hazy distortions of the senses. The eternity that 'stands beyond' our time-bound world is 'Invisible, as Music —/But positive, as Sound'. The diffuse waves of sound floating in the ether of the next world are less angelic harmonies than a kind of white noise that 'beckons, and ... baffles'.

The extraordinary last lines are a (literally) biting gloss on the evangelical zeal of her grandfather's traditional Revivalist religion:

> Much Gesture, from the Pulpit —
> Strong Hallelujahs roll —
> Narcotics cannot still the Tooth
> That nibbles at the soul —

In this year of her most prodigious prolificity, in which she produced 365 poems, the bloodiest war ever waged by human-kind hitherto was raging through the nation. The Civil War, along with traumatic transformations of industrialization and urbanization, was striking hammer blows against the faith of her grandfather's generation in God's luminous and benign ordering of the world. The turbulence and horror of these seismic upheavals can be seen and heard in the poems' jarring rhythms and suffocating imagery. Still, we might wonder at how such historically urgent events gave rise not to her active public contribution, but to a retreat into what she called, in a late poem of 1877 (no. 1695), 'That polar privacy/A soul admitted to itself'. Why would you daydream in a locked room while the world outside burns?

Alternatively, why wouldn't you? Daydreaming, as I've tried to show, isn't always an expression of melancholy resignation and despair. In her life and work alike, Dickinson reveals the daydream to us as means to the deepest expressions of love, doubt and defiance.

Chapter 4

The Slacker

In the mid-1980s, I made much-anticipated termly trips to Carnaby Street to stare furtively at punks and sift through the records and memorabilia of my favourite bands. It was during one of these trips that I was stopped in my tracks by a poster: a woman, lying on her back, tilted languidly to the left. Peeking out of the black swamp of bedding, bleached shoulders hinted at nakedness. But she was as oblivious as Sleeping Beauty to the desire she might be arousing. Her body was a cancelled erotic promise radiating indifference. Stare long enough at the dense shock of hair and it became the dark void of night, swallowing everything but sleep itself.

The poster was tacked to the wall, bordered above and below by spiky letters, spelling out a confession, an injunction, a seduction of sorts: 'I DIDN'T GO TO WORK TODAY . . .' and '. . . I DON'T THINK I'LL GO TOMORROW / LET'S TAKE CONTROL OF OUR LIVES AND LIVE FOR PLEASURE NOT PAIN'.

The picture plunged me into sadness and panic, as though an invisible missile had been launched into the heart of my adolescent life, polluting my sense of meaning and purpose. The pleasure of a long lie-in, suggested the girl, might conceal a wish for the renunciation of the world beyond my bed.

Heading home, my gloom began to dissipate. The words I'd read as a rejection of life now sang with a strange hope: you do not

160

have to live under the tyranny of the world's, or your own, expectations. You are not obliged to comply with the daily agenda set by your parents or your school or your boss or you own head. If you don't like the day that's been doled out to you, erase it and choose another one, one you like better.

'Live for pleasure, not pain' – that was a mind-blowing slogan of practical philosophy, a spur to do the thing I'd been told my whole life I couldn't, namely whatever felt good. And then came the thrilling recognition of a deep secret, that the freedom I really craved was the freedom to do nothing, to throw off the burdens of duty and necessity. Refusing to leave my bed might seem like depressive withdrawal, but from a different angle it was a release of the imagination and a recovery of the day's potential. Clear the day of tasks and commitments, and its canvas is invitingly blank, available to anything. Of course, 'anything' could include wasting the day in bed, but unlike going to school or work that at least would be a choice. Going to work yesterday meant going today, which in turn meant going tomorrow. Going back to sleep, on the other hand, committed you to nothing beyond the next few hours. Working killed off the day's openness; dozing preserved it.

The girl was suspended at the threshold of sleep and wakefulness, where solid reality quivers like projected images on a shaken screen. Perhaps her preference for sleep over the regimented consciousness of the working day wasn't nihilism but an affirmation of human possibility. To think of my daily routine as optional dissipated its suffocating givenness, loosened the real world's constrictive grip on my young body and mind.

The burnout also chooses sleep and withdrawal over work and social life. But to speak of choice here is misleading. The burnout's predicament is that she can bear neither necessity nor freedom. If going to work is a consignment to the repetitive punishment of hell, staying in bed is no tranquil idyll. For the burnout, the possibilities conferred by a so-called free day are more persecutory than liberating. Every choice, if it is meaningfully a choice, needs a desire to animate it, and this is precisely what the burnout is lacking. She lies in bed because she cannot think of anywhere she'd want to go.

The slob, in contrast, enjoys sinking into the delicious torpor of an unmade bed, while the daydreamer, escaping into the fancies of his imagination, hovers over it. But these are all different ways of inhabiting the same immobile position. Exhaustion, lassitude and dreaminess can ensure that all my choices are preserved, but only at the expense of action. Stranded at the point where the road of life forks, the burnout, slob and daydreamer dare not take any one path for fear of losing access to all the others.

Their fear is well founded, as almost anyone who's had a regular job, bound by the requirement to be at work for specified hours each day, will know. As you tire yourself out litigating for corporations or emptying bins or inputting data or healing the sick, you may find yourself dreaming of a freer existence, in which you too could decide you won't go to work today, or tomorrow, that you will live for pleasure not pain, only to run up resentfully against that brick wall of obligations to your family, employer, customers, patients, not to mention yourself.

So you abandon wage slavery for some long-term freelance project – a novel or invention or fast fortune or cult blog. You wake up now to vast expanses of time, craving the relief of the regular hours and definable tasks you stupidly gave up, feeling chronically deprived of the urgency, direction and clarity of purpose you'd taken for granted when you'd had somewhere to go and something to do every day.

When our time doesn't belong to us, we demand it back; get it back and we want to return it, so that it becomes a perpetually recycled gift, immensely desirable when not in our possession, an unbearable burden when it is.

This brings us to a fourth way, and perhaps the one in which I find the deepest personal resonance: the way of the slacker.

Seven years after seeing the poster of the dozing girl, I was finding myself more attuned than ever to her state of mind. I was beginning a PhD, and a research council award meant I could pursue it free from the sordid obligation to earn an income, a privilege more ambiguous than I could have anticipated. Even as an English Lit undergrad, I needed to be at the odd lecture and seminar. Now I was stranded in a zone off any institutional or personal radar, where no one seemed to expect me to do anything or be anywhere. I could have gone days, weeks, perhaps even months without my absence being noticed by a soul.

During those first autumnal weeks, I would wake up to the unbidden thought, at once glorious and tormenting, that if I didn't read or write a single word, it would make no difference to anyone. Even as anxiety clawed at the front of my head and the pit of my stomach, I was aware of a quietly voluptuous, outlaw pleasure in being bound to nothing and nobody. Like the dozing girl, I could absent myself from the overbearing congestion of the world beyond my bed merely by closing my eyes.

But as weeks went by, the pleasure of inaction, precarious from the first, was diminished by anxiety. With much of the morning slept off, I would sit immobile on a straight-backed living-room chair, staring groggily into the shadows until jolted into awareness by a train rattling past my kitchen window. I showered, ate and drifted aimlessly around the grey Neasden streets, my inner voice churning out a fog of nonsense to obscure my one clear thought: I have no idea what I'm doing.

Around four years earlier, I'd been unexpectedly lifted out of my inertia by the story of the cadaverous young legal copyist. This time a lifeline came from the cinema. Richard Linklater's *Slacker* was one of those handful of films that, like the first breathless sight of a lover's face, you know immediately will never leave you. I paid £2.50, roughly £10 less than admission to the same cinema today, albeit to sit on a tattered seat, soles lightly soldered to the sticky floor. For this film, a run-down fleapit felt like a carefully designed immersive environment.

It didn't take me long to see the aimlessness of my own life reflected in the funhouse mirror of Linklater's film, comprised of weird, randomly connected episodes from the makeshift subcultures of Austin, Texas, teeming with amateur metaphysicians and madmen, conspiracy theorists and street entrepreneurs, tinkerers and petty criminals, anarchists and poseurs, linked only by their uncompromising renunciation of 'the kind of work you have to do to earn a living'.

I slouched in my seat, staring in enraptured lassitude from the opening shot of the amiable-looking young guy, the director himself I later found out, arriving at a bus station and sauntering over to a cab with his backpack. Within seconds he was delivering a monologue in an unbroken shot trained through the windscreen on both occupants of the cab, the guy's drawling fantasia in cahoots with the silent blankness of the driver, as though total disconnection were a form of connection. Sharing the same tight space, they occupy different universes.

The young guy spoke of dreams and fantasies and the daily forking paths of life. Just now, he might have stuck around at the bus station and been picked up and taken home by a beautiful stranger, a version of events which at this very moment might be unfolding in some alternate reality. The camera leaves him as he exits the cab, arriving at the next scenario before strolling casually minutes later to the next, each scene in a relation of random disconnection from and intricate connection to the last. Stories begin, break off, begin again, over and over, but this breathless sequence of abortive stories seems to be a way of telling one and the same story.

Rambling through the grass and concrete landscape of Austin, the camera runs up against its own forking paths, each scene implicitly forsaking a different one, so that the film I was watching seemed haunted by any number of films I didn't get to watch. Not that this was a privative experience; on the contrary, the spectral presence of other scenes gave me a delirious sense that each moment is pregnant with other moments. For someone so abjectly empty of purpose, so 'unpregnant of my cause' (in the words of Hamlet), there was something crazily enlivening about such a thought, which the film's drawling, listless bodies and voices paradoxically enhanced.

It wasn't that I identified with the fleeting characters, or aspired to their comically aimless lives. I wasn't going to play in a band called The Ultimate Losers or write a book called *Conspiracy-a-Go-Go*, and I wasn't the type to berate his girlfriend with a line like, 'Every single commodity you produce is a piece of your own death.'

It was more the spirit of the camera that inspired me, in its radiation of laziness, distraction, curiosity and freedom. I was entranced by its movement between the loosely connected scenes, its hesitant, sluggish drift from the departing back of one character to the indifferent person of the next, as though it only just bothered to keep going. The film's title seemed to allude less to its characters than to itself, its own slack relationship to its subjects, at once fascinated and distracted, alive and lackadaisical.

The term 'slacker' was coined to disparage draft dodgers during the Second World War, gradually evolving to encompass all forms of apathy and indifference towards life and work. The slacker would seem to be the exemplary naysayer, a connoisseur of all forms of refusal – work, activity, emotional agitation, choice and belief swallowed into the black hole of his indifference. So how could these vignettes in lassitude and stagnation feel so intensely affirmative?

Watching *Slacker* opened up a different way of relating to my own life, one that wasn't measured and valued by the externally imposed targets and achievements. It offered a glimpse of what Roland Barthes termed 'idiorrhythmy', 'where each subject lives according to his own rhythm'. To live life in this way means to refuse the regimentation of your time and space by the impersonal forces of work and leisure, giving yourself over to the pace and style of the impulses, curiosities and desires unique to you. But it is equally a social ideal, whereby the rhythms of all our individual lives coexist without encroaching on each other.

The landscape of *Slacker* was no utopia if by that we mean a community in which all work in concert to achieve the same moral, social and economic ideals. But it gave a sense of what our lives might look like when lived at once singularly and together, without the demand to comply with a single, overarching physical and psychic rhythm or ethos. It encouraged me to find my own idiorrhythm, the discovery of which it turned out I'd been in real need.

I had long been mired on waking by feelings of overwhelming shame. I would accuse myself of casually wasting the privilege of time and money to read and write. The problem, as *Slacker* helped me see, was that the rhythms of my curiosity didn't comply with the format of the standard working day. An open-ended, self-managed project was best served by adapting itself to the unpredictable flows of my mind.

If I sat down at a set time of the morning to read, I was liable within minutes to be staring into the middle distance, or else endlessly reading over the same paragraph. On the other hand, a new thought could take me by surprise as I was washing the dishes late in the evening.

Over the years that followed, I realized my productivity was best stimulated not by discipline, but by a kind of sustained indiscipline. I read and thought and wrote in sharp bursts or epic all-nighters, between fifteen-minute tea breaks or spontaneous week-long hiatuses of inactivity. I was doing what I'd dreamed of doing on my walk back from Carnaby Street seven years previously, namely whatever felt right. The revelation was that if I let myself work idiorrhythmically, if I followed the unpredictable drift of my desire, I didn't get lost in some inertial void; in fact, that was much more likely if I forced the work.

No doubt there comes a time when your idiorrhythm can no longer be isolated from everyone else's, when it must reckon with the externally imposed rhythms of an institutional day or the competing idiorrhythms of lovers or children or pets. But perhaps this is when it is most important to keep hold of its spirit of indiscipline and refusal, its commitment to activity, and inactivity, without purpose or aim. If you allow your whole self to be absorbed by the demands and agendas of a persecutory to-do list scribbled by others, you will quickly lose the very dimension of life that makes it liveable.

Recall the ridiculous lengths to which Pyrrho, the ancient Greek forebear of today's philosophical scepticism, would go to evade the lure of commitments and the seductions of belief. Straying to the edges of cliffs, in sight of dangerous animals, he defied the law of nature and risked his life rather than acknowledge its reality. Pyrrho's scepticism is radically debilitating, as it doggedly evades all decisive action, consigning the self to ataraxia, or unconcern, towards its own fate.

The key premise of Pyrrhonism is that experience tells us there is no reliable measure for natural or moral truth: the air a young person finds mild will make an old person feel cold, the act one individual considers wicked another considers virtuous. Pyrrho had extrapolated from this condition of cosmic undecidability that we may as well allow ourselves to be blown willy-nilly by the winds of chance, as no positive action or state of being is preferable to any other, including existence itself.

For most people, this is hardly a viable way to live. Around 500 years later, when the medic and philosopher Sextus Empiricus codified scepticism as a body of thought, he adapted Pyrrhonic thinking to the ordinary demands of daily life. While still oriented towards the ataraxia achieved by suspending all judgements and rejecting all definitive claims to truth, Sextus recognized the pragmatic requirement to act in accordance with 'guidance by nature, necessitation by feelings, handing down of laws and customs, and teaching all kinds of expertise'. In other words, if we cannot know which truth to live by, we can at least have rules.

The true and the good may not be knowable to us, but custom and feeling allow us to live as though they were. There is no way of determining if it really is cold, but I can certainly tell if I feel cold, and this is sufficient motive for putting on a coat. Thus, without contesting Pyrrho's radically sceptic stance, Sextus found a way to moderate its extreme implications for how we live. Like the good medic he was, he pointed out that 'we are not able to be utterly inactive'; by extension, we cannot let ourselves sink into total indifference towards ourselves.

As with the wild speculations and schemes of Linklater's slackers, so uncannily evocative of sceptic thought in their feeling for undecidability as a basic condition of life, the appeal isn't the content of the argument, which seems absurd from our smug retrospective vantage point (which affords us, for example, scientific methods and instruments to measure air temperature). Scepticism's appeal today, especially in a culture that encourages the narcissistic drip feed of preferences and opinions, lies in its stance of reticence, its wariness of mouthing off. In our social media landscape, opinion has become the currency and substance of our selfhood. The positions we publicize have become a way of affirming the reality of our existence to the world. We pontificate therefore we are.

Sextus tells a story that illustrates the sceptics' more modest relationship to truth and rightness. The painter Apelles was painting a horse and wanted to render accurately the lather on his mouth. In frustration at his failure to get it right, he flung his wet sponge at the picture; 'and when it hit ... it produced a representation of the horse's lather.'

As long as we actively seek the state of ataraxia, by trying to decide or resolve a given problem we only exacerbate our feelings of tension and frustration. But let go of the zeal to be right and ataraxia will come to us 'as it were fortuitously, as a shadow follows a body'. There is an unmistakable psychoanalytic resonance to the story in its suggestion that what we most want to say or do slips out of us in spite of our conscious intention. But it hints by the same token at a link between scepticism and ethics. Sextus shows us that the most desirable orientation to life, the one least likely to tie us in knots of irritable dissatisfaction, is one that renounces the illusion that we are master of the truth.

It was this aspect of scepticism that spoke to Roland Barthes, who found in it an expression of what he called the 'Neutral' state: 'the Neutral ... is good for nothing, and certainly not for advocating a position, an identity.' This neutrality is not some bland mean point between political or ethical extremes. It is a state of being, an orientation to life, implying the existence in us of what the aphoristic Romanian philosopher E. M. Cioran calls a '*faculty of indifference*' (the emphasis is his).

Deadly ideologies and movements take root, argued Cioran, when ideas are animated with the same impassioned zeal human beings once invested in gods: 'Once man loses his *faculty of indifference* he becomes a potential murderer.' Indifference is not simply an attitude we assume, but a fundamental dimension of our being, which struggles to avoid being submerged by the violence of dogma and ideology.

For Cioran, there are no virtues nobler than the so-called vices of 'doubt and sloth', for these preserve us from the terrors of fanaticism and the exclusive claim to truth. 'Only the sceptics (or idlers or aesthetes) escape' the contagion of fanaticism, 'because they *propose* nothing, because they – humanity's true benefactors – undermine fanaticism's purposes . . . I feel *safer* with a Pyrrho than with a Saint Paul, for a jesting wisdom is gentler than an unbridled sanctity.'

The sceptic stance, at least as Cioran interprets it, is a quiet resistance to the conception of the human as a propositional animal, a being defined by his proclaimed beliefs and public actions. To recognize a faculty of indifference or neutrality is to insist on the human being as irreducible to these badges of identity. Doubt and sloth, the twinned moods of the slacker, protect us from the terrors of unbridled sanctity.

The slacker challenges the unquestioned privilege of action and purpose in our culture of relentless accumulation and competition. She confronts the fundamental question of what makes a life worth living. For example, in the name of what do we protest neoliberalism's creation and exacerbation of social division, economic inequality, inhumanity and chaos? We can respond to such evils with a raft of worthy progressive aims and policies: protecting the welfare safety net, redistributive taxation, living wages and so on. Such policies may rightly seek to improve the conditions under which we live; but they do not address what we might want to live for. Social policy propositions address the needs of the human being as a creature of action, as a product of particular affiliations and identities. The quiet virtue of 'proposing nothing' is that it encourages us to think about and experience ourselves as irreducible to the sum of what we do and opine, as creatures who, beyond any action or achievement, simply *are*.

From this perspective, the slacker's life of sloth and doubt is a protest not in the name of this or that cause, but for the very right to be, to exist in what philosopher Frédéric Gros calls a 'suspensive freedom', outside the confines of personal, professional or any other identities. In the modern age, this right is under threat. The manic productivity of capitalism, the demands and aspirations of social status and the mechanical rhythms of industrialism all corral the individual into a perpetual state of anxious and compliant activity.

The so-called 'countercultures' that have sprung into being at every stage of modern history are models of living forged in opposition to these alien mechanical rhythms. The Romantics of the latter part of the eighteenth century, the aestheticists and decadents of the nineteenth, the beatniks and hippies and punks of the twentieth, all conceived new modes of social, creative and sexual life, encompassing what we might call idiorrhythmic experiments in communal living, opiate consumption, artistic forms and everyday fashion.

The Romantics were the first in this long chain, protesting against the coercive demand to do and comply with industrial society and its regime of permanent productivity. In Romantic poetry and prose, such protest often takes the form of episodes of reverie in which the writer, transported by a sublime landscape into the depths of the self, floats free of the external world and its encumbrances. In such moments, the nervous agitations of reality dissolve, leaving him in a bubble of perfect, though necessarily transient, tranquillity.

While there are many such episodes in Romantic literature, few are more definitive or more transfixing than the 'Fifth Walk' of Rousseau's last, unfinished masterpiece of 1776, *Reveries of the Solitary Walker*. Now in his final years, Rousseau meditated in these 'walks' on his state of solitary exile, the ideal remedy for the traumatic blows of intrigue and treachery he has endured through his life.

The Fifth Walk sees Rousseau taking refuge on the tiny Île de Saint-Pierre, set in the middle of the Swiss Lac de Bienne, following the stoning of his house by a mob in the nearby village of Môtiers. The quiet and solitude of the island prove the ideal balm for his state of persecuted agitation. Dedicating himself to 'precious *far niente* [doing nothing]', he embraces a daily life of inactivity – idly gathering botanical specimens, sitting on the banks of the lake or drifting in a little boat into the middle of it. This mode of minimal activity induces a perfect inner state:

> But if there is a state where the soul can find a position solid enough to allow it to remain there entirely and gather together its whole being, without needing to recall the past or encroach upon the future, where time is nothing to it, where the present lasts for ever, albeit imperceptibly and giving no sign of its passing, with no other feeling of deprivation or enjoyment, pleasure or pain, desire or fear than simply that of our existence, a feeling that completely fills the soul; as long as this state lasts, the person who is in it can call himself happy, not with an imperfect, poor and relative happiness, such as one finds in the pleasures of life, but with a sufficient, perfect and full happiness, which leaves in the soul no void needing to be filled.

There is a painful paradox about this moment of happiness: perfect and eternal it may be, but it cannot last. The sensation of nirvanic bliss, of permanent liberation from the ups and downs of daily life, is an effect of the moment's transience. This bubble of pure selfhood retains its timeless perfection only for as long as one is sealed inside it, immobile and indifferent to the world outside. But as Sextus had already noted over 1,500 years earlier, 'we are not able to be utterly inactive.' As soon as the sun starts to set, as soon as the breeze on the lake blows us awake and reminds us that the boat needs taking ashore, we are back in the workaday world of passing time and its frustrations.

Still, the fact that this moment must pass is no reason to dismiss it as trivial. Something profoundly significant happens in that boat; the drifting Rousseau discovers a radically free region of the self, defined, in the words of contemporary German philosopher Peter Sloterdijk, by 'its ecstatic unusability for any purpose'. From the perspective of an instrumental world bent on exhausting the physical and creative resources of individuals in being useful, this region of the self is very dangerous. The Rousseau 'of the Fifth Walk,' writes Sloterdijk, 'is like a nuclear reactor that suddenly radiates pure anarchic subjectivity into the environment'.

Useless, shiftless, good-for-nothing – the contemptuous words and phrases we use to denigrate the slacker attest to the secret fear he induces in us. No sooner does his 'anarchic subjectivity' appear, whether in the form of Romantic reverie, Bohemian intoxication, hippy freak-out or punk nihilism, than it's attacked for its brazen parasitism, irresponsibility and delinquency. So invested is our manically productive culture in the image of us as active and purposeful beings that we seek to erase or destroy all evidence to the contrary – the slacker must put on a suit, get a job, lose his benefits and make himself useful. Harmlessly ineffective as he may be, we hate and fear him for showing us the useless dimension of our own selfhood, for voicing our own impulse not to go to work today, or tomorrow.

That impulse to recover the personal rhythms of our own being from the imposed rhythms of the modern world continues to haunt us. For those of us caught up in this world's twin demands of permanent activity and distraction, all the basic elements of everyday being – sleep, eating, sex, movement, thought – survive in a state of chronic deprivation. Disturbed, accelerated, truncated and confused, our bodily and mental lives seem barely to belong to us. The consulting room is only one of many spaces in which I'm made aware of this predicament; every tube carriage or social gathering or office seems to hum with declarations of exhaustion and time poverty – of sleep interrupted, of electronic devices intruding themselves between couples and family members at the dinner table or in bed, of evenings and weekends swallowed up in work.

Into this enervated culture steps the so-called 'slow movement', a loose affiliation of practical advocates for slowing the pace of daily activities from cooking and gardening to design and medicine. As crystallized in its informal bible, Carl Honoré's *In Praise of Slow* (2005), the aim of the movement is not to promote slowness for its own sake, but to allow the activity itself, rather than some imposed schedule, to set the speed at which we perform it. A slow-braised stew, a yoga pose, a kiss or a chat will tell us, if we allow them to, the time for which they should be cooked, assumed and enjoyed.

Taken in this way, the ordinary pleasures of the world are felt rather than consumed, giving us the joy of an actual experience rather than the grim satisfaction of the next task executed. It isn't hard to see the appeal of slowness, the promise it offers of recovering the fullness and depth of real life from the manically accelerated impersonation of life dictated by consumer capitalism.

But there is another strain of argument audible in the proliferation of books, TED talks and blogs promoting the ethos of slow: the assurance that slowness will make us not only happier but more productive. To do things slowly is to do them properly rather than in the mode of resentful carelessness fostered by the rage for speed. Honoré cites the IBM manager who encourages employees 'to make the most of email (and life) by using email less'. More haste, less speed; the quality of email use as well as its efficacy is maximized by placing limits on it.

With such counsel, the imperatives of purpose and productivity, which slowness seemed at first to subvert, are returned to the driving seat. Slowness ceases to be its own justification and instead becomes a means to the end of a healthy work–life balance. And what's wrong with that? Surely to remedy the pervasive malaise of exhaustion and agitation by resetting priorities and recovering a measure of control over the pace of daily life can only be sensible and humane?

It also keeps intact, and indeed bolsters, a conception of us as essentially instrumental, task-driven creatures. Slowness, no longer a brake on productive efficiency, is instead put in its service, cultivating the healthier bodies and clearer minds we need to become better workers, parents, lovers, cooks. Like most self-help movements, the argument for slowness is liable to get pulled between a fundamental challenge to the status quo and cosmetic amelioration of it.

Rousseau's mid-lake reverie, after all, doesn't end with his declaring himself newly invigorated for his return to work and society. It isn't an early version of the yoga retreat or mindfulness course that recharges the batteries for those twelve-hour days at the office, but a plunge into 'pure anarchic subjectivity' – a dangerous energy that resembles the defiant dozing of the girl on the poster, corroding the will to serve as a good worker and citizen. It is slowness as the enemy rather than ally of social responsibility and cohesion.

In today's overworked executive culture, there is a striking contemporary analogue for Rousseau's drifting boat: the flotation tank. In their 2012 book *Dead Man Working*, Carl Cederström and Peter Fleming observe the increasing popularity of this elaborate device among 'over-worked, hyper-stressed employees of London who simply cannot turn off'. They describe the experience of entering the tank and floating in the warm salt water. In the darkness, the contours of the body seem to dissolve, so that 'you can no longer distinguish between your different body parts. As you lie there, in the dark, hearing the ambient music slowly fading out, your brain activity slows down and you willingly surrender to a dream-like state. Then, finally, you have become no one.'

As in Rousseau's reverie, the self here feels neither surfeit nor deficit of pleasure, dissolving instead into a state of pure anonymity, a nirvanic emptiness more perfect than any worldly happiness. But the differences are at least as instructive as the resemblances. Where for Rousseau the state of blissful self-sufficiency cannot be reconciled with the workaday world lurking at its edges, the flotation centre sells itself on its positive effect on our dynamism and productivity. 'A float session,' says Floatworks' PR, 'is guaranteed to eliminate stress, leaving you with a clear mind to concentrate 100% on the matter in hand. It increases creativity, the ability to solve problems, concentration span, personal motivation and energy levels.'

Corporate workplaces have become increasingly invested in pressing such fleeting experiences of pure being, including mindfulness meditation and yoga as well as flotation, into their service. If the worker is to be made maximally productive, then the slacker in him must become subservient. The corporate strategy isn't to dismiss the slacker as some loser wandering the streets outside its shiny glass towers but to recognize him as a dimension in all of us. In encouraging the employee to cultivate inner peace, it acknowledges an inertial tendency, an anarchic refusal of the demand to be useful, or, in today's dehumanizing parlance, a 'net contributor'. The clever ruse of sending the employee to a flotation tank during their lunch hour marshals this outlaw region of selfhood for the corporation's own uses.

In Slow TV we are faced with a strand of the slow movement that isn't so easily co-opted. Slow TV is a style of broadcast inspired by Andy Warhol's experiments in long-form cinema recording a continuous static or near-static entity – his sleeping lover, the Empire State Building. Its earliest experiment was contemporaneous with Warhol's films. At Christmas 1966, WPIX showed the famous 'Yule Log', a looped film of a burning fire set against a festive music soundtrack and broadcast without commercial interruption. But it wasn't until 2009 that a series of programmes produced by the Norwegian Broadcasting Corporation (NRK) turned Slow TV into a fully fledged television subgenre.

The NRK's first foray into Slow TV was a real-time record of the seven-hour train journey between Oslo and Bergen, using four alternating cameras fixed on both exterior and interior viewpoints. Its popular success, which saw 1.25 million viewers tune into some portion of the programme, has since led to the commissioning of similar broadcast events, among them further train as well as boat rides, a salmon fishing expedition, a compilation of three months of recorded bird life, a night of chopping and burning firewood, and a knitting marathon.

Ever since television insinuated itself into our homes and lives, it has been the object of bitter polemic from cultural critics lamenting its stupefying effects on our moral, intellectual and political faculties. TV, we are told, renders us docile, pliable, credulous. It drip-feeds the new opiate of the masses, a pappy diet of vapid entertainment and pseudo-information. Fictional or factual, its flow of programming is tacitly directed towards entrenching and normalizing moral depravity (for its conservative critics) and political subservience (for its revolutionary enemies).

These critics point to TV's capacity to induce a collapse of the erect and alert bodily and mental stance we're supposed to maintain during the working day, striding down corridors or seated at desks. In this state of exhaustion, our weary bodies are massaged and our drained minds filled with stories, opinions and information. TV, in other words, exploits the inertial region of our selfhood. For us on the sofa as for Rousseau on the lake, the sorrows of the day past and the anxieties of the day to come seem to dissolve. But where the beautiful vista before Rousseau wants nothing from him, and so leaves him to sink into his blissful oblivion, the vista on our screens seduces our attention, pleasure and interest.

Slow TV is different in this regard, closer to a 'Fifth Walk' for our times. It lets us experience the stupor induced by the medium of TV, without the stimulus aroused by the message. Instead of filling up empty time with content, it encourages us to keep it empty, without past or future, to let ourselves waste time watching next to nothing.

The pioneering NRK Slow TV producer Thomas Hellum tells of a man of eighty-two who sat enraptured for a full five days in front of a real-time fjord cruise. What was he looking at? Was he, as Hellum jocosely suggests, not wanting to leave his chair in case he missed something? Or was the catatonic fascination more an effect of the absence of anything to miss, the increasing loss of any sense of differentiation between moments, places, images?

Watch the Oslo–Bergen train journey for long enough, staring into the endless yards of track rolling toward the horizon,
bathed in the shadow of the driver's car, and the contents of the
scenery – the fitfully illuminated pitch black of rail tunnels, the
grey mountain rock bathed in the resplendent glare of the sun,
the towering pylons and hulking shipping containers dotting
the station yards, the flat stretches of sea and sand, of blindingly
white snow and lush grasses and glassy lakes nestled under the
same expanse of cloudless blue sky – will eventually dissolve into
a single, endless flow of colour and sound.

It isn't the landscape so much as your own mind that you're
immersed in by this point. The things looked at become secondary to the act of looking. The effect of real slowness is to pull us
away from our everyday view of the world as a series of discrete
objects and events, and recall to us an experience of the world as
the undifferentiated stream of sensory effects it once was, when
we first arrived in it.

From Rousseau to Slow TV, reverie has served as a kind of silent
protest, a yearning to live within the indifferent region of ourselves that can't be used or put to work. The obvious objection
to reverie is that it's profoundly antisocial. It models happiness
on narcissistic withdrawal, in which the basic conditions of the
external world – time, space, the presence of others – have melted
away. This is probably why slacker types are so often accused of
'living on another planet', the indignant contempt provoked by
their apparent unconcern for the rules and norms that govern
this planet.

Like scepticism, Epicurus's doctrine of hedonism promoted
ataraxia, or tranquil unconcern, as the highest good of life. Its
route to this goal was not, as the term hedonism now connotes,
endless pleasurable indulgence, but the avoidance of the physical

and psychic pressures that induce tension and pain. In Rousseau's boat or the Slow TV viewer's armchair is experienced 'no other feeling of . . . pleasure or pain . . . than simply that of our existence'. It's hard to imagine a fuller realization of Epicurus's counsel: 'Live in hiding and do not care about the world.'

Perhaps anticipating the strange pleasures of Slow TV, David Foster Wallace's epic 1996 novel *Infinite Jest* centres on the clandestine circulation of a film so captivating it causes its viewer, unable to wrench himself away from it, to expire in a state of stupefied bliss. This is the logical outcome of surrendering oneself to a state of pure ataraxia. If you stay in the boat or chair long enough, you'll die; perfect tranquillity must at some point give way to biological necessity. But is the slacker tendency in us so thoroughly incompatible with the reality of existence in a world of others? Why is it so difficult to imagine a world in which my own personal rhythms can exist peaceably alongside yours?

A good part of this difficulty can be chalked up to the need to procure and sustain the means of our survival, an imperative which imposes on us the obligation to adapt ourselves to rhythms that are not our own – those of the field, the street, the factory, the office. Our survival requires work, or more precisely labour. Hannah Arendt argues that what we call work gives rise to a tangible product. Labouring, in contrast, is an endless process, a matter of surviving rather than making. We labour for the means to feed, clothe and shelter ourselves and our dependants, meaning the cycle must begin again the next day and the next. When it comes to labour, writes Arendt, 'what makes the effort painful is not danger but its relentless repetition'.

Relentless repetition is painful because it means submitting to a rhythm imposed on us from without. It means sitting in stationary traffic or waiting for overdue trains on overcrowded platforms; adapting mind and body to the rhythms of keyboards, power drills, conveyor belts, cash registers; executing tasks to tight deadlines that override any urge to, say, have a nap or go for a stroll. We dislike labour because it makes us experience the day on terms that are not our own.

For more than two centuries, anarchists and socialists have sought to imagine forms of work that would put an end to the drab tyranny of labour, among them Charles Fourier, the utopian socialist who inspired a string of communitarian experiments across the nineteenth century; Paul Lafargue, son-in-law of Karl Marx and author of an inspired polemical defence of 'The Right to Be Lazy'; Mikhail Bakunin and Peter Kropotkin, the major theorists of Russian anarchism; and William Morris, leader and activist of the English Arts and Crafts movement.

Many of these ideas and impulses are distilled in Wilde's famous 1891 essay 'The Soul of Man Under Socialism', written immediately after reading Kropotkin. Wilde's essay provokes us into examining our assumptions about what matters most in life. We tend to assume unthinkingly that our primary concern in life should be with what is useful to us, and that beauty is mere embellishment or indulgence. Where the useful serves our deepest needs, the beautiful merely caters to our desires and whims.

Wilde asks us to imagine a self and a society governed instead by the primacy of beauty, where the soul-crushing burden of 'useful' labour is outsourced to commonly owned machines. Beauty in such a world consists in a person or thing 'being what it is', in manifesting its singular personality. Under socialism, the human personality 'will not be always meddling with others, or asking them to be like itself. It will love them because they will be different.'

The value of a person in such a society would consist not in how much she's like everyone else but how much like herself. Socialism as Wilde conceives it will foster the conditions under which singular individuals live side by side, without resentment or rivalry. The angry, dissident spirit is an effect of a society which will not let its members become who they are. 'The note of the perfect personality,' says Wilde, 'is not rebellion, but peace.'

Far from being the enemy of society, in this vision ataraxia becomes its very basis. A 'faculty of indifference', a slothful disinclination to dictate to others how they should be, helps us cultivate creative boldness, a fearless and joyful self-expression which is Wilde's very definition of beauty. In abolishing the tyranny of the useful and the 'relentless repetition' of labour, we clear the way for the reign of useless beauty over our daily lives.

Things haven't turned out as Wilde had hoped, at least not yet. In this age of 'strivers and skivers', the popular fantasy is of a parallel society of welfare cheats and layabouts enjoying easy lives at the expense of our hard ones. The tyranny of the useful seems as entrenched as it's ever been. A unique personality is more a marketing tool than an expression of beauty; 'be what you are' sounds more like an advertising slogan than a spur to social and individual transformation.

Wilde's socialist society was an aesthetic one, meaning that art alone, in his view, could express the unconstrained uniqueness of the human person. In our neoliberal society, art has become a means of buying and selling human uniqueness as a commodity like any other. Where Wilde anticipated a world of proliferating slackers doing whatever they wanted, our world is one in which would-be slackers are under compulsion to go wherever the Job Centre tells them.

Under such conditions, making a claim for art as authentic and spontaneous self-expression seems naive. Almost none of us live in a world that nurtures such spontaneity. The majority of artists are stuck between the rock of financial self-sacrifice for the sake of creative time and the hard place of sacrificing creative time to financial necessity. A minority can make a living from their art, while a tiny fraction of that minority are made wealthy by the inflation of their prices to obscene levels, fuelled by the status of art as the ultimate speculative commodity, frequently yielding profits that dwarf those of other sectors.

Far from contesting the tyranny of the useful, art today has become its great ally, put to the task of enhancing brands, adorning corporate boardrooms and boosting investment portfolios. How, then, is an artist meant to defy such uses of her work? The German artist Maria Eichhorn offered a memorable answer to this question in her 2016 show at London's Chisenhale Gallery, *5 weeks, 25 days, 175 hours*.

The show opened with a one-day symposium, featuring lectures and discussions of the ideas and questions it raised. The following day, a sign was placed outside the gallery entrance:

> For the duration of Maria Eichhorn's exhibition, *5 weeks, 25 days, 175 hours*, Chisenhale Gallery's staff are not working. The gallery and office are closed from 24 April to 29 May 2016. For further information please visit www.chisenhale.org.uk.

Eichhorn's 'exhibition' put the gallery's entire staff on five weeks' fully paid leave, during which no phone calls were taken and all emails were deleted. Staff were requested to do no work relating to their roles at the gallery throughout the duration of the show (or no-show).

Eichhorn wasn't the first artist to have made art out of a refusal to display anything. Robert Barry's 1969 exhibition in Amsterdam consisted of a sign on the gallery's locked door reading, 'During the exhibition the gallery will be closed', while in his LA show of 1974 Michael Asher removed the partition wall between the gallery's empty exhibition space and its office, exposing its everyday operations to the public.

But the emphasis of Eichhorn's show was markedly different. The previous two artists placed the focus on the viewer's desire, thwarted by Barry and gratified by Asher, to see the very spaces blocked off to him. Eichhorn, in contrast, drew our attention to the gallery being closed because the staff were 'not working'.

In so doing, she channels Wilde's utopian spirit. The symposium prior to the gallery closure spent a good portion of its time detailing the huge volume of administrative labour and fundraising activity that goes into the gallery's survival. Eichhorn's gesture orchestrated a break into this painful labour of survival, using the funds raised for the show to release its staff from work. The gift of their freedom, and the implicit plea for the value of not working, became the invisible content of the show. For those five weeks, she realized in practice what Wilde envisioned in theory: the human being, liberated from the everyday tyranny of labour, could be experienced as what he is rather than what he does or has. We can imagine how the staff might have used or wasted their freed-up time, but we cannot see it or make an image of it to display and sell. The staff, in other words, were released from the bonds of action and into the freedom of being.

We don't get to see what the staff did with their free time. A display of images of the staff sleeping, strolling in the park, watching daytime TV or falling into massive existential self-doubt would extract a product from their freedom and so compromise it. On the terms set by Wilde, it is a work of art precisely because there is nothing to see, because it isn't a thing to put in a gallery for others to visit. It suspends art as we know it, a discrete commodity produced to be circulated and looked at, in order to get us to imagine life itself as art – that is, life no longer in thrall to the labour of survival.

For Wilde, life and art could only be worthy of themselves when released from instrumental bonds, when they became ends in themselves rather than the means to something else (money or fame). This is impossible as long as art consists of objects made to buy and sell. Eichhorn is the latest in a long chain of modern artists who have asked how it is possible, if at all, to produce a work of art that wouldn't immediately be commodified. In 1961, the Italian artist Piero Manzoni produced a series of cans containing, so he claimed, his own shit (the claim can only be verified by opening the tin, thereby destroying its market value). The last auction of one of the Manzoni cans, in 2016, fetched around £250,000.

Manzoni showed the alchemy whereby the art market turned waste into gold. Eichhorn's alchemy is different, taking funding that would ordinarily be put to work in the forms of curation, publicity, security, administration and public education, and transforming it into an unexpected and abundant gift of free time. Those five weeks, twenty-five days and 175 hours are taken out of the circuit of productivity and purpose; from the perspective of work and profit, they are wasted. But this wasted time is alchemized by the work into the immaterial gold of non-work, giving us a glimpse of the world as it might look if left to the slackers.

Is psychoanalysis an ally of the slacker in us, or does it seek to discipline and 'cure' the non-working self? There are good reasons to suspect psychoanalysis of being on the side of work. 'Work', indeed, is one of the preferred synonyms of the psychoanalyst to describe the clinical process of seeing a patient and the gradual change it seeks to effect. And amplifying the qualities of pain and difficulty, one often hears the analogy made between this process and that of prenatal labour and birth, as though the emergence of a new and different self couldn't be authentic if it wasn't also excruciating.

And then there are the desired results of psychoanalytic work. Freud identified 'love and work' as the ideals of life and analysis alike, suggesting the ultimate aim of the process was to lift inhibitions on the energy we would want to invest in a productive and purposeful life. In mid-twentieth-century America, this conception of analysis drove its medicalization. In functioning as the dominant paradigm of psychiatry, it was pressed into the service of society's needs, its primary curative aim being the integration of the patient into the workplace and sanctioned forms of social and family life. In the 'ego psychological' tradition that dominated American psychoanalysis during this period, the essential clinical task was conceived as 'strengthening the ego', seat of active and rational selfhood, against the incursions of the unconscious and its debilitating conflicts.

Work, with its predictable routines and tasks, is perhaps the most reliable means of strengthening the ego. Like all regular work, psychoanalytic work has something of this predictability, the 'relentless repetition' of which Arendt speaks. One of the most difficult demands of clinical practice, at least for me, is the simple maintenance of its routines – beginning and ending the sessions at the appointed times with the same individuals, being no more or less available and attentive to each of them for one session than you were the previous session or will be the next. Of course, the professional requirements of punctuality and consistency are hardly exclusive to psychoanalysis. But in psychoanalysis good timing is not merely a means to the end of efficiency, but a source of therapeutic value, a way for a patient to experience a reliability and regularity they might never have previously enjoyed. Perhaps because it's a clinical necessity and ethical obligation, the repetitiousness of psychoanalytic routine can feel peculiarly burdensome.

Paradoxically, the purpose of this labour it to protect a space for non-labour, a temporary suspension of the working self and its effort of organized, logically sequential thinking. The assurance of the constancy of the space and time of the session licenses a certain slackening of the mind, a mode of speaking – and, indeed, of not speaking – which doesn't need to know what it's saying or where it's going.

In today's accelerated culture, most of daily life is experienced in drive mode, seeking the fastest and most direct route from one task to the next (though it's worth recalling that driving often gets mired in congestion). The psychoanalytic session releases us from this purposive mode, ushering us into a time of aimlessness, a movement through thoughts and feelings and words directed less towards getting somewhere in particular than to cultivating curiosity about the mind itself.

Walking, suggests Frédéric Gros, is a kind of non- or even anti-work. Work privileges doing over being, the single-minded action over a more diffuse receptivity. One works to produce, whereas in conventional economic terms walking is 'time wasted, frittered away, dead time in which no wealth is produced'. It isn't a coincidence that the experience of watching *Slacker* most immediately evoked in me a long and lackadaisical walk.

The reverse side of the aim-oriented tendency of psycho-analysis is its insinuation into a person's daily life of designated periods of time freed from the imperative to do or say anything in particular. Certainly one addresses one's inhibitions, frustrations, guilt, shame, inadequacy and other forms of suffering, but the curative force of a session lies not in finding the most effective solution to these problems, but in rousing the kind of interest in, and intimacy with, our own minds that daily life typically blocks off. In this sense, it is another way of cultivating idiorrhythmy, of slowly discovering the pace and style of one's own particular walk.

This is why, especially when seen from the perspective of more time-limited, quick-fix psychotherapies, it is so often accused of frittering away time, with failing to turn a psychic profit with sufficient quickness and efficiency. Psychoanalysis, in this view, doesn't get anywhere, is talk for the mere sake of it. Which is not altogether wrong, but misses the point nonetheless: in one way or another, a patient comes to psychoanalysis to be relieved of the pressure to produce, to formulate a solution, to get somewhere. It offers the experience, as Winnicott hints, of discovering the layer of pure being buried under the surface of daily doing.

~

For as long as I could remember, each of Jerome's three weekly sessions had brought dispatches of some new outrage perpetrated against his dignity and intelligence by one or other venal, vulgar colleague at his accountancy firm. Listening to him, I'd catch myself wondering caustically how on earth, given the chronic and pervasive mediocrity of its personnel, it got any business at all, let alone serviced the massive roster of corporate clients it boasted.

Filled with his cold rage and hate, the room quickly turned airless, sticky. At first, and without realizing it, I survived his contempt by letting myself become infected with it. I quickly learned to expect some tirade against the ignorance and sycophancy of the junior and senior partners promoted over his head. 'They haven't a fucking clue,' he'd say in a tone of theatrically hopeless exasperation, to which I'd once, early on, replied in a tone of spiteful impatience, 'No. It's lucky they have you.' His comeback, after several minutes of freezing me out, was merciless: 'If your clinical ability is on a par with your wit, I'm wasting my time here.'

It was a useful if harsh bit of instruction. With a different patient, my response might have presented a gently ironic mirror to his self-regard and the self-hatred it concealed. But Jerome was too attuned to its tone of scratchy one-upmanship, and duly punished me for it. He hardly needed me to point out his attitude of enraged superiority; he had to live with it every minute of the day.

No, what he needed now was precisely the opposite: a place to bring his hate, to spew it unsparingly until he could trust it wouldn't provoke my retaliation. And so for six, ten, twelve, eighteen months, I took in his contempt and disgust towards his work, his colleagues, towards the wife who so quickly lost patience, the young children who demanded the one thing he couldn't offer – his happiness – and towards his analyst, who just sat there 'listening to my tedious bullshit with practically nothing to say'.

For close to three hours a week, I inhabited a world peopled by cocks and arseholes, bitches and harridans and brats, a world of sadistic enslavement, of gratuitous meanness and disrespect, of perpetual demands and failed communication. I could find little to say beyond some variation on how difficult it must be to live in a world so bereft of joy or love or fulfilment.

In spite of his regular swipes at me, I had the sense he was helped by the assurance of someone knowing how unrelievedly lousy it felt to be him. As the story of his childhood emerged, it became difficult to imagine how it could have been any other way. His father, manager of a local retail franchise, transmitted nervous disdain for the imaginative precocity and intellectual curiosity of his youngest son. What kind of kid stayed home to draw and listen to music, when he could be out cheering the local non-league football team with his dad, sister and brother?

His father's distance found its mirror image in his mother's proximity. He would feel her peer over his shoulder at the picture he was drawing and half needily, half resentfully await its pronouncement as a masterpiece. Frustrated by her premature exit from formal education, she lived her son's schooling as though it were her own second chance. At a certain point, Jerome told me, he no longer knew whose homework he was doing or whose piano he was practising.

His father looked askance on this alternative couple, more puzzled than concerned, perhaps relieved they'd both found someone who seemed to make them happy. Jerome thus lost the last line of defence against the intrusions of his mother's desire, against her claustrophobic investment in his life. His only refuge during his largely friendless, joyless adolescence was his kitschy fantasies of escaping to Paris to paint in a garret. He would stare longingly at photographs of Cézanne, Matisse and especially Picasso, placing himself amid the breathless hum of brilliance, agony, absinthe and women.

The discussion with his mother about college was swift and brutal. 'Actually,' he'd gathered the courage to tell her, 'I want to go to art school.' Her laugh in response, he said, was one of the worst moments of his life. 'You can paint to your heart's content when you're earning a decent living!' she told him. 'I can see now how profoundly I hated her at that point,' he told me. So profoundly that his unconscious revenge was to be unhappy for the rest of his life, to spoil her life by spoiling his own. When she told him he should study for accountancy, he simply acquiesced in steely resentment and silent loathing.

She had wanted him to have a life better than hers, a life less blighted by blind compliance and unfulfilled promise. Instead, the two of them had unwittingly colluded to ensure that his life would repeat the very same patterns. She had married a man as unable as her own father to acknowledge the substance of her desire; Jerome, or so he told himself, had married a woman with the very same blind spot. Thus he found himself stuck in an existence whose chief and profoundly perverse pleasure was hating it.

One of the favoured forms of this hate was to sink into fantasies of quitting the firm, coming home to his wife and telling her gleefully he'd chucked it in, watching her mounting anxiety as he gave his days over to lounging around in assorted hideous Hawaiian shirts, not shaving, going to matinees, getting fat, vaguely contemplating enrolling on a painting course. 'I can just see her screaming at me, "*You're a fucking useless waste of space!*" and giving her the great Lebowski comeback, "Yeah, well, that's just, like, your *opinion*, man."' That would set him laughing uncontrollably for a minute, until he calmed down and stared at the ceiling in eerie silence.

I wondered aloud what might be needed to get him to take his anger and sadness and longing seriously, as opposed to drowning them in trivializing contempt. Wasn't that why he had come to me? He wanted to experience a life set to the rhythm of his own curiosity, shaped by his own desire, and with me he could begin to discover what this might be like. For a few hours a week, he could simply be, without having to do anything. His fantasies of becoming a slacker had for too long served his hate, his image of himself as ridiculous, pathetic; perhaps they could now begin to serve life.

He began to see a couples therapist with his wife and was astounded to hear her say she didn't care what he did, she just wanted him to be happy, or at least not so relentlessly wretched. 'But,' he had weakly responded, 'you and the kids, you need me to support you . . .' 'You will *not*,' she had yelled back, 'pin your misery on me and the kids. After all the shit we've put up with, that is one insult too far.'

It was a critical intervention, shaking him angrily and lovingly out of his toxically aggressive self-pity and forcing him into a reckoning with his own role in the traumatic loss of his creative and imaginative life. It ushered in a phase of fierce self-reflection in the analysis, in parallel with a new and serious contemplation of the kinds of psychic and external changes he dared to hope for. Then, disaster, cruel and sudden.

In his autobiographical preface to *The Scarlet Letter*, Nathaniel Hawthorne told of the strange coincidence of being abruptly dismissed from the post he'd long hated. 'In view of my previous weariness of office,' he wrote, 'and vague thoughts of resignation, my fortune somewhat resembled that of a person who should entertain an idea of committing suicide, and, altogether beyond his hopes, meet with the good hap to be murdered.'

The unfolding of Jerome's story would soon cast the wit of that sentence into severe relief. After years of extravagant fantasies of resignation, he too had the good hap to be murdered. He announced to me flatly one morning that he'd been handed his notice. When he said nothing more, I asked how he was feeling about it. 'Intelligent question,' he replied. 'You must have guessed what a boon it was to my sense of security and self-worth.' The old Jerome was, all too literally, back with a vengeance.

Even now, two years on, it is difficult for me to understand why Jerome experienced his dismissal as such a final and irrecoverable blow. The weeks following it saw a fierce surge in the contempt we had been working so hard to understand and transform. Nothing could shift him from the grim conviction that he'd lost all claim on the love and respect of anyone who mattered. When I tried to remind him of the inner transformation he'd begun to experience in the weeks prior to losing his job, he told me dolefully that he'd been a fool to believe all that shit. He was brutally and casually murdering the new self he'd been ushering into being before it could assume real existence.

The analysis had helped free him to imagine a life in which he was licensed to not work, to define himself outside the standards and metrics set by his mother's wishes and spurred by his father's indifference. At forty-four years old, he wouldn't be enrolling in art school and searching Paris Gumtree for a dilapidated garret. But at least the possibility of creative life was no longer being entirely suffocated by cynical self-irony.

Being fired laid waste to these changes in a moment. All that ludicrous guff about painting and living the dream, he declared, had betrayed his mother's dedication to him and confirmed his father's belief in his overreaching pretention. And I had *encouraged* him to think it.

It seemed he couldn't forgive me. Two weeks later, the first morning after the Easter break and minutes before his session was due to start, I picked up a message on my voicemail. It was Jerome. He wouldn't be coming this morning. He had decided, in fact, that he wouldn't be returning to analysis. He thanked me for my help.

Stung by the sheer coldness of a curt farewell voice message after five years of analysis, I returned his call and told him I thought, after all this time, it was worth coming to discuss his decision and, at very least, to say goodbye in person. 'Sorry, I can't face that . . . I don't know what it is. I think with me, in the end, nothing works.'

I wanted to respond, 'OK, but hadn't you started to discover that this desperate zeal for things to "work" is the problem? What happened to letting things, and you, not work for a while and seeing what unfolded?' But I didn't get the chance. Jerome had replaced the handset, leaving me to listen to dead air.

'Enduring tedium': David Foster Wallace

On the night of 12 September 2008, Karen Green returned to the home she shared with her husband, David Foster Wallace, to find him hanging dead on the patio.

In the nearby garage, she discovered the two-page note he had left her, along with 200 pages of his novel in progress, to be published three years later as *The Pale King*. Nearby, on the hard drives of two computers and floppy disks in his draws were stored hundreds more pages, 'drafts, character sketches, notes to himself, fragments', accumulated, according to his biographer D. T. Max, over the decade he'd been working on the novel.

The posthumous publication of *The Pale King* casts poignant retrospective light on this juxtaposition of patio and garage: in the first room, the irrevocable and enraged renunciation of a life defeated by the impossibility of living; in the second, an unfinished project imagining how this impossibility might be endured, even affirmed.

Wallace had killed himself, in other words, while engaged in a compulsive and unresolved creative struggle with the question of how to go on living.

Wallace had survived previous episodes of suicidal depression, a state he described, with the unmistakable intimacy of inside knowledge, through various of his fictional characters. His inquisitive and jocose non-fiction voice, in contrast, betrayed almost no hint of this terrible despair.

Perhaps real proximity to that despair was bearable only from the distance afforded by fiction. But as he wrote to his agent, Bonnie Nadell, nine months before he died, in the grip of such severe depression, he simply could not attain that distance, could not 'remotely expect anything of myself' as far as writing fiction was concerned. He was, effectively, too ill to access the imaginative life that might have helped him go on living.

The depression that finally killed Wallace had begun in the summer of 2007, following his decision to come off Nardil, an antidepressant on which he'd been dependent for twenty-two years, now considered by psychiatrists to be dated and ridden with bad side effects. Originally intending to switch to a different drug, once he'd come off Nardil he sought to live drug-free. He was hospitalized soon after with severe depression, resulting in the kind of knotted predicament that resurfaces so persistently in his life and his writing: 'If he tried an antidepressant,' writes Max, 'he would read that a possible side effect was anxiety, and that alone would make him too anxious to stay on the drug.'

In the ensuing months, different drug combinations and a course of ECT failed to restore any semblance of internal equilibrium. He was, suggests Max, reduced to the life of a 'shut-in', or long-term inactive recluse, a term often used to translate the Japanese *hikikomori*. Fearful of bumping into his Pomona College students in town, barely able to read much less write, he reverted to the habit of compulsive TV watching, an established default of his depressive episodes since his first breakdown in college. But this inertial collapse belied an internal state of constant, tormented agitation from which the prospect of suicide offered some, albeit thin relief. In the months before he finally succeeded, he had made one attempt and planned others.

In *Infinite Jest,* the massive dystopian epic for which Wallace continues to be most famous, the suicidal state is described by the '"psychotically depressed person"' Kate Gompert as an escape in the most literal sense. Death holds no special appeal for the would-be suicide. Instead, the victim of what she calls *It*, a level of psychic pain too extreme for life to support, 'will kill herself the same way a trapped person will eventually jump from the window of a burning high-rise ... when the flames get close enough, falling to death becomes the slightly less terrible of two terrors'.

Months before his death, Wallace wrote to a friend that he felt thirty years older, while his editor spoke of the 'haunted' look in his eyes. Seen in the light of Gompert's *It*, this state of radical exhaustion, of having come to the end of all internal resources, starts to look like the necessary culmination of living in proximity to an inferno no one else can perceive. The 'emotional character' of *It*, reflects Gompert, 'is probably mostly indescribable except as a sort of double bind in which any/all of the alternatives we associate with human agency – sitting or standing, doing or resting, speaking or keeping silent, living or dying – are not just unpleasant but literally horrible'.

This is very far from the nirvanic inertia of a rabbit, the unbroken peace of non-desire. The torpor of the suicidal depressive is the effect of a permanent but invisible enervation, a malignant pull between the undecidable claims of action and inaction, being and non-being.

Taken together, Wallace's life and work tell the story, or stories, of the quest for a way out of this state of permanent agitation. One iteration of the story ends that September night on the patio; another begins, and continues to circulate among his readers, in the garage. In one very literal sense, the scene on the patio is the seal of Wallace's defeat in the struggle to go on living. In another more speculative but no less real sense, the pages left in the garage are a tentative and ambiguous victory in that same struggle.

Wallace's writings, fictional and non-fictional alike, are pervaded by inertial images, states and characters, imbued variously with qualities of apocalyptic horror, contented bliss, complacent self-satisfaction, catatonic blankness and stoic quietude. The expressionless faces of animals, the deadened passivity of TV watchers, the numb contentment of holidaymakers, the oblivion of opiate addicts, the grinding boredom of office workers: different faces of the same fascination for a near-zero point of consciousness, an emptying of mental activity that might at one moment be felt as a blessing, at another a curse.

Perhaps Wallace invested so much creative energy in trying to imagine states of quiescence because he was unable to experience them directly. Standing in the way of both the compliant mindlessness he disdained and the transcendent quiet he yearned for was an insistent undertow of anxiety that had accompanied him since childhood.

There is no obvious source for this anxiety in his early life. Growing up in the Midwestern university town of Champaign-Urbana, 'Wallace's childhood,' remarks Max, 'was happy and ordinary'. He did not want for the affection, interest or admiration of either his mother, a community college teacher of English composition, or his father, an academic philosopher. His family and earliest schoolfriends recall a bright, outgoing and funny kid, a fan of American football, adventure and fantasy stories, TV sitcoms and soaps.

But a summary of his medical history written towards the end of his life yields a more troubling picture of his childhood; Wallace recalled experiencing his first bouts of depressive anxiety at the age of nine or ten. Gripped by contempt for the inadequacies of his boyish body and emotional vulnerability, he bore the secret conviction that no one who really knew him could like him.

The years that followed saw a dramatic uplift in his academic performance and the burgeoning of an impressive junior tennis career. But as the external markers of esteem proliferated, his inner state deteriorated. The anxiety attacks became worse and more frequent, at times manifesting as full-blown panic attacks. 'He was not sure what set them off,' writes Max, 'but he saw that they quickly became endless loops, where he worried that people would notice he was panicking, and that in turn would make him panic more.' These ever more tortuous loops induced him into the nightmare of aggravated self-consciousness he would eventually come to see as the malaise of his culture as well as his own psyche.

At Amherst College, Wallace's dazzling academic achievement continued to run in parallel with increasingly virulent bouts of depressive anxiety. In a 1989 interview with its house journal, *Amherst Magazine*, he spoke of the ambiguous effect of his voracious desire to learn: 'The same obsessive studying that helped me come alive also kept me dead.' His immersion in the pages of books fed his deep social reticence; reading and thinking at once woke him up to and sealed him off from the world beyond. At Amherst he suffered two separate breakdowns that returned him for long periods to a confined and sedentary existence at home in Illinois, delaying his graduation by a year.

In the aftermath of recovery from the second, near-suicidal breakdown, Wallace wrote to a friend, 'One hideous symptom of severe depression is that it is impossible both to do anything and to do nothing.' The tone of the letter is one of forced good-humour, but the insight is indispensable as a characterization of his lifelong predicament.

Why should Wallace have been so devastatingly vulnerable to the vagaries of the emotional pressures engendered by the progress of a life – ambition, envy, competitiveness, love, hate, desire? When, at the end of the first term of his sophomore year, he received A grades for his Philosophy and English courses, he told friends that 'he wanted to please both parents'. But this was not the statement of a child meeting his parents' punitively high expectations. While encouraging of his intellectual curiosity and creativity, Sally and Jim Wallace were not, as far as we can discern, especially pushy. They seem to have weighed if anything towards permissiveness, cultivating the young David's sense of his own autonomy and responsibility in managing his life and work.

But as Freud pointed out, the correlation between the actual parents we experience and the internal parents we come to invent is surprisingly unpredictable. Wallace took up with a special zeal of his own his mother's 'grammatical militancy' and demanding standards of English usage. This was no bitter, resentfully assumed maternal inheritance, but an evident source of self-enrichment and pleasure. But it points to how readily, even competitively, the child will identify with the ideal of the parent.

Such parental ideals seem benign for as long as the child feels he is worthy of them, often helping to drive him to great heights of intellectual and creative achievement. But their obverse is that the fear of falling short, of failing 'to please both parents', can just as easily plunge him into the depths of inadequacy and despair.

Towards the end of his life, Wallace had confessed to his wife that he had no idea why he had spent his third decade in such a rage with his parents. It may not be a coincidence that it was in this decade he had struggled so intensely with his outsize creative ambitions, and his agonizing hopes and fears for literary fame. Wanting badly to please both parents is a hair's breadth away from the terrible fear of disappointing, and so being unlovable to, them – not to mention the more unconscious desire and fear of triumphing over them.

As psychoanalysis conceives it, the life drive exerts a demand on us almost as soon as we come into the world to reach outward, to obtain the satisfactions and gratifications of love. Freud would come to call this drive Eros, a force for the expansion and development of both the individual and the species. Eros is a breeder of desire, and so of envy, rivalry, longing, greed, of all those turbulent feelings we're forced to suffer for as long as we are in the grip of the will to live.

The scale of Wallace's literary ambition intimates just how overbearingly the pressures of the life drive weighed on him. The universal desire to be loved and admired seems to have worked on him with a virulence that left him wishing life could stop persecuting him and leave him in peace. For decades before he gave the most concrete and tragic expression to this wish for an undisturbed state, he had mined its imaginative possibilities.

In the years since Wallace's death, his suicide has increasingly come to be absorbed into a sentimental mythology of the writer as sage, a fount of hard-won, earnest life wisdom, martyr to the corruptions and cynicism of his age. It is difficult to object to the popular diffusion of this dubiously sanctified persona without acknowledging that, as the critic Christian Lorentzen observes, 'Wallace started the process himself.'

It began with the delivery of his now famed 2005 commencement speech at Kenyon College, which for more than a decade has circulated virally in both text and video formats. In an irony Wallace might have appreciated, an author identified in life with a forbidding, formally ambitious 1,079 page epic whose guiding theme was the contracting American attention span, achieved posthumous fame with a hastily scrawled, twenty-two-minute speech.

The Kenyon address, along with *The End of the Tour,* the 2015 movie based on *Although of Course You End Up Becoming Yourself* (2010), David Lipsky's verbatim account, originally commissioned by *Rolling Stone*, of his conversations with Wallace over the course of a five-day road trip, established Wallace in the contemporary imagination as a beacon for mindful living and a hero of the struggle to maintain personal integrity and authenticity in the face of the moral and spiritual corrosions of the surrounding culture.

Within a few months of his death, the Kenyon address was published as a glossy slim volume, *This Is Water: Some Thoughts, Delivered on a Significant Occasion, about Living a Compassionate Life*, the sort impulse-bought at chain bookshop payment desks, piled alongside pocket-sized compendia of Eastern wisdom or Jewish humour. And it cannot be denied that it lent itself all too well to this kind of marketing.

It is the concentrated distillation of an ethical attitude present in much of Wallace's writing, both fictional and non-fictional, since the mid-1990s, most notably in *The Pale King*, which Wallace had been working on at the time. But there is a big difference between a novel and a speech. Where *The Pale King* turns over the same question – how to live meaningfully with the lonely self-absorption inimical to our culture and perhaps to human life itself – its responses are layered, looping, paradoxical. The Kenyon address seemed to give very straight answers to the same question, as though in delighted relief from the suffocating strictures of literary nuance and ambiguity.

Indeed, the speech is something like a repudiation of ambiguity, of the dead end of 'over-thinking'. This, Wallace told his rapt audience, was the first drawback of a strong academic education, 'my tendency to over-intellectualize stuff ... instead of paying attention to what is going on in front of me, paying attention to what is going on inside me'.

The speech opens with the homily of two young fish who swim past an older one, who asks them how the water is. After swimming on for a while, one turns to the other and asks, 'What the hell is water?' Unaware of the very element in which he's immersed, and by which his life is sustained, the young fish stands for our failure to notice the essential facts of the world before us.

The remainder of the speech is an extended riff on this homily. It enjoins us to find paths out of the prison of our self-centred perception, our unconscious habit of filtering all our responses through the lens of our own interests and preferences. This shift of perspective will nourish our capacity for empathy, for inhabiting perspectives other than our own.

The same enhanced consciousness will put in question the unthinking veneration of those objects – bodily beauty, money, power, intellect – most valued by the 'real world'. 'The so-called real world of men and money and power,' says Wallace, 'hums merrily along in a pool of fear and anger and frustration and craving and worship of self.'

The manifest argument of the speech, then, is unexceptionable. It is also, and no one makes this point more emphatically than Wallace himself, thoroughly trite. As though pre-empting the criticism, he tells us his proffered wisdom is 'banal platitude', 'liberal arts cliché', 'totally obvious'. But banal platitudes 'can have a life or death importance', and it is these untapped profundities of the obvious that he wants us to be alive to.

It is difficult, at least for me, to read the Kenyon address closely without feeling that what makes it compelling is not the unremarkable content of the speech but the disruptive presence of the speaker. Wallace pleads repeatedly throughout not to be misunderstood as preaching – he is not the wiser older fish, has no wish to lecture his audience about 'the so-called virtues', is not dispensing moral advice.

We might recognize this disparagement of his own wisdom as one of the oldest rhetorical tricks in the sage's book, well known to readers of the Socratic dialogues. But something about

Wallace's zealous insistence on the point suggests he is gripped by the very anxious self-consciousness he wants us to escape. Why is someone extolling the values of directness and sincerity so concerned to anticipate and pre-empt our responses?

Perhaps because he needs us to take him at his word; he is not dispensing wisdom from above, but trying to imagine from below what it might be. The state of mindful attention, peace and compassion to which he is pointing us is one he found difficult, if not impossible, to attain. His central counsel, to make conscious choices as to how we see and think, is one he typically found himself hopelessly unable to follow.

The mind is 'an excellent servant but a terrible master': what makes this more than a tired old saw is that it reads as barely disguised self-description. One doesn't need to have read very far in Wallace's life and work to recognize that he's speaking from inside knowledge of a mind's tendency to get caught in the snares of its own thinking.

From this perspective, the speech becomes less a pious sermon than a tortured self-reproach and a desperate bid to imagine a different mode of relating to oneself and the world. This is nowhere more evident than in a key passage in which Wallace imagines different ways of experiencing the everyday frustrations of queueing in a crowded supermarket or heavy traffic.

Our first impulse in such situations is to resent the chain of people in the long queue before us as mere obstacles in our path. But this quickly presents us with a choice; the preferable option, the way of mindful consciousness and empathy, would be to recognize that the crowds are made up of individuals, each of whom may have a need to get home at least as urgent as mine, if not more so. This is the response Wallace urges us to cultivate.

But the option Wallace presents far more vividly is our default mode of casual outrage at the very fact of the existence of others:

'And who are all these people in my way? And look at how repulsive most of them are, and how stupid and cow-like and dead-eyed and nonhuman they seem in the checkout line, or at how annoying and rude it is that people are talking loudly on cell phones in the middle of the line.'

It is hard to read this without feeling the response described is rather less general than Wallace wants to acknowledge, without noticing just how acutely he voices the nihilistic despair of the severe depressive. The sentiments are expressed in the service of a plea for tolerance and compassion, but there is no disguising its intimacy with the disgust the passage expresses at the basic fact of humanity.

Our relationship to major figures of our culture is apt to be shaped by a compulsion to idealize, a tendency complicated in Wallace's case by a mix of collusion and resistance. An intriguing subplot hums beneath the surface of the conversations recorded by Lipsky in *Although of Course You End Up Becoming Yourself*, whereby Wallace is perpetually trying to second-guess how what he's just said or is about to say might come across to the *Rolling Stone* readership. In another prime instance of his loops of tortured self-consciousness, he wonders aloud whether his insistence on his 'regular guy' status will be read as proof of his authenticity or his disingenuousness.

The Kenyon address is shot through with a similarly ambivalent bid for its audience's love; even as he seduces his audience into awed veneration of his hard-won wisdom, he warns them off, willing them to hear how deeply implicated he is in the self-involved misanthropy he decries. Ostensibly offered and aggressively marketed as a general lesson in finding inner peace, the speech is more convincing and more interesting as an oblique confession of his own despair of the very possibility.

*

The tormenting elusiveness of that peace was Wallace's abiding obsession throughout his life and writing, manifesting most emphatically in his personal and literary struggles with various kinds of addiction.

Addiction is the model of the mind as terrible master, a condition of bodily and psychic dependency that ruins the self's conviction in its own freedom. Among many other things, *Infinite Jest* is a portrait of addiction as a state of permanently agitated stasis, shrinking daily life to the dimensions of an airless cell holding only the addict and her substance, from which she can only helplessly watch her life collapse.

Wallace drew on his own recent experiences for *Infinite Jest*'s portrayal of the culture of addiction and recovery. Over the course of his time in Tucson, enrolled on the University of Arizona's graduate creative writing programme, he had spent increasing amounts of time in a pot-induced haze or alcoholic stupor, oscillating between periods of recovery and recidivism before moving to Boston in April 1989. By November he had been admitted to the McLean rehabilitation facility, where he was resident for six weeks before being moved to Granada House, the halfway house that inspired the fictive Ennet House of *Infinite Jest*.

The recovery process left Wallace emotionally and imaginatively drained, and unable to face contact with literary friends. In 1990, he cancelled a planned meeting with Jonathan Franzen, writing to him that he felt unworthy of their burgeoning rivalry. 'All I can tell you,' he wrote, 'is that . . . right now I am a pathetic and confused young man. He was 'a failed writer at 28', 'so jealous, so sickly searingly envious of you' and other young writers as to make suicide seem 'a reasonable – if not at this point a desirable – option'.

The sense of fulfilment and 'near-genital pleasure' he'd once gained from writing now gave way to a kind of creative inertia, he told Franzen: 'I have in the last two years been struck dumb . . . Not dumb, actually, or even aphasic. It's more like, w/r/t things I used to believe and let inform me, my thoughts now have the urgent but impeded quality of speechlessness in dreams.'

The imagery used to describe the damage addiction inflicts on the mind and nervous system is unmistakably traumatic. The urgent need to speak is also felt as a gag on speech, a scream both desperate and inaudible. This is inertia as enraged paralysis, shutting down the channels of creative expression that might relieve or redeem it.

But in *Infinite Jest*, Wallace would forge a creative vehicle to channel the trauma of addiction. The novel's recovering addicts are the mouthpieces for a revived 'communism of spirit'. More than a mere treatment centre for substance abuse, *Infinite Jest* imagines Ennet House and the AA meetings its residents attend as an antidote to the spiritual malaise of consumer capitalism. Scribbled in the margins of Wallace's copy of Lewis Hyde's 1983 book *The Gift*, Max tells us, was a note reading, "'AA's = those driven mad w/ fear by the paradigm of scarcity in a commodity/capitalist economy; require return to basically 21st-century communism of spirit.'"

In one tour de force sequence, the attendees of the White Flag AA meeting anatomize the deadly predicament of the addict at the lowest point (or 'Bottom') of addiction: 'Doing the Substance now is like attending Black Mass but you still can't stop, even though the substance no longer gets you high. You are, as they say, Finished. You cannot get drunk and you cannot get sober; you cannot get high and you cannot get straight. You are behind bars; you are in a cage and can see only bars in every direction.'

Addiction, as Wallace's scribbled note had hinted, is the end point of consumerism, in which wanting what we don't have morphs from nagging desire to state of emergency. 'Scarcity' is now felt as a fatal incapacity to obtain the one thing that would make life bearable, a condemnation to an interminable state of lack. It is a state of neurasthenic agitation far from the blissful opiate fantasias of Thomas De Quincey or The Beatles.

To the seductive oblivion of opium or heroin, the narrator of *Infinite Jest* (in one of its notorious long endnotes, or, more precisely, an endnote to a footnote) contrasts the enervated inertia of 'Marijuana Thinking'. Every mental step forward taken by the dope (or, in Bostonian argot, Bob Hope) stoner immediately activates the opposite movement, as though the secret motive of his thinking were to stay forever stuck: 'it is not that Bob Hope-smokers lose interest in practical functioning, but rather Marijuana-Think themselves into labyrinths of reflexive abstraction that seem to cast doubt on the very possibility of abstract functioning, and the mental labor of finding one's way out consumes all available attention and makes the Bob Hope-smoker look physically torpid and apathetic and amotivated sitting there, when really he is trying to claw his way out of a labyrinth.'

The dope smoker sends himself to sleep in the act of trying to force himself awake, just as – to recall Wallace's college reminiscence – 'The same obsessive studying that helped me come alive also kept me dead.' Wallace could not seem to stop stumbling into the same treacherous topography, signposting the explorer towards vitality only to lead him into deadness and shuttling him interminably between the two. 'Narcotics cannot still the Tooth/That nibbles at the soul –'.

As Wallace had attested to Franzen in 1990, when the dope smoker finally emerges from the labyrinth, his inner resources have been radically depleted. The clawing is over, but so is any capacity for struggle, leaving him vulnerable to the temptation of pure lethargy. The ultimate transmitter of this state is not dope or any other sedative; it is television, for Wallace both a specific medium and a synecdoche for the terminal decadence of American culture.

As he told the critic Larry McCaffery in 1993, Wallace had been intimate since childhood with the 'schizogenic experience' of both reading voraciously and 'watching grotesque amounts of TV', as though his inner life were split irrevocably between active curiosity and passive indifference. The seduction of TV, he told Lipsky years later, is that it offers 'entertainment and stimulation' while asking nothing but 'the most tangential kind of attention' in return. Dope may render one inactive in the world, but it turns the mind into an excitable hub of labyrinthine abstraction. TV is in this sense a much more effective narcotic, catering near perfectly to the impulse to bring life and all the work it involves to a stop.

Perhaps this is why, as Max writes, 'during periods of collapse he seemed almost literally attached to it'. Each of his breakdowns saw him reduced to a state of chronic torpor that expressed itself above all in blank and wordless absorption by the TV screen. This was 'his drug of last resort', the means by which he held himself together once reading, writing, sex or drugs no longer worked. The TV, we recall, was Wallace's regular companion during the final weeks of his life.

The close affinity between TV and death turns out to be more than a fanciful throwaway speculation; it was an abiding motif of both his writing and his life. In his much-cited 1993 essay on television and American fiction, 'E Unibus Pluram', he formulates again the recurring paradox of an entity that at once gives life and kills it. TV feeds off our yearning to escape into other worlds and lives, while riveting us helplessly to our own. He cites the 'fat, cynical, gloriously decadent puppet (so much like Snoopy, like

Garfield, like Bart, like Butt-Head)', titular hero of the sitcom *Alf*, 'advising me to "Eat a whole lot of food and stare at the TV"'.

All of these cartoon icons of slobbish abandon license us to take refuge in 'a pose of passive reception to comfort, escape, reassurance', cancelling out all demands and pressures on body and psyche to work. This was the same deep-rooted fantasy Wallace unearthed in perhaps his best-loved essay, 'A Supposedly Fun Thing I'll Never Do Again', his account of a week on a luxury cruise liner.

The painstakingly pursued goal of the luxury cruise, Wallace suggested there, is to realize the cruiser's primary unconscious wish – to be maintained in a state of pure, gapless gratification. It is a kind of revival of what Winnicott would call the fantasy of infantile omnipotence, the newborn baby's conception of the world around him as a round-the-clock service for the meeting of his every need. Winnicott's point, though, is that the inevitable failure of this service is the necessary and universal destiny of every human infant.

The luxury cruise is in this regard a kind of corrective emotional experience, creating a sealed-off time and space that simulate the unerring attunement of the perfect mother without the ensuing disillusion. It revives the infantile dream of total satisfaction while fending off the distressing intrusions of desire and choice. Wallace, the addict and compulsive TV watcher, is alive to the power of this fantasy and wants desperately to believe it could be fulfilled: 'And of course I want to believe it . . . I want to believe that maybe this Ultimate Fantasy Vacation will be *enough* pampering, that this time the luxury and pleasure will be so completely and faultlessly administered that my Infantile part will be sated.'

But the essay's running gag is Wallace's hapless inability to comply with the cruiser's regime of mandatory comfort and fun. Staff are everywhere concealed, handing him towels at the exact moment he needs one, cleaning his room during the brief window he leaves it. All these ministrations cause him a discomfort that prevents his achieving the relaxed state they're supposed to induce.

And so, in his magnum opus, he imagines an onslaught of pleasure so total as to overwhelm any possible resistance to it. The febrile plot of *Infinite Jest* has militant Québécois separatists seeking the master copy of 'Infinite Jest', a late offering of the late-twentieth-century experimental film-maker James O. Incandenza, rumoured to entertain its viewer to the point of blissful catatonic oblivion.

Its first victim is the 'Near Eastern medical attaché', whose wife returns home one evening to find him slumped immobile before the Interlace cartridge viewer (Wallace's futurist vision is oddly old-tech) in a puddle of his own waste, noting in the midst of her alarm 'that the expression on his rictus of a face nevertheless appeared very positive, ecstatic even'.

In the scattered dialogues between Québécois agent Marathe and his ONAN (Organization of North American Nations) counterpart Steeply, the film is talked about as the concentrated symptom of America's terminal decadence, its society's defencelessness in the face of an insidious and ultimately lethal drip feed of pleasure. Steeply tells Marathe of an experimental Canadian research programme to discover the means for the permanent stimulation of 'the various neurotransmitters of pleasure'. Rigging an 'auto-stimulation lever' in a rat cage, the researchers found that the rat would 'press the lever to stimulate his p-terminal over and over, thousands of times an hour ... stopping only when the rat finally died of dehydration or simple fatigue'.

The prospect now is of the same p-terminal, adapted to human stimulus response, circulating around underground markets, engendering a new population of pleasure-addled zombies, 'Bug-eyed, drooling, moaning, trembling, incontinent, dehydrated. Not working, not consuming, not interacting or taking part in community life.'

Wallace's dystopian vision was a magnification on the grandest scale of the personal fate he most dreaded. His own experience of 'not working' was not a giddy freedom but a brutal hollowing out of mind and body. The wrecked psychobiological function-ing of Steeply's abject p-terminal addict reads irresistibly like an amplified representation of Wallace's extended post-breakdown periods of lethargic TV viewing.

More than a cheap piety, the earnest enjoining of the Kenyon audience, echoed in many of the later interviews, 'to stay con-scious and alive in the adult world day in day out' is an expression of Wallace's horror of reversion to this state of traumatized indif-ference. It helps explain why, beyond mere literary temperament, he never affected the blank, torpid writerly voice of so many of his contemporaries, notably his long-time antagonist Brett Easton Ellis, who in 2012 lambasted his late peer on Twitter as 'the most tedious, overrated, tortured, pretentious writer of my generation'.

It isn't difficult to see why, beyond embittered pique at Wallace's posthumous literary canonization, Ellis might consider his prose tedious and pretentious; its deliberately frenetic, not to say neu-rotic, prolixity is the very antithesis of Ellis's glassy minimalism.

But the contrast is not as straightforward as it may seem. While very different in tone and texture from Ellis's anomic voice, Wallace's writing has its own quality of lassitude. It is the voice not of boredom but of a kind of slackness, in the sense conveyed by Linklater's film. 'And but so', many of his sentences begin, an incoherent tumble of adjacent conjunctions mimicking the contrived indiscipline of slacker speech. The characters in *Slacker* often express their slackness in a kind of drawling incessance, as though they can't quite be bothered with the labour of specifying what they want to say.

Like Proust, Wallace's extravagantly long sentences are peopled by chains of associative clauses, but the resemblance ends there, and the contrast is instructive. In Proust's method of *correspondances*, the first object of a sentence finds a correspondence in another object, which in turn finds another, so that the whole sentence forms an intricate weave of parallel thoughts and sensations.

Wallace's long sentences don't work so hard. They go on as long as they do because the observing eye of the writer seems not to want to select, juxtapose or distinguish but simply to record one thing after the other, without the obligation to say what does and doesn't matter. Take this example from an early sequence in *Infinite Jest*, in which the dope addict Ken Erdedy is awaiting the visit of his dealer:

> His last piece of contact from the appropriation artist, with whom he had had intercourse, and who during intercourse had sprayed some sort of perfume up into the air from a mister she held in her left hand as she lay beneath him making a wide variety of sounds and spraying perfume up into the air, so that he felt the cold mist of it settling on his back and shoulders and was chilled and repelled, his last piece of contact after he'd gone into hiding with the marijuana she'd gotten for him had been a card she'd mailed that was a pastiche photo of a doormat of coarse green plastic grass with *WELCOME* on it and next to it a flattering publicity photo of the appropriation artist from her Back Bay gallery, and between them an unequal sign, which was an equal sign with a diagonal slash across it, and also an obscenity he assumed was directed at him mag- isculed in red grease pencil along the bottom, with multiple exclamation points.

The 'appropriation artist' will disappear from the book forth-with. The fact of her intercourse with Erdedy may be passingly relevant, the perfume she sprayed from a mister much less so. But in what sense do we need to know in which hand she held the mister? The accumulations of detail don't have the effect of organizing the scene, but of dispersing its elements and so loosening our focus.

Where Proust's multiple correspondences sharpen our sense of a scene's centre of gravity, Wallace's diffusion of a scene's disparate elements leaves us uncertain of where we're supposed to direct our attention. The effect is heightened by the fact that the weird vignette compressed in the sentence is a red herring, adding noth-ing to the progress of the overarching narrative (in fact, the phrase 'red herring' itself is misleading – a red herring, if you will – in that it assumes a forward narrative thrust that simply isn't there). This loose focus is the comic frustration and serious pleasure of slacker speech – look at this, and that, and there, it encourages us, without telling us how to do so. It imposes no hierarchy on the proliferation of facts, invites us to take pleasure in incident for its own sake, not because it tells us something or takes us somewhere.

In a striking paradox, the pyrotechnical energy animating Wallace's sentences issues from a voice apparently depleted of vitality and passion.

It is as though minimizing the work of thinking – organizing, differentiating, directing – releases the writer's voice to uninhib-ited insight, a capacity, as his editor Michael Pietsch put it after his death, 'to see everything on every level all at once'. Or as one of his former students put it, Wallace was 'a noticing machine'.

Wallace put this paradox, of an internal slackness that gives rise to an unfettered creativity, into play in his writing. But he found it at work in many other forms of activity – most notably in tennis, a sport he'd played at a high competitive level in his youth and about which he wrote some of his finest non-fiction (as well as a central strand of *Infinite Jest*).

In his 1992 essay 'Derivative Sport in Tornado Alley', an account of how, as a boy, he'd harnessed the unpredictably windy conditions of central Illinois to his competitive advantage, he speaks of 'my Taoistic ability to control via noncontrol'. His beautiful 2006 essay on Roger Federer, 'Federer Both Flesh and Not', described the internal setting of the greatest player of our time as one of pure unselfconsciousness. His apparently infallible reflexes are the effect of an elimination of the cumbersome labour of thinking, of an impossible coincidence of body and mind to the point where 'he looks like what he may well (I think) be: a creature whose body is both flesh and, somehow, light'.

The best tennis brings an unexpected sense to the phrase 'not working'; Federer's prodigious athletic prowess is the counter-part of his psychic and fleshly lightness, his miraculous freedom from the physical and mental loads the rest of us are made to lug around so gracelessly. Wallace's own tennis career, he recounted on many occasions, foundered on his inability to shed his self-consciousness, on his proneness, at the most decisive moments, to the fatal intrusions of thinking.

This is the lot of the rest of us, the non-Federers, consigned to the disappointing reality of being all flesh and no light. We do not get to defy gravity, to do the impossible and make it look effortless. When we work, it shows in our straining faces and limbs, in the inelegance or mediocrity or ordinarily good quality of the results. We get tired and frustrated and bored and have somehow to endure it day after day, an achievement as ordinary as it is (to cite the Kenyon address once more) 'unimaginably hard'. It was certainly unimaginably hard for Wallace, as he so brutally informed the world that September night.

*

In the hours preceding that night, he also made sure to let the world know that he could imagine an alternative, even if he hadn't been able to avail himself of it. At the point he gave up on it (along with everything else), *The Pale King* comprised a series of loosely overlapping chapters centred on the eerily solitary and strange inner lives of a series of employees of the IRS. Each of them has given up their daily life to a perpetual, grinding tedium, and each of them must find their own way to endure, perhaps even affirm it.

Stated this baldly, the novel's organizing dilemma sounds suspiciously like the one Wallace had addressed at Kenyon. But where at Kenyon he reduced the remedy to a series of tidy prescriptions, *The Pale King* renders the achievement, at once unremarkable and deeply elusive, of bearing the burden of every-day life a mystery of near-theological proportions.

No character conveys this mystery more vividly than the substitute lecturer for the Advanced Tax course, the final class of which Chris Fogle, the narrator of the long personal memoir at the centre of the book, stumbles into by accident. The substitute's bearing conveys to Fogle, then a callow, nihilistic waster who's spent most of his college years umbilically attached to the TV, a quality of 'indifference' markedly different from his own: 'What he seemed to be was indifferent – not in a meaningless, drifting, nihilistic way, but rather in a secure, self-confident way.' It is from the substitute that Fogle hears the truth that will transform his life: '"Enduring tedium over real time in a confined space is what real courage is."'

Fogle has spent years drifting listlessly between options for work or study, none more or less urgent or meaningful than the next. The array of choices in front of him induces a debilitating lethargy. Sitting dead-eyed in front of a lunchtime soap, it dawns on him, 'That I drifted and quit because nothing meant anything, no one choice was really better. That I was, in a way, too free, or that this kind of freedom wasn't actually real – I was free to choose "whatever" because it didn't really matter.'

Fogle's story tells of his slow awakening from his own, nihilistic mode of indifference into the substitute's more affirmative one. The process begins, surprisingly enough, with a change in narcotic preference from pot to Obetrol, an amphetamine-based prescription drug. Obetrol engenders a new self-awareness he calls 'doubling', a heightened clarity in the texture of moment to moment experience, 'a sort of emergence, however briefly, from the fuzziness and drift of my life'.

Doubling is not an overcoming of inertia in the sense of a sudden rush of energy and can-do spirit, but something more enigmatic: an internal transformation of inertia, infusing the moment's lassitude and boredom with an unsuspected fullness and intensity. Routine, monotony and dullness are gravitational forces that pull life down into a self-perpetuating depressive indifference. But this, suggests the substitute lecturer, is precisely the potential of an enterprise as grindingly joyless as tax examination 'for actual heroism, and therefore . . . a denomination of joy unequalled by any you men can imagine'.

In a 2011 article for the *New Yorker*, Jonathan Franzen raised the brutal possibility that Wallace had 'died of boredom'. Fiction writing had long been his path out of the prison of his own painful solitude, his gesture of solidarity with the world beyond himself. Fiction was Wallace's Obetrol, the means by which he doubled his isolated existence, transfiguring his deep reserves of nihilistic indifference into a kind of fragile affirmation.

But this was always a precarious lifeline. If fiction failed him, as Franzen suggested, it also removed his primary hope of mitigating his loneliness, and the gnawing emptiness that followed in its wake. 'When his hope for fiction died,' writes Franzen, 'after years of struggle with the new novel, there was no other way out but death. If boredom is the soil in which the seeds of addiction sprout, and if the phenomenology and the teleology of suicidality are the same as those of addiction, it seems fair to say that David died of boredom.'

Franzen's two 'if's are very large ones and a speculation of this kind will always risk revealing more about the bitterness and rage of the bereaved friend than the motive of the dead one. Yet I can't help finding some silent corroboration of Franzen's thesis in the juxtaposed scenes Wallace, with a cruelty peculiar to the abandonment of hope, left his wife to discover that September night.

'There is hope,' Franz Kafka famously told his friend Max Brod, 'but not for us.' On his patio, Wallace attested to the truth of the aphorism's second half; for himself, life had stopped working. But he did not instruct Green, as Kafka had Brod, to burn his unpublished writings. Instead he left an unfinished novel for her and the world to find, and with it the ambiguous gift of an unresolved question: might there be hope, even if not for me?

Conclusion

The bald assertion of this book's subtitle that 'we have to stop' begs the obvious question: stop *what*? We read 'to stop' as a transitive verb, which implies that stopping is imaginable only in relation to a specified activity or entity – smoking, say, or Brexit, or some other target of a New Year's resolution or political agenda.

But 'to stop' can be read also as an intransitive verb, one with no direct object. Here the meaning of the word changes. Instead of being defined as the cessation of something we dislike or know is bad for us, stopping becomes a choice.

Daily life in this culture is governed by a permanent compulsion towards frenetic activity and distraction. The void of time must be filled with something, anything. Even the decision to stop smoking or lose weight turns the aim of not doing something into something that must be done (and indeed, done obsessively and anxiously). The transitive sense of stopping ('I must stop sleeping in till ten on the weekend and get to the gym early') is another way of adding items to the to-do list.

To stop in the intransitive sense – to say no not to doing this or that but to doing anything, to *just stop* – is an assertion of autonomy, an invisible act of resistance against the tyranny of action. To make this claim raises an apparent contradiction – how can stopping be an act? In what sense are we doing something when we do nothing?

218

Stopping is a necessary condition for any and every meaningful activity. We acknowledge this when we describe thoughtless, automatized or blind activity (or speech) as 'going on and on without stopping'. Aimlessness, as I've tried to show, can nurture our creative freedom when it helps us to stop and to ask where it is we want to go or what it is we want to do. Blind activity is aimless in a more malign sense that it is bent only on perpetuating itself, blocking entrances for the new or surprising. The Duracell Bunny is an emblem of our culture because neither he nor we can imagine him stopping – which also means we cannot imagine him doing anything else.

'We have to stop' should be heard both descriptively and imperatively. Descriptively in that it refers to a basic fact of our psychic and biological constitution. As an organism, the human being is as much given to saying no as to saying yes, as much to rest as to motion, as much to being as to doing. Our minds and bodies find ways of reminding us of this when we feel tiredness, pain and apathy.

The American cultural critic Mark Greif has written about the overload of our nervous systems by what he calls the 'omnipresence of *drama*' in contemporary culture – referring as much to the trauma of nightly news as to the TV dramas we consume voraciously in 'box-set binges', a striking allusion to the over-satiation experienced in some eating disorders. This supersaturation of 'strong experience', far from intensifying our feeling capacity, has what Greif calls an 'anaesthetic' effect: 'Watching *enough* represented strong experience is associated with states of relaxation and leisure, the extreme loosening and mellowness in which we find a person deliberately "vegetating" in front of the TV.'

This brings out the second, imperative sense of 'having to stop'. Blind activity and distraction impoverish our lives, turning them into a permanent quest to shut down the barrage of stimuli and feelings assailing us. These stimuli train us to live by partially dying to ourselves. Stopping is essential to the feeling of being alive.

But stopping is difficult and even perilous. At one extreme are the *hikikomori* for whom stopping comes to be an end in itself, miring them in a kind of death in life. At the other, the corporate executive's mindfulness or flotation tank session is slotted into the lunch hour of her gruelling working day, as though stopping were simply a way of ensuring the long-term efficiency of the working machine.

Both these examples remind us that the real value of stopping lies in its cultivation of interior freedom. The *hikikomori* seals himself in the prison of his bedroom because all the paths out of it seem to him to lead to another, perhaps even more inescapable prison. The executive spends his lunch hour in a flotation tank because it provides a temporary shutdown of the day's unforgiving demands. The long-term retreat of the one and the short-term relief of the other share a quality of last-resort desperation.

In this context of constrained possibility the idea of UBI – universal basic income – comes into its own. A liveable income provided by the government without questions or demands would enable stopping to be more than a reactive gesture to social and economic pressures. In untying the bonds of necessity, stopping becomes a step towards freedom. If the constraints of sheer survival are loosened, we can stop not because we're too frightened to move or too exhausted from doing too much, but to discover what it is we might want to do and who we might want to be.

This does not and should not exclude the choice to work very hard, to pursue large worldly ambitions and desires for oneself and others. But even a life of hard work looks and feels different when we know that we can stop it if we need to.

*

I haven't written this book to advocate for policy. Breaking the grip of compulsory activity on our culture will take more than the provision of a basic income. The idea of UBI is promising because it points us beyond a technocratic solution to specific problems of job scarcity and automation, and asks us to address more essential questions: what is a human being? What is a human life for? – questions a blindly overworked life never has the chance to stop and think about.

Schools and universities would be the ideal institutions to ask these questions. But our education systems have been ransomed to an anxious quantification of achievement that annuls the space for this kind of reflection. Recent years have seen proposals for literacy and numeracy assessments for children as young as two. At the other end of the system, students saddled with colossal debts are encouraged to think of their degrees as paths to the acquisition of transferrable skills for a shrinking labour market. In between lies a treadmill of assessment and evaluation in 'core' subjects, along with a marginalization or even exclusion of the arts – indeed, of all those areas of learning (philosophical, theological, political) which might encourage us to see life as more than a perpetual struggle to achieve and survive.

In *Civilization and Its Discontents*, Freud argued that the conflict between the claims of the individual and the group was fatally irresolvable; the pursuit of individual desires could never be reconciled with the enforcement of collective laws and conventions. The result, grimly confirmed as he was writing by the rise of fascism, was a society governed by a pervasive self-hatred, which puts us in an increasingly guilty and punitive relationship to our own wishes and impulses.

This war on the self continues today in our similarly punitive relationship to our need to stop. To challenge our idea of life as an unbroken state of work requires us to imagine a possibility

Freud dismissed: that collective needs and individual desires might sometimes converge.

Few political writings have spoken to me more resonantly than those of Oscar Wilde and the great nineteenth-century American nature writer H. D. Thoreau. Neither is a political theorist in any formal sense. Indeed, they share a vision of the best life as one in which politics least intrudes, in which the first and last goals of social justice are the realization of each person's capacity to become who they are. Like many of the best jokes, Wilde's famous quip that 'the problem with Socialism is that it takes too many evenings' masks a serious point. If the aims of legal, political or economic justice are isolated from the question of what makes a life worth living, they are liable to become just another set of items on an interminable and joyless to-do list.

In his famous 1862 essay 'Life Without Principle', Thoreau laments his nation's tendency to equate human worth with material productivity. 'I see advertisements for *active* young men,' he writes, 'as if activity were the whole of a young man's capital.' Young people are vulnerable to the lure of waged drudgery only because they have been taught to identify their entire selves with their active selves.

Thoreau invites us to imagine what it would mean for us to break with this conception of ourselves as working beings, and of the world as 'a place of business': 'I think that there is nothing, not even crime, more opposed to poetry, to philosophy, ay, to life itself, than this incessant business.' In the face of this unforgiving imperative of business, the practice of aimless drift, of straying from the path of activity and purpose, 'free from all worldly engagements' (in Thoreau's case, by spending half the day walking the woods), becomes an urgent political and existential task, a way of preserving 'life itself'. 'To have done anything by which you earned money *merely*,' writes Thoreau, 'is to have been truly idle or worse.'

I have turned repeatedly to art and artists in this book because they bring vividly to life the ways we might forge a different kind of aimlessness. But I hope I've also shown that art has no monopoly on this experience, that it can be had during a walk, before a window, in conversation or in shared silence. This is an aimlessness attuned to a profound but all too unrecognized need in us to be left not to work.

In acknowledging this need, we glimpse a way out of the repetitive circuits in which our overworked lives are today so easily caught, and into a life and a world we don't yet know. Once we can see that we have to stop, we may soon find that we want to.

Notes

Introduction

p. xiv   Sigmund Freud's postulation of a 'death drive' . . .: Freud
introduced the idea in *Beyond the Pleasure Principle* (1920) and
continued to develop it until the end of his life. See *The Standard
Edition of the Complete Psychological Works of Sigmund Freud*, trans.
and ed. J. Strachey, Volume 18 (London: Vintage, 2001).

p. xvii   'Even groups that have been traditionally exempted . . .': David
Frayne, *The Refusal of Work* (London: Zed Books, 2015), p. 16.

p. xvii   'ego ideal': Freud introduces the idea in the last part of his 1914
essay 'On Narcissism: An Introduction', *Standard Edition*, Volume
14, pp. 93–101. The term has been obscured by his later concept
of the superego, introduced nearly a decade later.

p. xviii   'Each worker is taught . . .': Frayne, *Refusal*, p. 77.

p. xx   In *The Republic* . . .: Socrates's famous impugning of the falsity
and uselessness of art occurs in Book 10 of *The Republic*, trans.
D. Lee (London: Penguin, 1986). The passage alluded to is on
pp. 427–8.

p. xx   'a life that has for its aim . . .': Oscar Wilde, 'The Critic As Artist',
The Major Works, ed. I. Murray (Oxford: OUP, 2010), p. 277.
Wilde goes on: 'We might make ourselves spiritual by detaching
ourselves from action, and become perfect by the rejection of
energy.'

p. xxi   'Art acts poorly and little . . .': Maurice Blanchot, *The Space of
Literature*, trans. A. Smock (Lincoln, NE: University of Nebraska
Press, 1989), p. 213.

p. xxi   T. W. Adorno argued that art . . .: Adorno makes the argument in a number of places, but most explicitly in his essay 'Commitment', *Notes to Literature Volume 2*, trans. S. W. Nicholsen (New York: Columbia University Press, 1992).

p. xxi   'the least divine of the god's functions . . .': Blanchot, *Space*, p. 219.

p. xxiv   'culminating in a work . . .': ibid., p. 220.

p. xxiv   'the sordid perils of actual existence': Wilde, 'Critic', p. 274.

p. xxiv   'Holding back, freezing . . .': Alain Ehrenberg, *The Weariness of the Self: Diagnosing the History of Depression in the Contemporary Age*, trans. E. Caouette, J. Homel, D. Homel and D. Winkler (Montreal: McGill–Queens University Press, 2010), p. 22.

p. xxv   'an eternally suspended future': Emmanuel Levinas, 'Reality and Its Shadow', *Collected Philosophical Papers*, trans. A. Lingis (Pittsburgh: Duquesne University Press, 1998), p. 9.

p. xxv   'The characters of a novel . . .': ibid., p. 10.

p. xxvi   'And at that moment . . .': Schnabel's interview with Emin appeared in the January 2006 issue of *Interview* magazine.

p. xxvii   'If a man will not work . . .': 2 Thessalonians 3:10, *The New Testament in Modern English*, trans. J. B. Phillips (London: HarperCollins, 1972), p. 434.

p. xxviii 'to live in the manner . . .': Max Weber, *The Protestant Ethic and the 'Spirit' of Capitalism* (1895), trans. P. Baehr and G. C. Wells (London: Penguin, 2002), p. 106.

p. xxix   'Keep up a high esteem of Time . . .': ibid., p. 178.

p. xxix   'According to God's . . .': ibid., p. 106.

p. xxx   'debility of all the functions . . .': quoted in Ehrenberg, *Weariness*, p. 32, from Beard's original article, 'Neurasthenia, or Nervous Exhaustion', which appeared in *The Boston Medical and Surgical Journal*, 29 April 1869.

p. xxx   'An entire battery . . .': Nick Srnicek and Alex Williams, *Inventing the Future: Post-Capitalism and a World Without Work* (London: Verso, 2016), p. 64.

p. xxxii   'natural human aversion': Sigmund Freud, *Civilization and Its Discontents, Standard Edition*, Volume 21, p. 80.

p. xxxii   Freud had hinted . . .: Sigmund Freud, 'Creative Writers and Daydreaming', *Standard Edition*, Volume 9.

p. xxxv   the Icarus myth ...: of the many versions, the greatest is surely
Ovid's in Book 8 of the *Metamorphoses*, trans. M. M. Innes
(London: Penguin, 2000).

Chapter 1: The Burnout

p. 2   'fettered to the moment ...': Friedrich Nietzsche, 'On the
Uses and Disadvantages of History for Life' (1874), *Untimely
Meditations*, trans. R. J. Hollingdale (Cambridge, CUP, 1997),
p. 60.

p. 3   'We become who we are ...': Freud develops the idea of
judgement as formative of selfhood in his 1925 essay 'Negation',
*The Standard Edition of the Complete Psychological Works of Sigmund
Freud*, trans. and ed. J. Strachey, Volume 19 (London: Vintage,
2001), p. 237.

p. 5   'come to the end of desire': Graham Greene, *A Burnt-Out Case*
(1951) (London: Vintage, 2004), p. 42. Greene's narrator writes
of his protagonist's flickering interest in his own life, 'He had
lived with inertia for so long that he examined his "interest"
with clinical detachment' (p. 48).

p. 6   'Just like neurasthenics ...': Anna Katharina Schaffner,
Exhaustion: A History (New York: Columbia University Press,
2016), p. 33.

p. 6   'Like an eremite ...': J.-K. Huysmans, *Against Nature*, trans. R.
Baldick (London: Penguin, 2004), p. 63.

p. 7   'Nirvana principle': Freud makes the reference to Low in 'Beyond
the Pleasure Principle', *Standard Edition*, Volume 18, p. 56.

p. 7   'Pain had no sting ...': John Keats, 'Ode on Indolence', *The
Complete Poems*, ed. J. Barnard (London: Penguin, 1977),
pp. 349–51.

p. 7   'desire for non-desire': Piera Aulagnier, *The Violence of
Interpretation: From Pictogram to Statement*, trans. A. Sheridan
(London: Routledge, 2001), p. 17. Aulagnier calls this
paradoxical tendency 'the major scandal of psychic functioning'.

p. 8   'a little safe shelter ...': Kamo no Chōmei, *Hōjōki* (1210), Kenkō
and Chōmei, *Essays in Idleness* and *Hōjōki*, trans. M. McKinney
(London: Penguin, 2013), p. 12.

p. 8   'The Buddha's essential teaching ...': ibid., p. 18.

p. 9   'a cognitive space ...': Franco Berardi, *The Soul at Work: From Alienation to Autonomy*, trans. J. Smith (New York: Semiotexte, 2009), p. 108.

p. 10   'the tyranny of choice': Renata Salecl, *The Tyranny of Choice* (London: Profile, 2011).

p. 13   'thunderstruck ... like the man ...': Herman Melville, 'Bartleby, the Scrivener' (1853), *Billy Budd and Other Stories* (New York: Signet, 1961), p. 128.

p. 13   'to invade my peace': ibid., p. 104.

p. 14   not 'cheerfully industrious': ibid., p. 111.

p. 14   'in a singularly mild, firm voice ...': ibid., p. 112.

p. 14   'alone, absolutely alone ...': ibid., p. 134.

p. 16   'Dollars damn me ...': Melville, letter to Nathaniel Hawthorne, 1851, quoted in Cindy Weinstein, 'Artist at Work: *Redburn*, *White-Jacket*, *Moby-Dick* and *Pierre*', in W. Kelly (ed.), *A Companion to Herman Melville* (New York: Wiley-Blackwell, 2015), p. 386.

p. 17   'their fits relieved each other ...': Melville, 'Bartleby, the Scrivener', p. 109.

p. 17   Edward Tronick's famous 'still-face' experiment ...: Tronick describes and elaborates the experiment in *The Neurobehavioral and Social-Emotional Development of Children* (New York: W. W. Norton, 2007).

p. 18   'Ah! Bartleby ...': Melville, 'Bartleby, the Scrivener', p. 140.

p. 18   'wagons ... and precipices ...': Diogenes Laertius, 'Pyrrho', in *Lives of the Eminent Philosophers*, trans. C. D. Yonge (London: H. G. Bohn, 1853), p. 402.

p. 18   'he carried his indifference ...': ibid., p. 404.

p. 18   'saying that it became ...': ibid., p. 405.

p. 19   'a thing can never be apprehended ...': ibid., p. 415.

p. 19   'According to some authorities ...': ibid., p. 420.

p. 19   '"three positive things per week"': Ivor Southwood, *Non-Stop Inertia* (Alresford, Hants: Zero Books, 2010), p. 44.

p. 21   Japan's rigidly disciplined industrial 'monoculture': Michael Zielenziger, *Shutting Out the Sun: How Japan Created Its Own Lost Generation* (New York: Vintage, 2007).

p. 22   'In reality, they are spending ...': Saitō Tamaki, *Hikikomori: Adolescence Without End*, trans. J. Angles (Minneapolis: Minnesota University Press, 2013), p. 48.

p. 26   'His Majesty the Baby': the phrase appears towards the end
         of Freud's 'On Narcissism: An Introduction', *Standard
         Edition*, Volume 14, p. 91. In a footnote, Freud's translator,
         James Strachey, speculates that the phrase may have been
         lifted from an Edwardian cartoon which 'bore that title
         and showed two London policemen holding up the crowded
         traffic to allow a nursery-maid to wheel a perambulator
         across the street'.

p. 27   '*the feeling of having achieved ...*': Byung-Chul Han, *The Burnout
         Society*, trans. E. Butler (Stanford: Stanford University Press,
         2015), pp. 39–40.

Andy Warhol

p. 31   'the painting was horrific ...': Victor Bockris, *The Life and Death
         of Andy Warhol* (London: Fourth Estate, 1998), p. 88.

p. 33   'I would spend ...': Andy Warhol, *The Philosophy of Andy Warhol:
         From A to B and Back Again* (1975) (London: Penguin, 2007),
         p. 21.

p. 34   'His fear of death ...': Bockris, *Life and Death*, p. 46.

p. 35   'Fearing illness and medicine ...': Brian Dillon, *Tormented Hope:
         Nine Hypochondriac Lives* (London: Penguin, 2010), p. 265.

p. 36   'An expression of indifference': Bockris, *Life and Death*, p. 170.

p. 36   'You see, I think every painting ...': Warhol, *Philosophy*, p. 149.

p. 37   'Vacant, vacuous Hollywood ...': Andy Warhol with Pat
         Hackett, *POPism: The Warhol Sixties* (London: Penguin, 2007),
         pp. 51–2.

p. 37   'happy ending': Bockris, *Life and Death*, p. 217.

p. 38   'A very sexless impression': ibid., p. 69.

p. 38   'Sex takes up too much time': ibid., p. 163.

p. 38   'It was almost ...': ibid., p. 185.

p. 38   'Sex is more exciting ...': Warhol, *Philosophy*, p. 44.

p. 38   'Personal love ...': ibid., p. 46.

p. 38   'gave him enormous ...': Bockris, *Life and Death*, p. 185.

p. 38   'You can be ...': Warhol, *Philosophy*, p. 46.

p. 39   'Andy was frightened ...': Bockris, *Life and Death*, p. 93.

p. 39   'The acquisition ...': Warhol, *Philosophy*, p. 26.

p. 40   'Just play it all on one level': ibid., p. 111.

p. 41   'When the action ...': Wayne Koestenbaum, *Andy Warhol: A Biography* (New York: Open Road Media, 2015), pp. 47–8.

p. 42   'Andy, like Hitler ...': Bockris, *Life and Death*, p. 205.

p. 43   '"Why didn't he tell me ..."': ibid., p. 208.

p. 43   'so that Herko ...': ibid., p. 209.

p. 44   'envy of every hip girl ...': ibid., p. 222.

p. 44   '"Everybody in New York ..."': ibid., p. 230.

p. 45   '"I wonder if Edie ..."': ibid., p. 236.

p. 46   '"Somehow I felt that Andy ..."': ibid., p. 317.

p. 46   '"just a kid who worked ..."': ibid., p. 438.

p. 47   'Profoundly disembodied already ...': Koestenbaum, *Andy Warhol*, p. 149.

p. 48   'just being alive ...': Warhol, *Philosophy*, p. 96.

p. 48   'The negative message ...': Bockris, *Life and Death*, p. 264.

p. 49   'At last Andy ...': Koestenbaum, *Andy Warhol*, p. 30.

p. 50   'Spying on motionlessness ...': ibid., p. 30.

p. 50   'Dreams only show us ...': Sigmund Freud, 'A Metapsychological Supplement to the Theory of Dreams', *The Standard Edition of the Complete Psychological Works of Sigmund Freud*, trans. and ed. J. Strachey, Volume 14 (London: Vintage, 2001), p. 223.

p. 50   'Machines have less problems ...': Bockris, *Life and Death*, p. 163.

p. 51   'As soon as you have to decide ...': Warhol, *Philosophy*, p. 149.

p. 51   'Everything is nothing ...': Bockris, *Life and Death*, p. 390.

Chapter 2: The Slob

p. 53   'Genuine *force of habit* ...': Arthur Schopenhauer, *Essays and Aphorism*, trans. R. J. Hollingdale (London: Penguin, 1976), p. 166.

p. 55   'with their feet in mud ...': Georges Bataille, 'The Big Toe', *Visions of Excess: Selected Writings 1927–1939*, trans. A. Stoekl (Minneapolis: University of Minnesota Press, 1985), p. 20.

p. 56   'rises in the direction ...': Georges Bataille, 'The Solar Anus', ibid., p. 7.

p. 59   '"Nothing so aggravates ..."': Herman Melville, 'Bartleby, the Scrivener' (1853), *Billy Budd and Other Stories* (New York: Signet, 1961), p. 115.

p. 60   'I refute it *thus*!': James Boswell, *Life of Johnson* (1791), ed. R. W. Chapman (Oxford: OUP, 2008), p. 333.

p. 60   'the compulsion to work': Sigmund Freud, *Civilization and Its Discontents, The Standard Edition of the Complete Psychological Works of Sigmund Freud*, trans. and ed. J. Strachey, Volume 21 (London: Vintage, 2001), p. 101.

p. 61   'when a love relationship . . .': ibid., p. 108.

p. 61   a perversion expresses . . .: Freud discusses perversion in forensic detail in the first of his *Three Essays on the Theory of Sexuality, Standard Edition*, Volume 7.

p. 61   'disinclination to give up . . .': Sigmund Freud, *Civilization and Its Discontents, Standard Edition*, Volume 21, p. 108.

p. 62   'the inertia of the libido': Strachey translates Freud's word *Trägheit* as both 'inertia' and 'sluggishness'.

p. 62   'the simplest of all experiences . . .': D. W. Winnicott, 'Creativity and Its Origins', *Playing and Reality* (London: Routledge, 1971), p. 80.

p. 63   'some mental activity . . .': Jonathan Lear, *Happiness, Death, and the Remainder of Life* (Cambridge, MA: Harvard University Press, 2002), p. 80.

p. 66   'nothing is ever fundamentally "off" . . .': Jonathan Crary, *24/7: Late Capitalism and the Ends of Sleep* (London: Verso, 2014), p. 13.

p. 66   'his normal condition': Ivan Goncharov, *Oblomov* (1859), trans. D. Magarshack (London: Penguin, 2005), p. 14.

p. 67   'the fairy-tale had become . . .': ibid., p. 119.

p. 67   'Oblomov would have liked . . .': ibid., p. 22.

p. 68   'two principles . . .': Sigmund Freud, 'Formulations on the Two Principles of Mental Functioning', *Standard Edition*, Volume 12.

p. 70   'a numbness, a despondency . . .': Pierre Saint-Amand, *The Pursuit of Laziness: An Idle Interpretation of the Enlightenment*, trans. J. C. Gage (Princeton: Princeton University Press, 2011), p. 2.

p. 70   'the necessity of *doing*': ibid., p. 3.

p. 71   the author of *Jacques the Fatalist* . . .: Denis Diderot, *Jacques the Fatalist* (1796), trans. D. Coward (Oxford: OUP, 2008).

p. 71   'one of the weirdest characters . . .': Denis Diderot, *Rameau's Nephew* (1805), trans. L. Tancock (London: Penguin, 1976), p. 23.

p. 71   'an idler, greedy . . .': ibid., p. 123.

p. 72   'worthy use . . .': ibid., p. 64.

p. 72   'drink good wine . . .': ibid., p. 65.

p. 72   'you . . . are not even capable . . .': ibid., p. 70.

p. 73   'Whatever produces . . .': Schopenhauer, *Essays*, p. 61.

p. 74   'seems to be subjected . . .': Maurice Blanchot, 'Literature and
          the Right to Death', trans. L. Davis, *The Work of Fire* (Stanford:
          Stanford University Press, 1995).

p. 75   'Sovereign Man': Bataille writes that this man's sovereignty
          'destines him, in a privileged way, to that glorious operation,
          to useless consumption', *The Accursed Share*, Volume 1, trans. R.
          Hurley (Cambridge, MA: Zone Books, 1991), p. 23.

Orson Welles

p. 82   'trying to be old . . .': David Thomson, *Rosebud: The Story of
          Orson Welles* (London: Vintage, 1996), p. 400 .

p. 84   'The one thing Welles . . .': Simon Callow, *Orson Welles, Volume
          3: One-Man Band* (London: Vintage, 2015), p. 59.

p. 86   'Any form of limitation . . .': Simon Callow, *Orson Welles, Volume
          2: Hello Americans* (London: Vintage, 2007), p. 444.

p. 88   'Now, Faustus . . .': Christopher Marlowe, *The Tragical History
          of Doctor Faustus*, *The Complete Plays*, ed. J. B. Steane (London:
          Penguin, 1969), p. 274.

p. 88   'I charge thee . . .': ibid., p. 275.

p. 90   'too gigantic . . .': Jorge Luis Borges, 'An Overwhelming Film',
          Selected Non-Fictions, trans. E. Allen and S. J. Levine, ed. E.
          Weinberger (London: Penguin, 2000), p. 258.

p. 90   'but shadows, not substantial': Marlowe, *Doctor Faustus*, p. 310.

p. 91   'When he was hungry . . .': Simon Callow, *Orson Welles, Volume
          1: The Road to Xanadu* (London: Vintage, 1996), p. 326.

p. 92   'On a purely quantitative level . . .': Callow, *Hello Americans*, p. 7.

p. 92   'then hustle back . . .': ibid., p. 314.

p. 93   'a kind of enemy . . .': Callow, *One-Man Band*, p. 358.

p. 97   'he retired into . . .': quoted in Callow, *Road to Xanadu*, p. 387.

p. 98   'deny real feeling . . .': ibid., p. 366.

p. 98   'He played the entire scene . . .': Callow, *One-Man Band*, p. 281.

p. 99   'at a time when . . .': Callow, *Hello Americans*, p. 306.

p. 102   'were a complaint against . . .': Peter Conrad, *Orson Welles: The
          Stories of His Life* (London: Faber & Faber, 2004), p. 40.

Chapter 3: The Daydreamer

p. 114   'just try acting': Hoffman discusses the story during
a 2015 interview. See https://www.youtube.com/
watch?v=Ss7F8BCrNz0.

p. 114   'Don't talk about action ...': Oscar Wilde, 'The Critic as Artist',
The Major Works ed. I. Murray (Oxford: OUP, 2010), p. 256.

p. 115   'is the refuge ...': ibid.

p. 115   Freud was speculating ...: Freud's first published discussion of
obsessional neurosis occurs in his 1896 paper 'Further Remarks
on the Neuro-Psychoses of Defence', *The Standard Edition of the
Complete Psychological Works of Sigmund Freud*, trans. and ed. J.
Strachey, Volume 3 (London: Vintage, 2001), pp. 168–74.

p. 115   'To do nothing ...': Wilde, 'Critic as Artist', p. 275.

p. 116   'I loved you ...': Oscar Wilde, *The Picture of Dorian Gray*, *The
Major Works*, p. 112.

p. 116   'Without your art ...': ibid., p. 113.

p. 118   'Let all the wretched ...': Xavier de Maistre, *Voyage Around My
Room*, trans. S. Sartarelli (New York: New Directions, 1994), p. 5.

p. 118   'Today is the day ...': ibid., p. 81.

p. 119   'there is no work ...': Desiderius Erasmus, *The Praise of Folly*,
trans. C. H. Miller (New Haven: Yale University Press, 2003),
p. 17.

p. 120   With *Don Quixote* ...: Miguel de Cervantes, *Don Quixote*, trans.
J. Rutherford (London: Penguin, 2003).

p. 121   'Everything you can imagine is real': more precisely, the quote is
always ascribed to Picasso, but no one seems to have located the
source.

p. 123   'we maintain a real relationship ...': Emmanuel Levinas, 'Reality
and Its Shadow', *Collected Philosophical Papers*, trans. A. Lingis
(Pittsburgh: Duquesne University Press, 1998), p. 3.

p. 123   'a continuation of ...': Sigmund Freud, 'Creative Writers and
Daydreaming', *Standard Edition*, Volume 9, p. 152.

p. 126   'The vision of him ...': Wilde, 'Critic as Artist', p. 275.

p. 127   'he begins to select ...': Sigmund Freud, 'Recommendations to
Physicians Practising Psycho-Analysis', *Standard Edition*, Volume 12,
p. 112.

p. 128   'like a receptive organ': ibid., p. 115.

p. 130   'the one that was shining . . .': Georges Bataille, 'Rotten
            Sun', *Visions of Excess: Selected Writings 1927–1939*, trans.
            A. Stoekl (Minneapolis: University of Minnesota Press, 1985),
            p. 58.

p. 131   'the main part . . .': D. W. Winnicott, 'Dreaming, Fantasying
            and Living: A Case-History Describing a Primary Dissociation',
            Playing and Reality (London: Routledge, 1971), p. 40.

p. 132   'lying all her life . . .': ibid.

Emily Dickinson

All quotations of Dickinson's poems are taken from *The Poems of Emily
Dickinson: Including Variant Readings Critically Compared with All Known
Manuscripts*, ed. T. Johnson (Cambridge, MA: Harvard Belknap, 1955).
As each poem is numbered, I have not provided page references.

p. 135   '. . . the sister Vinnie . . .': quoted in Lyndall Gordon, *Lives Like
            Loaded Guns: Emily Dickinson and Her Family's Feuds* (London:
            Virago, 2010), p. 228.

p. 135   'I have done with guises . . .': quoted in Cynthia Griffin Wolff,
            Emily Dickinson (New York: Perseus Books, 1988), p. 401.

p. 135   'Don't you know . . .': ibid., p. 402.

p. 136   'It is strange . . .': ibid.

p. 136   'Emily "Jumbo" . . .': ibid., p. 403.

p. 137   'We have met with little . . .': Richard B. Sewall, *The Life of Emily
            Dickinson* (Cambridge, MA: Harvard University Press, 1980),
            p. 642.

p. 138   'It would be difficult . . .': Wolff, *Emily Dickinson*, p. 3

p. 138   'Other all-time poets . . .': Gordon, *Lives*, p. 82.

p. 140   'intensely rigid': Gregorio Kohon, 'Louise Bourgeois and
            Franz Kafka: Of Lairs and Burrows', *Reflections on the Aesthetic
            Experience: Psychoanalysis and the Uncanny* (London: Routledge,
            2016), p. 26.

p. 140   'still, silent spot': Winnicott posits the existence of this spot in
            his essay, 'Communicating and Not-Communicating, Leading
            to a Study of Certain Opposites', *The Maturational Processes and
            the Facilitating Environment: Studies in the Theory of Emotional
            Development* (London: Karnac, 1990).

p. 142   'Perhaps you thought . . .': March 1862, Emily Dickinson, *The*

Letters of Emily Dickinson, ed. M. L. Todd (Mineola, NY: Dover, 2003), p. 169.

p. 142   'I cannot see you': quoted in Wolff, *Emily Dickinson*, p. 399.

p. 142   'Emily, you damned wretch . . .': ibid.

p. 142   'She always wears white . . .': quoted in Gordon, *Lives*, p 14.

p. 143   'a much-beloved local dignitary': Sewall, *Life*, p. 650.

p. 143   'a man of more than . . .': ibid., p. 653.

p. 146   'Nothing in Edward's life . . .': Wolff, *Emily Dickinson*, p. 35.

p. 146   'I always ran Home . . .': both Dickinson and Higginson are quoted in Sewall, *Life*, p. 74.

p. 147   'a distant figure . . .': André Green, 'The Dead Mother', *Life Narcissism, Death Narcissism*, trans. A. Weller (London: Free Association Books, 2001), p. 170.

p. 148   'nameless, disabling apathy': Wolff, *Emily Dickinson*, p. 133.

p. 148   'Mother lies . . .': January 1856, Dickinson, *Letters*, p. 139.

p. 153   'In the poet . . .': Wolff, *Emily Dickinson*, p. 362.

p. 155   Freud's definition . . .: Freud's fullest discussion of the timelessness of the unconscious is in his 1915 paper 'The Unconscious', *The Standard Edition of the Complete Psychological Works of Sigmund Freud*, trans. and ed. J. Strachey, Volume 14 (London: Vintage, 2001).

p. 155   'to say if my Verse . . .': April 1862, Dickinson, *Letters*, p. 253.

p. 156   'foreign to my thought . . .': June 1862, ibid.

Chapter 4: The Slacker

p. 166   'where each subject . . .': Roland Barthes, *How to Live Together: Novelistic Simulations of Some Everyday Spaces*, trans. K. Briggs (New York: Columbia University Press, 2013), p. 6.

p. 168   'guidance by nature . . .': Sextus Empiricus, *Outlines of Scepticism*, trans. J. Annas and J. Barnes (Cambridge: CUP, 2000), p. 9.

p. 168   'we are not able . . .': ibid.

p. 169   'and when it hit . . .': ibid., p. 10.

p. 169   'as it were . . .': ibid., p. 11.

p. 169   'the Neutral . . .': Roland Barthes, *The Neutral: Lecture Course at the Collège de France (1977–1978)*, trans. R. Krauss and D. Hollier (New York: Columbia University Press, 2008), p. 80.

p. 170   'Once man loses . . .': E. M. Cioran, *A Short History of Decay*

(1949), trans. R. Howard (New York: Arcade Publishing, 1998), p. 3.

p. 170   'Only the sceptics ...': ibid., p. 4.

p. 171   'suspensive freedom': Frédéric Gros, *A Philosophy of Walking*, trans C. Harper (London: Verso, 2015), p. 3.

p. 172   'precious *far niente*': Jean-Jacques Rousseau, *Reveries of the Solitary Walker*, trans. R. Goulbourne (Oxford: OUP, 2011), p. 51.

p. 172   'But if there is a state ...': ibid., p. 51.

p. 173   'its ecstatic unusability ...': Peter Sloterdijk, *Stress and Freedom*, trans. W. Hoban (Cambridge: Polity, 2015), p. 23.

p. 173   'is like a nuclear ...': ibid., p. 33.

p. 174   its informal bible: Carl Honoré, *In Praise of Slow: How a Worldwide Movement Is Challenging the Cult of Speed* (London: HarperCollins, 2005).

p. 175   the IBM manager: 'Kill the smartphone: the slow fight against the rat race', *Independent*, 1 October 2010. See https://www.independent.co.uk/life-style/kill-the-smartphone-the-slow-fight-against-the-rat-race-2095847.html.

p. 176   'over-worked, hyper-stressed ...': Carl Cederström and Peter Fleming, *Dead Man Working* (Alresford, Hants: Zero Books, 2012), p. 51.

p. 176   'A float session ...': ibid., p. 52.

p. 180   'Live in hiding ...': The best selection of Epicurus's thought can be found in Epicurus, *The Art of Happiness*, trans. and ed. J. K. Strodach (London: Penguin, 2013).

p. 180   'what makes the effort ...': Hannah Arendt, *The Human Condition: A Study of the Central Dilemmas Facing Modern Man* (New York: Doubleday Anchor, 1959), p. 101.

p. 181   'will not be always ...': Oscar Wilde, 'The Soul of Man Under Socialism', *The Collected Works of Oscar Wilde* (Ware, Herts: Wordsworth, 2007), p. 1,046.

p. 182   'The note of the perfect ...': ibid.

p. 183   'her 2016 show': Maria Eichhorn, *5 weeks, 25 days, 175 hours*, exhibition catalogue (Chisenhale Gallery, 2016).

p. 187   'time wasted ...': Gros, *Philosophy*, p. 89.

p. 192   'In view of my ...': Nathaniel Hawthorne, *The Scarlet Letter* (Oxford: OUP, 1990), p. 42.

David Foster Wallace

p. 194   'remotely expect ...': D. T. Max, *Every Ghost Story Is a Love Story: A Life of David Foster Wallace* (London: Granta, 2012), p. 298.

p. 195   'If he tried ...': ibid.

p. 195   'will kill herself ...': David Foster Wallace, *Infinite Jest* (London: Abacus, 1997), p. 696.

p. 196   'emotional character ...': ibid.

p. 197   'Wallace's childhood ...': Max, *Every Ghost Story*, p. 4.

p. 198   'He was not sure ...': ibid., p. 12.

p. 198   'The same obsessive ...': David Foster Wallace, *The Last Interview and Other Conversations* (New York: Melville House, 2012), p. 57.

p. 198   'One hideous symptom ...': Max, *Every Ghost Story*, p. 34.

p. 198   'he wanted to please ...': ibid., p. 21.

p. 200   'Wallace started ...': Christian Lorentzen, 'The Rewriting of David Foster Wallace', *New York* magazine, 29 June 2015. See http://www.vulture.com/2015/06/rewriting-of-david-foster-wallace.html.

p. 200   'the 2015 movie based on ...': David Lipsky, *Although of Course You End Up Becoming Yourself: A Road Trip with David Foster Wallace* (New York: Broadway Books, 2010).

p. 201   'my tendency to over-intellectualize ...': David Foster Wallace, *This Is Water: Thoughts, Delivered on a Significant Occasion, About Living a Compassionate Life* (New York: Little, Brown, 2009), p. 2.

p. 201   'What the hell ...': ibid., p. 1.

p. 202   'The so-called real world ...': ibid., p. 7.

p. 202   'banal platitude ...': ibid., p. 1.

p. 203   'an excellent servant ...': ibid., p. 3.

p. 203   'And who are ...': ibid., p. 5.

p. 205   'All I can tell you ...': Max, *Every Ghost Story*, p. 143.

p. 206   '"AA's = ..."': ibid., p. 316.

p. 206   'Doing the Substance ...': Wallace, *Infinite Jest*, pp. 347–8.

p. 207   'it is not that ...': ibid., p. 1,048.

p. 208   'schizogenic experience ...': quoted in Max, *Every Ghost Story*, p. 6.

p. 208   'entertainment and stimulation ...': Lipsky, *Although of Course*, p. 85.

p. 208   'during periods of collapse . . .': Max, *Every Ghost Story*, p. 149.

p. 208   'fat, cynical . . .': David Foster Wallace, 'E Unibus Pluram: Television and US Fiction', *A Supposedly Fun Thing I'll Never Do Again: Essays and Arguments* (London: Abacus, 1997), p. 41.

p. 209   'And of course I want . . .': David Foster Wallace, 'A Supposedly Fun Thing I'll Never Do Again', ibid., p. 316.

p. 210   'Near Eastern medical attaché': Wallace, *Infinite Jest*, p. 79.

p. 210   'the various neurotransmitters . . .': ibid., p. 474.

p. 210   'Bug-eyed, drooling . . .': ibid.

p. 211   'to stay conscious . . .': Wallace, *This Is Water*, p. 8.

p. 211   'the most tedious . . .': 'Bret Easton Ellis launches broadside against David Foster Wallace', *Guardian*, 6 September 2012. See https://www.theguardian.com/books/2012/sep/06/bret-easton-ellis-david-foster-wallace.

p. 212   'His last piece of contact . . .': Wallace, *Infinite Jest*, p. 24.

p. 213   'to see everything . . .': quoted in 'David Foster Wallace: "a mind that seemed to see everything on every level all at once"', *Chicago Tribune*, 15 September 2008. See http://featuresblogs.chicagotribune.com/entertainment_popmachine/2008/09/after-david-fos.html.

p. 213   'a noticing machine': ibid.

p. 214   'my Taoistic ability': David Foster Wallace, 'Derivative Sport in Tornado Alley', *A Supposedly Fun Thing I'll Never Do Again*, p. 12.

p. 214   'he looks like what . . .': David Foster Wallace, 'Federer Both Flesh and Not', *Both Flesh and Not* (London: Penguin, 2013), p. 20.

p. 215   'What he seemed to be . . .': David Foster Wallace, *The Pale King* (London: Penguin, 2012), p. 228.

p. 215   '"Enduring tedium . . ."': ibid., p. 231.

p. 215   'That I drifted . . .': ibid., p. 225.

p. 216   'a sort of emergence . . .': ibid., p. 183.

p. 216   'for actual heroism . . .': ibid., p. 232.

p. 216   'When his hope . . .': Jonathan Franzen, 'Farther Away', *New Yorker*, 18 April 2011. See https://www.newyorker.com/magazine/2011/04/18/farther-away-jonathan-franzen.

p. 217   'There is hope . . .': quoted in Max Brod, *Franz Kafka: A Biography* (Boston: Da Capo Press, 1995), p. 227.

Conclusion

p. 219   'Watching *enough* represented strong experience . . .': Mark Greif, 'Anaesthetic Ideology: The Meaning of Life, Part III', *Against Everything: Essays* (London: Verso, 2016), p. 238.

p. 222   'I see advertisements . . .': H. D. Thoreau, 'Life Without Principle', *Essays*, ed. J. S. Cramer (New Haven: Yale University Press, 2013), p. 350.

p. 222   'I think that there is nothing . . .': ibid., p. 347.

p. 222   'To have done anything . . .': ibid., p. 349.

Bibliography

Adorno, T. W., 'Commitment', *Notes to Literature Volume 2*, trans. S. W. Nicholsen (New York: Columbia University Press, 1992)

Arendt, Hannah, *The Human Condition: A Study of the Central Dilemmas Facing Modern Man* (New York: Doubleday Anchor, 1959)

Aulagnier, Piera, *The Violence of Interpretation: From Pictogram to Statement*, trans. A. Sheridan (London: Routledge, 2001)

Barthes, Roland, *The Neutral: Lecture Course at the Collège de France (1977–1978)*, trans. R. Krauss and D. Hollier (New York: Columbia University Press, 2008)

Barthes, Roland, *How to Live Together: Novelistic Simulations of Some Everyday Spaces*, trans. K. Briggs (New York: Columbia University Press, 2013)

Bataille, Georges, *Visions of Excess: Selected Writings 1927–1939*, trans. A. Stoekl (Minneapolis: University of Minnesota Press, 1985)

Bataille, Georges, *The Accursed Share*, Volume 1, trans. R. Hurley (Cambridge, MA: Zone Books, 1991)

Berardi, Franco, *The Soul at Work: From Alienation to Autonomy*, trans. J. Smith (New York: Semiotexte, 2009)

Blanchot, Maurice, *The Space of Literature*, trans. A. Smock (Lincoln, NE: University of Nebraska Press, 1989)

Blanchot, Maurice, 'Literature and the Right to Death',
        trans. L. Davis, *The Work of Fire* (Stanford, CA: Stanford
        University Press, 1995)

Bockris, Victor, *The Life and Death of Andy Warhol* (London:
        Fourth Estate, 1998)

Borges, Jorge Luis, *Selected Non-Fictions*, trans. E. Allen and
        S. J. Levine, ed. E. Weinberger (New York: Penguin,
        2000)

Boswell, James, *Life of Johnson*, ed. R. W. Chapman (Oxford:
        OUP, 2008)

Brod, Max, *Franz Kafka: A Biography* (Boston: Da Capo Press,
        1995)

Callow, Simon, *Orson Welles, Volume 1: The Road to Xanadu*
        (London: Vintage, 1996)

Callow, Simon, *Orson Welles, Volume 2: Hello Americans*
        (London: Vintage, 2007)

Callow, Simon, *Orson Welles, Volume 3: One-Man Band*
        (London: Vintage, 2015)

Cederström, Carl, and Fleming, Peter, *Dead Man Working*
        (Alresford, Hants: Zero Books, 2012)

Cioran, E. M., *A Short History of Decay*, trans. R. Howard
        (New York: Arcade Publishing, 1998)

Conrad, Peter, *Orson Welles: The Stories of His Life* (London:
        Faber & Faber, 2004)

Crary, Jonathan, *24/7: Late Capitalism and the Ends of Sleep*
        (London: Verso, 2014)

de Cervantes, Miguel, *Don Quixote*, trans. J. Rutherford
        (London: Penguin, 2003)

de Maistre, Xavier, *Voyage Around My Room*, trans. S. Sartarelli
        (New York: New Directions, 1994)

Dickinson, Emily, *The Poems of Emily Dickinson: Including
        Variant Readings Critically Compared with All Known*

Manuscripts, ed. T. Johnson (Cambridge, MA: Harvard
Belknap, 1955)

Dickinson, Emily, *The Letters of Emily Dickinson*, ed. M. L.
Todd (Mineola, NY: Dover, 2003)

Diderot, Denis, *Jacques the Fatalist*, trans. D. Coward (Oxford:
OUP, 2008)

Diderot, Denis, *Rameau's Nephew* and *D'Alembert's Dream*, trans.
L. Tancock (London: Penguin, 1976)

Dillon, Brian, *Tormented Hope: Nine Hypochondriac Lives*
(London: Penguin, 2010)

Ehrenberg, Alain, *The Weariness of the Self: Diagnosing the
History of Depression in the Contemporary Age*, trans. E.
Caouette, J. Homel, D. Homel and D. Winkler (Montreal:
McGill-Queens University Press, 2010)

Eichhorn, Maria, *5 weeks, 25 days, 175 hours*, exhibition
catalogue (London: Chisenhale Gallery, 2016)

Epicurus, *The Art of Happiness*, trans. and ed. J. K. Strodach
(London: Penguin, 2013)

Erasmus, Desiderius, *The Praise of Folly*, trans. C. H. Miller
(New Haven, CT: Yale University Press, 2003)

Frayne, David, *The Refusal of Work* (London: Zed Books, 2015)

Freud, Sigmund, 'Further Remarks on the Neuro-Psychoses of
Defence', *The Standard Edition of the Complete Psychological
Works of Sigmund Freud*, trans. and ed. J. Strachey, Volume 3
(London: Vintage, 2001)

Freud, Sigmund, *Three Essays on the Theory of Sexuality*, *Standard
Edition*, Volume 7 (London: Vintage, 2001)

Freud, Sigmund, 'Creative Writers and Daydreaming', *Standard
Edition*, Volume 9 (London: Vintage, 2001)

Freud, Sigmund, 'Formulations on the Two Principles of
Mental Functioning', *Standard Edition*, Volume 12
(London: Vintage, 2001)

244   *Not Working*

Freud, Sigmund, 'Recommendations to Physicians Practising Psychoanalysis', *Standard Edition*, Volume 12 (London: Vintage, 2001)

Freud, Sigmund, 'On Narcissism: An Introduction', *Standard Edition*, Volume 14 (London: Vintage, 2001)

Freud, Sigmund, 'The Unconscious', *Standard Edition*, Volume 14 (London: Vintage, 2001)

Freud, Sigmund, 'A Metapsychological Supplement to the Theory of Dreams', *Standard Edition*, Volume 14 (London: Vintage, 2001)

Freud, Sigmund, 'Beyond the Pleasure Principle', *Standard Edition*, Volume 18 (London: Vintage, 2001)

Freud, Sigmund, 'Negation', *Standard Edition*, Volume 19 (London: Vintage, 2001)

Freud, Sigmund, *Civilization and Its Discontents, Standard Edition*, Volume 21 (London: Vintage, 2001)

Goncharov, Ivan, *Oblomov*, trans. D. Magarshack (London: Penguin, 2005)

Gordon, Lyndall, *Lives Like Loaded Guns: Emily Dickinson and Her Family's Feuds* (London: Virago, 2010)

Green, André, *Life Narcissism, Death Narcissism*, trans. A. Weller (London: Free Association Books, 2001)

Greene, Graham, *A Burnt-Out Case* (London: Vintage, 2004)

Greif, Mark, *Against Everything: Essays* (London: Verso, 2016)

Gros, Frédéric, *A Philosophy of Walking*, trans C. Harper (London: Verso, 2015)

Han, Byung-Chul, *The Burnout Society*, trans. E. Butler (Stanford, CA: Stanford University Press, 2015)

Hawthorne, Nathaniel, *The Scarlet Letter* (Oxford: OUP, 1990)

Honoré, Carl, *In Praise of Slow: How a Worldwide Movement Is Challenging the Cult of Speed* (London: HarperCollins, 2005)

Huysmans, J.-K., *Against Nature*, trans. R. Baldick (London: Penguin, 2004)

Keats, John, *The Complete Poems*, ed. J. Barnard (London: Penguin, 1977)

Kenkō and Chōmei, *Essays in Idleness* and *Hōjōki*, trans. M. McKinney (London: Penguin, 2013)

Koestenbaum, Wayne, *Andy Warhol: A Biography* (New York: Open Road Media, 2015)

Kohon, Gregorio, *Reflections on the Aesthetic Experience: Psychoanalysis and the Uncanny* (London: Routledge, 2016)

Laertius, Diogenes *Lives of the Eminent Philosophers*, trans. C. D. Yonge (London: H. G. Bohn, 1853)

Lear, Jonathan, *Happiness, Death, and the Remainder of Life* (Cambridge, MA: Harvard University Press, 2002)

Levinas, Emmanuel, 'Reality and Its Shadow', *Collected Philosophical Papers*, trans. A. Lingis (Pittsburgh, PA: Duquesne University Press, 1998)

Lipsky, David, *Although of Course You End Up Becoming Yourself: A Road Trip with David Foster Wallace* (New York: Broadway Books, 2010)

Lorentzen, Christian, 'The Rewriting of David Foster Wallace', *New York* magazine, 29 June 2015

Marlowe, Christopher, *The Complete Plays*, ed. J. B. Steane (London: Penguin, 1969)

Max, D. T., *Every Ghost Story Is a Love Story: A Life of David Foster Wallace* (London: Granta, 2012)

Melville, Herman, 'Bartleby, the Scrivener', *Billy Budd and Other Stories* (New York: Signet, 1961)

The New Testament in Modern English, trans. J. B. Phillips (London: HarperCollins, 1972)

Nietzsche, Friedrich, 'On the Uses and Disadvantages of

History for Life', *Untimely Meditations*, trans. R. J. Hollingdale (Cambridge: CUP, 1997)

Ovid, *Metamorphoses*, trans. M. M. Innes (London: Penguin, 2000)

Plato, *The Republic*, trans. D. Lee (London: Penguin, 1986)

Rousseau, Jean-Jacques, *Reveries of the Solitary Walker*, trans. R. Goulbourne (Oxford: OUP, 2011)

Saint-Amand, Pierre, *The Pursuit of Laziness: An Idle Interpretation of the Enlightenment*, trans. J. C. Gage (Princeton, NJ: Princeton University Press, 2011)

Salecl, Renata, *The Tyranny of Choice* (London: Profile, 2011)

Schaffner, Anna Katharina, *Exhaustion: A History* (New York: Columbia University Press, 2016)

Schopenhauer, Arthur, *Essays and Aphorism*, trans. R. J. Hollingdale (London: Penguin, 1976)

Sewall, Richard B., *The Life of Emily Dickinson* (Cambridge, MA: Harvard University Press, 1980)

Sextus Empiricus, *Outlines of Scepticism*, trans. J. Annas and J. Barnes (Cambridge: CUP, 2000)

Sloterdijk, Peter, *Stress and Freedom*, trans. W. Hoban (Cambridge: Polity, 2015)

Southwood, Ivor, *Non-Stop Inertia* (Alresford, Hants: Zero Books, 2010)

Srnicek, Nick, and Williams, Alex, *Inventing the Future: Post-Capitalism and a World Without Work* (London: Verso, 2016)

Tamaki, Saitō, *Hikikomori: Adolescence Without End*, trans. J. Angles (Minneapolis: Minnesota University Press, 2013)

Thomson, David, *Rosebud: The Story of Orson Welles* (London: Vintage, 1996)

Thoreau, H. D., *Essays*, ed. J. S. Cramer (New Haven, CT: Yale University Press, 2013)

Tronick, Edward, *The Neurobehavioral and Social-Emotional Development of Children* (New York: W. W. Norton, 2007)

Wallace, David Foster, *A Supposedly Fun Thing I'll Never Do Again: Essays and Arguments* (London: Abacus, 1997)

Wallace, David Foster, *Infinite Jest* (London: Abacus, 1997)

Wallace, David Foster, *This Is Water: Thoughts, Delivered on a Significant Occasion, About Living a Compassionate Life* (New York: Little, Brown, 2009)

Wallace, David Foster, *The Last Interview and Other Conversations* (New York: Melville House, 2012)

Wallace, David Foster, *The Pale King* (London: Penguin, 2012)

Wallace, David Foster, *Both Flesh and Not* (London: Penguin, 2013)

Warhol, Andy, *The Philosophy of Andy Warhol: From A to B and Back Again* (London: Penguin, 2007)

Warhol, Andy, with Hackett, Pat, *POPism: The Warhol Sixties* (London: Penguin, 2007)

Weber, Max, *The Protestant Ethic and the 'Spirit' of Capitalism*, trans. P. Baehr and G. C. Wells (London: Penguin, 2002)

Weinstein, Cindy, 'Artist at Work: *Redburn, White-Jacket, Moby-Dick* and *Pierre*' in W. Kelly (ed.), *A Companion to Herman Melville* (New York: Wiley–Blackwell, 2015)

Wilde, Oscar, 'The Soul of Man Under Socialism', *The Collected Works of Oscar Wilde* (Ware, Herts: Wordsworth Library Collection, 2007)

Wilde, Oscar, 'The Critic As Artist', *The Major Works*, ed. I. Murray (Oxford: OUP, 2010)

Wilde, Oscar, *The Picture of Dorian Gray*, *Major Works* (Oxford: OUP, 2010)

Winnicott, D. W., *Playing and Reality* (London: Routledge, 1971)

Winnicott, D. W., *The Maturational Processes and the Facilitating Environment: Studies in the Theory of Emotional Development* (London: Karnac, 1990).

Wolff, Cynthia Griffin, *Emily Dickinson* (New York: Perseus Books, 1988)

Zielenziger, Michael, *Shutting Out the Sun: How Japan Created Its Own Lost Generation* (New York: Vintage, 2007)

Acknowledgements

My thanks to my excellent editor, Bella Lacey, as much for the long and stimulating conversations as for her exact and incisive work on the page; to my agent, Zoe Ross, as informed and fierce a champion of my work as a writer could wish for; to Lesley Levene, once again an exceptionally thorough and thoughtful copy-editor; and to the readers of the work in progress, careful and incisive in equal measure, Devorah Baum and Lara Feigel.

I was also lucky enough to have an ideal reader in Abigail Schama, who has little choice in the matter. She keeps me inspired, in writing and all else; as do Ethan, Reuben and Ira Cohen.

This book is dedicated to my parents, Raquel Goldstein and Edward Cohen, who were sufficiently exasperated by my dreaminess to make me notice it, and sufficiently tolerant to ensure I stayed curious about it.

Permissions

Extracts from *Untimely Meditations* by Friedrich Nietzsche, edited by Daniel Breazeale, translated by R. J. Hollingdale, copyright © 1997 by Cambridge University Press. Reproduced by kind permission of Cambridge University Press.

Extracts from *Reveries of the Solitary Walker* by Jean-Jacques Rousseau,, translated by Russell Goulbourne, copyright © 2011 by Oxford University Press. Reproduced by kind permission of Oxford University Press.

Extracts from *Essays and Aphorisms* by Arthur Schopenhauer, selected and translated with an introduction by R. J. Hollingdale (Penguin Classics, 1970). Translation and introduction copyright © R. J. Hollingdale, 1970. Reproduced by kind permission of Penguin Random House UK.

Extracts from *Non-Stop Inertia* by Ivor Southwood, copyright © 2011 by Ivor Southwood. Reproduced by kind permission of John Hunt Publishing Ltd.

Extracts from *Inventing the Future: Postcapitalism and a World Without Work* by Nick Srnicek and Alex Williams, copyright © 2015, 2016 by Nick Srnicek and Alex Williams. Reproduced by kind permission of Verso Books.

Extracts from *The Philosophy of Andy Warhol: From A to B and Back Again* by Andy Warhol, copyright © 1975 by Andy Warhol. Reproduced by kind permission of Houghton Mifflin Harcourt Publishing Company.

Extracts from *Playing and Reality* by D. W. Winnicott, copyright © 1971 by D. W. Winnicott. Reproduced by kind permission of The Taylor and Francis Group.

Index

Keep in touch with
Granta Books:

Visit granta.com to discover more.

GRANTA

Also by Josh Cohen and available from Granta Books
www.granta.com

HOW TO READ
FREUD

'The whole trend of your previous education and all your habits of thought are bound to make you into opponents of psychonalysis ...'
Sigmund Freud

In this engaging introduction, Josh Cohen argues that Freud shows above all that any thought, word or action, however apparently trivial, can invite close reading. Indeed, it may be just this insight that provokes so much opposition to psychoanalysis.

By reading short extracts from across Freud's work, addressing the neuroses, the unconscious, words, death and (of course) sex, *How to Read Freud* brings out the paradoxical core of psychoanalytic thinking: that our innermost truths only ever manifest themselves as distortions. Read attentively, our dreams, errors, jokes, symptoms, in short, our everyday lives, reveal us as masters of disguise, as unrecognizable to ourselves as to others.

THE PRIVATE LIFE
Why We Remain in the Dark

'Elegant and suggestive . . . Cohen is equally at home discussing Katie Price as he is expounding the thoughts of Arendt' *Guardian*

Your privacy is under attack. Some seek to expose, invade and steal it, others to protect, conceal and withhold it. But what are we searching for and what are we hiding?

In this groundbreaking work, Josh Cohen draws on his experience as a psychoanalyst and literature professor to explore the 'private life'. Covering a wide array of characters and concerns, from John Milton and Henry James to Katie Price and Snoopy, from philosophy and the Bible to pornography and late-night TV, he asks: in a culture that floods our lives with light, how is it that we remain so helplessly in the dark?

'Highly topical and fascinating . . . Summoning literature from Milton to Sophocles, Cohen concludes that our only hope now may be to protect things that should remain unknown' *Daily Telegraph*

'Subtle and stimulating . . . Cohen gives us fascinating glimpses of cases [and] engages in some astute reading of literature and popular culture' Lisa Appignanesi, 'Books of the Year', *Observer*

'A work of real cultural importance, deserving of the widest readership' Rowan Williams

'Deserves . . . to be read and referred to again and again, and every time to provide something new to think about' *Jewish Chronicle*